D0201121

INSIDE
STORY

INSIDE
STORY
by
BRIT HUME

1974
DOUBLEDAY & COMPANY, INC.
Garden City, New York

ISBN: 0-385-06526-4
LIBRARY OF CONGRESS CATALOG CARD NUMBER: 73–83640
COPYRIGHT © 1974 BY BRIT HUME
ALL RIGHTS RESERVED
PRINTED IN THE UNITED STATES OF AMERICA
FIRST EDITION

For George Hume

INSIDE STORY

ONE

When I first went to work for Jack Anderson, I was assigned a desk in the back room of the office. The room was also the kitchen, supply room, file room and reference library, and it also contained the Xerox machine, which was in constant use. But there was a rug on the floor and I had the place to myself most of the time. For several years I had been working in the din and gloom of several newspaper city rooms and a wire-service bureau, and after that, my kitchen office seemed luxurious. Besides, I didn't go to work there for the physical surroundings. Jack Anderson was Drew Pearson's successor as proprietor of the most widely syndicated column in America, "The Washington Merry-Go-Round." I joined him because I expected Jack Anderson would be involved in some major stories about the misdeeds of those in power in Washington, and that was the kind of journalism that interested me.

I hadn't been there very long before one of those stories came along. I was sitting at my desk in the kitchen in early March, 1970, when Les Whitten, Jack's senior assistant, came across the hall from Jack's office wearing a sly grin.

"Hey," he said, "one of Jack's sources in California's on the phone. He says George Murphy's been on the Technicolor Company payroll ever since he's been in the Senate."

If true, that was quite a story. George Murphy was a Republican senator from California. A genial, likable man with a twinkle in his eye, he had once been a movie actor and song-and-dance man. Since his election to the Senate in 1964, he had been one of its most conservative members. Technicolor was owned by Patrick Frawley, a multimillionaire who had made a fortune in ballpoint pens, then acquired control of the Schick Razor company

1

before buying Technicolor, Inc., the firm that pioneered in color movies. He was a right-wing activist who had pumped large amounts of corporate money into his favorite political causes. Taking income from any corporation was an obvious impropriety for a senator. In this case, however, the conflict of interest was howling. Murphy's voting record and stands on issues would match Frawley's ideological predilections almost perfectly. Besides that, Frawley was widely regarded as an extremist.

"Does the source have proof?" I asked Les.

"I don't know, Jack's still talking to him," he replied, heading back across the hall.

I got up and walked into Jack's office. He had just gotten back from a lecture trip and his overnight bag was standing on his desk. He looked tired. The conversation was drawing to a close.

"Well, you've always been right before," he was saying. "I'll get to work on it right away. I hope you'll give us a chance to break this one before you say anything to anyone else . . . I know you will . . . Many, many thanks . . . I'll let you know right away . . . Good-by."

"What's he got?" Les asked eagerly once Jack had put down the phone.

Jack looked up and smiled. "Technicolor has been paying Murphy $20,000 a year as a consultant. They're also picking up Murphy's apartment rent here in town and giving him use of company credit cards."

"Does he have proof?" Les and I asked simultaneously.

"No, just the word of someone he says is reliable. I believe him, but we can't go on the strength of that. Apparently, Murphy got the arrangement cleared with the Senate Ethics Committee."

"What are you going to do?" I asked.

"Call Murphy and try to get him to admit it. I think that's the only way. What do you two think?"

"Suppose he denies it?" asked Les.

"Then we'll have to try something else. But if it's true, I don't think he'll deny it."

Jack picked up the phone and dialed the Capitol. "Senator Murphy's office, please . . . thank you . . . Is the senator in? This is Jack Anderson calling . . . Oh, he is. Do you know where I can reach him? . . . You will . . . Well, I'd appreciate it. Yes, 347-4325. Thank you."

Jack hung up the phone. "He's in California, but they said they'll be hearing from him this afternoon and they'll have him call me."

Opal Ginn, Jack's secretary, who had been standing in the doorway during the conversation, came in and shooed Les and myself out so that Jack could take a nap on his office sofa. A large, rangy woman with short, reddish hair, Opal had been with Jack for twelve years and she was loyal to him in a way that, at times, was almost maternal. Frequently, Jack and I would look up when I was in his office to find Opal standing in the doorway, hands on hips, wearing a reproachful expression. "Jack's got to get the column out," she would say, glancing at the clock on the wall. "And he can't do it with you in here taking up his time." Everyone was used to being chased out of Jack's office by Opal.

A couple of hours later, I heard Opal get up from her desk in the office next to Jack's and walk quickly the few steps down the hall to Jack's office. She opened the door. "Jack," she said, "it's George Murphy calling from California. He's on 26."

When I got across the hall, Opal had switched on the light and Jack, shoes off and necktie down, was squinting as he groped his way to the telephone. He cleared his throat.

"Hello," he said. "Oh, Senator, how are you? It's good to hear your voice."

This effusive greeting seemed a little much to me, under the circumstances, but this was characteristic of Jack. He was always palsy toward politicians on a personal level. He acted as if he liked them, and many of them, even those who fared badly in the column, seemed genuinely to like him.

"Senator," Jack was saying. "I've received information that for some years now, you've had an arrangement with Technicolor, probably something that carried over from your days in Hollywood, whereby they pay you $20,000 a year . . ."

Opal and I stood across the desk from Jack, staring intently at him for any sign of Murphy's reaction. When Jack stopped talking, he made no move to take notes, and his expression was downcast. It was evident that Murphy had interrupted with an outright denial. Disappointed, I turned and started to walk out of the room. Just then I heard Jack raise his voice as if to interrupt.

"Well, Senator," he said, "I think you should know that I've been talking to the Senate Ethics Committee. I don't want to say anything to give away my source, but I understand you have gotten clearance from them for this. I understand it involves $20,000 a year in consultant's fees, rent on your Washington apartment, and the use of some of the company's credit cards. Now, for all I know, this is perfectly proper, but I thought it my duty to at least look into it."

There was a brief pause, for effect, and then Jack went on.

"Now, Senator, you and I have been friends for a long time. I don't think you want to be quoted as denying this whole thing. So, because we've been friends, I'll forget what you said before and give you another chance, in fairness."

Jack lifted his left shoulder to hold the receiver to the side of his head and began hunting frantically for pen and paper. He never seemed to have a notebook handy. He found a felt-tip pen but no notebook, just an envelope. He began scribbling furiously on the back of it. Although I was standing over him on the other side of the desk, there was no way I could tell what he was writing because Jack made notes in an unintelligible mixture of shorthand, words spelled out, and abbreviations of his own invention. As he wrote, Jack interrupted only twice. The first time he said,

4

"What about the apartment rent?" and the second time he said, "And the credit cards?" There was more scribbling after each question, and I knew that Murphy was confessing.

I was amazed. There is nothing unique about a newsman trying to pretend he knows more than he actually does in the hope of coaxing an acknowledgment out of a guilty official. But it is rare that once a denial has been made that a person can be persuaded to reverse his field. Yet this is what Jack had done, with his white lie about talking to the Ethics Committee. If Murphy had had time to think, he might have realized that it was most unlikely that Jack had learned anything from the committee. It is one of the most tight-lipped operations in town and it exists to protect, not to investigate, senators. Its chairman, Mississippi's John Stennis, is a rock of integrity, but also of discretion. He would never tell a newsman about his confidential discussions of an ethical question with a fellow senator. The only other person privy to the Murphy arrangement with Frawley was committee counsel Ben Fern, a former navy captain who took his orders from Stennis and kept his mouth shut. Yet Jack's source had given him enough accurate detail, so that when he began reciting it, Murphy was impressed, and enough so that he was afraid Jack had all the facts anyway, so there was no use denying them. But Jack wasn't finished.

"You say there was no conflict and I've always known you to be honest," he was telling Murphy, "so I'm inclined to take your word for it. I'm not sure what I'm going to do with this information but I do want to look into it a bit further before I make a decision. I hope you will do me the favor of not saying anything about it until I've had a few more days to work on it."

Now this really took nerve. Murphy obviously knew his deal with Frawley was highly improper or he wouldn't have denied it when Jack first asked him about it. A United States senator is simply not supposed to be in the hire of anyone besides the taxpayers. What Jack was really asking Murphy, of course, was to

5

give him time to break the ruinous news exclusively. His comments about Murphy's honesty and his uncertainty about what to do with the information were intended to give the senator some hope Jack might decide not to publish it. How anyone could have believed such a thing is beyond me. Jack was the number-one muckraker in America, accused sometimes of finding impropriety where none existed. Could he possibly be expected to sit on a scandalous deal like this? All Jack wanted, of course, was to avoid having Murphy rush out a statement on the Frawley arrangement himself during the three or four days it would take to get a column into print. Such a statement by Murphy would rob Jack of his exclusive and get Murphy's version out first.

Jack hung up, leaned back in his chair, and grinned broadly. By now, everyone in the office was in the room. "It's all true," he said. "The salary, the credit cards, everything, except the company only pays *half* his apartment rent." Everyone laughed. Jack chuckled a little and shook his head. "He denied it at first, but after I told him I'd been talking to the Ethics Committee and gave some of the details, he said, 'Say, you really have been talking to the Ethics Committee?' "

"Do you think it'll hold for four days?" Les wondered.

"I don't know. I think I sewed him up. He's hoping we won't write anything. Opal, call the syndicate and tell them we won't have the Wednesday column today. Tell them we're going to put it out on Sunday. And get me those back columns on Dodd and Frawley and the one about [Senator Thomas] Kuchel and Frawley. Also, find out if Technicolor has any government contracts, particularly any with agencies that might be under the jurisdiction of the committees Murphy's on. I guess you'll have to come in Sunday to move the column."

Opal left the room, but Les and I stayed to hear more about Murphy. "You know," Jack said, "it's a funny thing about these conservatives. I've always found that they're more honest, or at least more candid, than the liberals. Even the crooks. A liberal might never have come out and admitted this the way Murphy did. But the conservatives don't seem to like to lie. Maybe they just don't feel as guilty about the things they do."

"What papers will this be in out there?" I asked. "I know we're not in the Los Angeles *Times* anymore."

"Oh, we're all over California," Jack said. "We've got something like fifty papers out there. We're in San Francisco, Fresno, Sacramento. We're in one of the San Diego papers but it's a Copley paper, so they just buy it but never run it. But we're all over the state. That's one of the things that worries me. One of the papers might just decide to call up Murphy, get him to confirm it, and publish their own story ahead of the column. It's so hot that I'm afraid it'll leak out. Especially with Murphy up for re-election this year. Well, we'll just have to hope it doesn't. That's one reason I'm just as glad we don't have time to mail it out today. If we put it out Sunday, the syndicate won't mail it until late that day and it probably won't get to most of the papers out there until Tuesday."

The column about Murphy was utterly typical of Jack's writing. Although it was the biggest story he had published in some time, he wrapped it up in thirteen paragraphs and devoted the rest of the column to two other stories. Jack never took any chances on boring his readers. The language was vintage "Washington Merry-Go-Round"—colloquial, irreverent, and not always grammatical. Patrick Frawley was described not as the Schick executive who contributed to conservative political causes, but as the "Schick razor king," who was a "sugar daddy for right-wing causes." The column told how Frawley's firm had been "helping to foot the bill for Murphy's plush Washington apartment." In the "Merry-Go-Round," people rarely paid for anything, they "footed the bill." No big shot ever had just an apartment, he had a "plush" apartment. And poor Murphy. Jack was not about to let him forget his days tap-dancing and making movies.

"The easy-smiling, light-stepping Murphy," he wrote, "appeared in 45 motion pictures, including a few Technicolor extravaganzas, before he traded in his box office appeal at the voting booth."

But for all the slang and the corny images about Murphy's Hollywood days, the column was not one-sided. The last four paragraphs were devoted to Murphy's explanation of the arrangement with Technicolor and his insistence that it involved no conflict of interest. No editor could complain that the story was unfair, or incomplete.

Over the weekend, I watched the papers apprehensively for some sign of the Murphy story. I spoke to Jack about it by phone. Nothing had broken by the time the column was transmitted to the syndicate in New York for mailing. Apparently Murphy was keeping quiet.

There was, of course, much more to our worry about losing the story than the ordinary journalistic desire to be first with the news. We all felt that the Murphy story would help to prove something, namely, that Jack Anderson had aimed "The Washington Merry-Go-Round" in a new direction since he had taken over after Drew Pearson's death the previous September—a direction that made its disclosures worthy of the close attention of other newsmen.

Under Pearson, the column had been an unpredictable mix of muckraking, crusading, and personal commentary. Corrupt officials had gone to jail because of Pearson's reporting and countless stories had been told that never would have without him. Even Pearson's enemies conceded that his mere presence made honest men of many officials who might otherwise not have been. With his distinctive appearance, dignified and gentle manner, he was an international celebrity and one of the journalistic giants of the century. His friendships reached the highest levels of government, to men like Chief Justice Earl Warren, Senator Wayne Morse, and, late in Pearson's career, President Lyndon Johnson. But Pearson was tendentious, an arch-liberal, at times a careless reporter. His friendships in high places sometimes made him appear an apologist, especially for Lyndon Johnson during the Vietnam

War. He had a sentimental streak and his writing could become almost mawkish. "Yes," he wrote after President Johnson left Washington, "Lyndon Johnson loved the White House."

Jack Anderson, by contrast, was almost purely a newspaperman. He had dug out many of the exposés that kept Pearson's name in the headlines, including the Sherman Adams–Bernard Goldfine case during the Eisenhower administration and, later, the Dodd case. He was perhaps the most resourceful reporter in Washington. "Drew was more of a reformer," Jack would say. "I think I'm more of a reporter."

But Jack was relatively unknown, and he seemed, as one friend put it, "sort of a pastel character" compared to Pearson. In the months since he had taken over the column, Jack had refrained from writing commentary or pure opinion, sticking instead to investigative reporting and inside stories, his strength. In hiring Les Whitten, he had obtained the assistance of a man of similar inclination and experience as well as prodigious energy. Neither was a pundit and neither wanted to be. As Jack once wrote of himself, "I do not observe the Washington scene from Olympian heights. I am neither historian nor scholar. I like to think I am an investigative reporter. I poke into the shadows of government, searching with a small light for the facts that officials would prefer to keep in the dark. I have a tendency to stray from orthodox news trails and I blunder into many dead ends. But while others are occupied with the imposing view out front, I catch an occasional glimpse behind the scenes."

When I had first read these modest words, in the preface to one of Jack's books, I had found them inspiring. They expressed precisely the feeling we all shared about the purpose of the column. Yet for all its circulation and popularity, the "Merry-Go-Round" frequently lacked the impact to create more than a one-day embarrassment for an official caught in some wrongdoing. This was because the reputation for factual carelessness and ideological bias the column had acquired under Pearson, in addition, no doubt, to a measure of professional jealousy, made other reporters reluctant to follow up the stories the column broke. The column was different, now, but there wasn't much evidence anyone had noticed. Numerous stories we had thought were important had passed seemingly unnoticed by the rest of the media, and many editors, such as those at the Washington *Post*, felt free to treat the column in as highhanded a manner as they pleased.

What was needed was stories so big they couldn't be ignored, which would call attention to the column and make it plain that Jack Anderson and those who worked for him were serious about investigative reporting and capable of doing it well. This is why there was such excitement about the George Murphy affair. It was a major story whose accuracy was unassailable, because Murphy had confirmed it himself.

Tuesday morning came without any word of leakage and everyone was relieved. Most clients would only then be getting the column, and, with its release set for the next day, there was little time for an effort to scoop it. No one even tried, however, and the Murphy story hit simultaneously in California and across the country. The reaction in Washington was modest, at first. But in California, the story was an instant sensation. The mighty Los Angeles *Times*, having dropped the column, found itself rushing to catch up with less esteemed publications such as the San Francisco *Chronicle*, which still subscribed. Murphy confirmed the facts to the *Times*, which carried a front-page story on it the next day. By this time, the wire services had picked it up, and their follow-up reports made the Washington papers. A few days later, Warren Weaver, national political reporter for the New York *Times*, wrote a lengthy, front-page story on the Murphy affair, crediting Jack for breaking it and suggesting that it would strongly affect Murphy's re-election chances.

Weaver was right. Murphy never recovered. Although he survived his Republican primary contest with industrialist Norton Simon, the Frawley scandal haunted him throughout the general election. Polls showed California voters overwhelmingly disapproved of it. Democratic Congressman John Tunney, Murphy's challenger, made one of his principal campaign promises that he would be "on only one payroll." Tunney won. The column had scored a direct hit.

But, in a sense, it turned out to be almost too direct. The story had been so unassailable, so easily confirmed by other media that there was never a moment of controversy over its credibility, never a period of doubt from which Jack could emerge vindicated. While the scandal lived on, people soon forgot who originally broke it. It certainly helped Jack's standing, especially in California. But it would take others like it to build the kind of reputation we all wanted.

TWO

The column's need to observe high standards and establish credibility had been drummed into me from the first day I walked into Jack Anderson's office looking for a job. I had heard that Anderson was looking for a young investigative reporter to fill out his staff, and so I telephoned him and asked to be considered. He asked me to come to his office right away. It was late in the afternoon of January 2, 1970, when I got off the elevator on the ninth floor of an office building a few blocks from the White House and began looking for a door with Anderson's name on it.

The door I was looking for was held open by a boyish-looking man who was talking to someone in the front room of the office. As I approached, he looked at me with an amused expression, smiled, stuck out his hand and said, "Hi, I'm Jack Anderson." Well, I knew what Anderson looked like and I knew this wasn't he, but I was nervous and I didn't know what else to do so I shook hands and said my name. He laughed and said he was Les Whitten. It was a name I had been reading often recently in Anderson's column, referred to by the columnist as "my associate."

I went in and found Anderson himself seated at a spare desk in the reception room of the office. He was in the midst of a phone conversation, which he had interrupted to bid Whitten good-by. He waved me to a chair and continued his call. He was wearing a dark suit, a chartreuse turtleneck jersey, and black slip-on shoes with short socks that matched his jersey. The reason I could tell the color of his socks was that he was sitting alongside the desk with one of his legs stretched across it and his shoe, partially off, dangled from the end of his foot. "Oh, I know all about it," he spoke up in his deep, loud, and slightly nasal voice. "Congressman Dante Fascell has promised to work with us exclusively on the story . . . Yes . . . Yes . . . Well, I appreciate it . . . You're great. Thanks. Bye."

He put down the receiver and stood up, wiggling his foot back into his shoe. As he had been talking, he looked and sounded like the man I thought him to be—confident, self-assertive, even boastful. There was a certain severity both in his voice and his expression. He looked much as he did in photographs, except for one thing. His hair, once parted near the middle, was now combed forward and across the front, apparently to conceal a receding hairline. He was just under six feet tall, with an athletic, muscular build, except for his ample waistline and a certain over-all fleshiness that might have been the result of his graduation from being Drew Pearson's legman to a full-fledged columnist. He had a pale complexion and his face was marked by a prominent nose and a stern expression. As we shook hands, though, the severe tone and stern expression vanished. He was suddenly warm and easygoing with a broad, genial smile. "I sure appreciate your coming down," he said. "Things have been kind of hectic here with Les and me trying to get out seven columns a week. We need some more help and I had been hoping to make a decision on hiring someone this week. Have you got any clippings that I can take a look at?"

Two months earlier, I had published a short article in the *Atlantic* on the United Mine Workers scandal, and I gave Jack a copy. He resumed his chair at the secretary's desk and began reading. After only a few minutes, he stood up and said, "Well, at least it looks like you can write well enough. Let's go back to my office."

I was struck by the decor of the suite, or the lack of it. The walls were white and largely bare. There was carpeting, but it was beige, stained and flattened by wear. In Anderson's own office there were none of the framed diplomas, awards, or photographs so common to the offices of prominent people, no mementos, no plaques, no knickknacks. The furniture appeared to be straight from the showroom of an office supply house, serviceable, but utterly impersonal.

The only unusual feature was a kitchen across the hall from Anderson's own office at the rear of the suite. It served also as a file room, Xerox copying room, storage room, and extra office. The kitchen, I learned, was left over from the days when Howard Hughes's organization had rented the entire floor of the building.

Anderson's office was dominated by a L-shaped desk littered with papers, some of them accumulated in stacks, others just lying about. Behind his swivel chair, against the wall, was a much smaller desk on which sat the one piece of equipment that might have identified this as the office of a newspaperman. It was an old Royal standard typewriter, brown with green keys. Once a day, Anderson would turn around in his chair, face the wall, and, in his stop-and-go fashion, pound out the column which would be read several days later by an audience that might number up to 45 million. When he talked of the column and its popularity, a little of the boastful, braying tone returned to his voice. I sat quietly while he lectured me.

"The column appears in six hundred newspapers," he said. "That's more than any other column. It has enormous impact. I would instantly fire anyone who ever used the column to threaten or blackmail anyone. But the power of the column is well known and the threat is felt although it is never stated. Sometimes we lose stories because once we start looking into something, action is taken to correct it before we can publish the story. Sometimes we lose stories because it takes three or four days from the time the column is written until it appears. That's one of the hazards of the column business. It happened recently in the McCormack case. We had the story about the influence-peddling operation being run out of the Speaker's office before anyone else, but after we sent the column out, he heard about it. He fired Martin Sweig, the aide who was the key figure. The Washington *Post* called to tell us the news had caught up with the column and they weren't going to run it. Instead, they ran a story about the firing on page one and used all of our information, without any credit.

"We have to work fast in this business, but we have to be careful, because the column has something of a reputation for inaccuracy and we need to overcome that. I've told Les and Joe Spear, who also works with me, time and again that a fact is not a fact for our column until it's been proven.

"I don't think anyone around here works a forty-hour week. When I worked for Drew, I was almost never in the office. I was up on Capitol Hill every day, and over at the Pentagon. I wrote the stories at night and turned them in the next morning. Drew never paid me more than $13,000 even after I became a full-fledged partner. Most of my income came from being the Washington bureau chief for *Parade*. I spent my weekends working on articles for *Parade* which I had been putting together in my spare time during the week. You have to learn to juggle a lot of things at once, because some stories fall through and you have to have others to turn to. And you should always keep one eye out for the really big story. I worked nights and part time on the Dodd case for almost a year before I even told Drew about it. By then, it was almost ready to go."

I interrupted to say that I knew the case of Senator Thomas Dodd well because I had been working for UPI in Connecticut during the height of the scandal—Dodd was from Connecticut. I told how I had done a three-part series on the case which UPI had killed, fearing a lawsuit.

"One of the reasons I'm interested in working here," I said, "is that in the other news organizations where I've worked, an investigative reporter spends half his time digging up information and the rest trying to get it published. I know I won't have that problem here."

Les Whitten had rejoined us by now and he was sitting on the sofa adjacent to the chair where I sat, his collar open and necktie down. The conversation rambled a bit, as Les and Jack talked about the column and its ability to get information the government would prefer to keep hidden.

"When I came here," Les said, "I was surprised to find out that Jack and I had many of the same sources. The difference now is that where these people used to give me their secondary stuff and save their better stuff for someone like Jack, I'm now getting the best stories, the ones I used to wonder why I couldn't get before when I worked for Hearst. Being with the column has opened a lot of doors. I've been in this business for twenty years and I've never worked harder or liked it more."

At one point, the discussion turned to the penchant of people in power for telling anything but the truth. Whitten said, "You know, Jack, I think Lyndon Johnson enjoyed lying. He used to lie when it didn't matter if he told the truth. He preferred to lie. It made him feel good."

I loved that. Most Washington reporters I had met, particularly those who had been around as long as Whitten, took the politicians they covered far too seriously to make such an irreverent crack. Even worse, they took themselves too seriously. But here were two veteran reporters kicking it around, laughing about the utter incorrigibility of a former President of the United States. This was the atmosphere I had been looking for.

It was long past dinnertime when I arrived in my battered Volkswagen convertible at the small house northwest of Washington where I lived with my wife and two children. Jack Anderson had not firmly offered me a job, but he had made it clear that I was his choice, barring some unexpected bad recommendation from the people he intended to ask about me over the weekend. He had seemed to like me, comparing me at one point to himself when he first went to work for Drew Pearson in 1947. I was now twenty-six, two years older than he was when he started with the column.

I had warned him that I could bring nothing like the sources of information to the column that someone like Whitten had brought when he came to work the previous fall, a few months after Pearson's death. Although I was born and raised in Washington, I had been back here working for only a year. My first two and a half years in the news business had been spent with the Hartford *Times* and with UPI in Connecticut. After that, we moved to Washington to live, but at first I had commuted to Baltimore to work for the *Evening Sun*. In early 1969, I had left there to go on a one-semester fellowship at the Washington Journalism Center. In my spare time, I began work on the book about the United Mine Workers. Now most of the research was done and the money the publisher had advanced me was running out. I needed a job for that reason, but that wasn't all. It had been frustrating to work on a major scandal, digging up material that might have made headlines without being able to do anything with it. I had longed to be back working for the daily press. Anderson had not seemed troubled that I didn't have an extensive collection of Washington sources. "Don't worry," he told me, "there's plenty of leads coming in over the transom to keep you busy." I was elated as I walked into the house that night. My wife, Clare, once she had been persuaded that I would still carry on with the book, shared my excitement.

I was still in bed when the phone rang the following Monday morning. "Hi," said a familiar deep voice cheerfully, "it's Jack. The people I've talked to gave you ringing endorsements. The job is yours if you want it."

"Well, that's wonderful," I said. "But when would you want me to start work?"

"As soon as possible. What about today? Come on in and we'll get you started and put you on the payroll right away."

I had expected I would have a couple of weeks more to work on the book, but I wasn't going to let that stand in the way now. I was in the office before noon.

I hadn't been at my desk in the multipurpose kitchen—it was the only space available—long before I got some shattering news. Joseph Yablonski, the reform candidate who had challenged United Mine Workers President Tony Boyle in the recent union election, had been found murdered, along with his wife and daughter, in his home in Pennsylvania. I had followed the campaign closely for my book and had come to know Yablonski and his family. It had been a bitter campaign, but no one expected the climax to be a triple murder. I was badly shaken.

I burst into Jack's office across the hall and told him the news. He reacted with concern, but I sensed this was more in deference to my feelings than a reflection of his own. It was not long before he was wondering what the column might be able to publish about the case.

"We can't let these buggers get away with this kind of thing. What can we do to help? Is there something that you know about because of your book that we can break?" he asked.

This, I soon found, was characteristic. The column was seldom far from Jack's thoughts. I told him how Yablonski had repeatedly sought a federal investigation of the way the union election was being conducted by Boyle and his men, how Yablonski had been beaten up at one campaign stop and asked for FBI protection afterward, all to no avail.

"I think that's a hell of a story," Jack said. "This guy wanted the government to enforce the law. Nobody paid any attention to him and now he and his wife and daughter are dead. That's a hell of a story. Do you think anyone else has this?"

"I doubt that anyone knows all this as well as I do," I replied. "The national press hasn't really paid much attention to the UMW scandal. Yablonski feared violence throughout the campaign."

"All right. I want you to give me a draft column on the way the government spurned Yablonski's requests for an investigation. Of course you'll have to check with his aides. Find out how they feel about it. If they are bitter about this, as I'm sure they are, we'll report that. Now we can't say the union had anything to do with this. But we can say that Yablonski's friends and supporters feared what union hotheads—use that word, hotheads—might do if there were no investigation."

The column I drafted for Jack was strongly worded. I had talked to Yablonski's lawyer and his campaign press secretary, who happened to be a close friend, and had gotten all the details of the repeated requests for action that had been made to the Labor and Justice Departments. And Jack was right about the attitude of the slain man's supporters. They were openly blaming the government. After Jack had finished editing the column the next day, it was even stronger, though no less accurate. It was satisfying to feel that at last my knowledge of this case would be used where it would have impact. Jack now had some more instructions.

"I want you to go up to the funeral," he said, "and while you're up there, approach the investigating authorities, whoever they are. In a case like this, they're bound to know more than they're saying publicly. Maybe they only have some theories about the killings. If you use my name, I think you'll get in to see whoever's in charge and I think you'll find they'll be willing to tell you things they aren't telling the rest of the press. That's always been my experience, anyway."

Jack explained how such a direct approach had enabled him to learn the inside story of the closed-door inquest into the death of Mary Jo Kopechne in Senator Edward Kennedy's car on Chappaquiddick Island. Jack had been severely criticized for some of the stories he had written about the Chappaquiddick incident by other reporters who thought his information most imaginary. I knew that his information about the inquest wasn't imaginary, though. I had already found copies of transcripts of the proceedings in my desk my first day on the job.

I tried my best with the Pennsylvania authorities, but I had no luck. They acted as though I was crazy. I just didn't have the hang of it. Still, I felt as I headed back to Washington on Friday that my first week with Jack Anderson had been a success. I had been able to give him a hard-hitting inside story on the biggest news event of the week. I wondered how Secretary of Labor George Shultz, the man who had decided that the Labor Department should take no action regarding the union election until it was over, had felt when he read the full story of his performance in Jack's column in the *Post* that morning.

But when I got back to Washington that night, I learned that Shultz did not read about himself in Jack's column that morning. Neither did anyone else who read the Washington *Post*, for the *Post* had called at the last minute to announce the column was being killed. No reason was given.

I was infuriated by the *Post*'s refusal to publish the Yablonski column, but Jack took it calmly. "We can't spend our time worrying about the Washington *Post*," he said. "We've got hundreds of other clients. The *Post* is important because it's our window in Washington, but if they dropped us tomorrow, we'd still be the biggest column in the country. They've got a bunch of Georgetown drawing room journalists over there who have never liked the column. They'd kick us out tomorrow if they thought they could get away with it. The only things that keep us in there is the column's popularity and the only way we can stay in there is to write the kind of column people read. Drew would never let the *Post* dictate the kind of column he wrote and I won't either. Usually when they kill a column like this, it backfires, because people find out about it and everybody wants to know why the *Post* wouldn't run it. We've got to try to get the kinds of stories they can't kill because it would be too embarrassing, the kinds of stories the rest of the press can't ignore."

THREE

One of Jack's operating principles was never to retreat from public controversy. He thought such fracases did the column good. Drew Pearson's public feuds with people like Harry Truman and Douglas MacArthur were as famous as any of his more conventional journalistic exploits: Jack did not find any adversaries as famous as Truman or MacArthur in the early days after he took over the column. But Jack did get into one scrape that grew out of a column no one in the office ever thought would stir more than a flicker of reaction. Instead, it drew Jack into the center of a 1970 election campaign.

The column in question was a jerry-built affair, put together from two separate stories, one developed by Joe Spear, the fourth member of Jack's reporting team, and the other by Jack himself. Spear's information concerned the lieutenant governor of Nevada, Ed Fike, a Republican, who was running for the governorship to succeed the retiring Paul Laxalt, also a Republican and one of the most popular politicians in the state's history. Fike appeared headed for an easy victory with a well-financed campaign in a Republican state against a relatively unknown Democrat named Donal "Mike" O'Callaghan.

Spear's story, based largely on official documents, showed that while in office, Fike had been an official of a company which bought some land from the state. The Nevada conflict-of-interest laws prohibit a state officer from being "in any manner interested" in any contract "authorized by or for the state." Since a sale contract technically fits the terms of the law, Fike had clearly violated it. The other facts, which Jack developed, were that a campaign appearance in Las Vegas by Vice President Agnew had been advertised on gambling-casino marquees, in violation of a state law against corporate participation in elections. Also, Jack found, Governor Laxalt had violated a state regulation by excusing state employees to greet the Vice President. These were hardly major disclosures and only Agnew's presence enabled Jack to weave them into a lead story for the column, pegged to the idea that these were "law and order" Republicans violating the law. We all considered it a weak column. But it appeared on Wednesday, October 14, just a few weeks before the elections, and created a terrific fuss in Nevada.

By coincidence, Jack flew into Reno, to give a lecture, two days after the column appeared. A group of newsmen greeted him at the airport to tell him that Governor Laxalt had denounced the column and charged that it was an outside effort to aid the Democrats. This was a familiar response to a newspaper exposé. We had all heard it dozens of times. It has two objectives. One is to avoid dealing with the specific charges, which are probably true, by making a blanket denial of wrongdoing. The other is to distract public attention from the issue by accusing the press of being in league with the political opposition. Jack had long since developed a stock rejoinder for such responses—he would challenge the accused official to a televised debate. This usually ended the controversy, because few intelligent politicians are willing to give Jack a forum even larger than the column to repeat his accusations, as well as appear side by side, and thereby implicitly on equal footing, with him. Naturally, Jack trotted out his debate challenge for Laxalt at the airport news conference in Reno. Then he went about his business, assuming that would end that.

But to his astonishment, Laxalt accepted the challenge readily. "I look forward to facing a man before the public who calls the President of the United States a liar," Laxalt told newsmen, apparently in reference to some earlier column challenging the truth of some presidential pronouncement. "This proves that the Democrats are turning to outside help in their political races, especially

Democratic gubernatorial candidate Mike O'Callaghan. O'Callaghan has spent too much time out of this state and he seems to forget that Nevadans don't like outside influence. Anderson's column was a planted smear by the O'Callaghan forces. I can't have too much respect for a man of this type, and I'm certainly looking forward to the confrontation on television. I just hope the details can be worked out."

All this occurred on a Friday, but I didn't hear about it until Monday. Jack returned from the West and began planning how to get the columns out early so that he could go back to Nevada for the debate. I heard the news from Opal. Jack, busy and unconcerned, didn't mention it. It worried me right away. Paul Laxalt was a handsome and poised man, in addition to being extremely popular. Besides that, he was a former trial lawyer who would obviously know how to handle himself in a debate. His eagerness was a further sign that Jack would need to be well prepared. But there was no sign that Jack was boning up, or that he even saw much need to. He had had Joe Spear gather his documentation for the charge against Fike, but it sat untouched on Jack's desk all day Monday and Tuesday. The debate was set for Wednesday evening. I called Jack at home the night before to see if he were ready.

"Well, I haven't had much time to prepare," he said, "I've had to rush to get the columns ready before I go."

"Aren't you worried about this?" I asked.

"No, not really," he said blandly. "I don't have anything to lose. I'm not running for anything. Any way I come out of this, I win, because this will be on state-wide television and the exposure will be good for the column."

"Yeah," I said, "but suppose you really come out of it looking bad?"

"I'm not too worried. I think I can do okay."

I called Opal to find out what she thought. She had been bombarded with calls from an aide to Senator Howard Cannon, the incumbent Democratic senator from Nevada, who was well ahead in his re-election bid but was afraid that this controversy could damage him. Cannon's man wanted Jack to withdraw. Opal was normally Jack's number-one booster, expressing almost unlimited confidence in him. But even she was concerned. The Republicans, brimming with confidence, had taken out large advertisements for the debate in the state's newspapers. Yet Jack was as blithe as ever when he left the office the next morning for the airport. I followed him into the hallway to say good-by and wish him luck. He must have seen concern in my expression.

"Hey, look," he said with a smile, "stop worrying. Anytime we can take on the governor of a state on television, we are winning, no matter what happens."

"But are you prepared?" I asked.

"Well, not yet. But I've got all of Joe's documents and I'm going to study them on the plane."

Terrific, I thought. Jack was going out to face an experienced, attractive, popular politician in his own home territory with him itching for the battle. And Jack was going to get ready on the way out. In retrospect, a showdown in a remote spot like Nevada doesn't seem so worrisome. But at the time, it made me uncomfortable just to think about it. With all of us striving to improve the column's credibility, the last thing we wanted was a televised fiasco, even in the nation's most sparsely populated state.

Of course, Jack did have one important ally in Las Vegas. He was Herman "Hank" Greenspun, a longtime personal friend, who was the editor and owner of the morning Las Vegas *Sun*. This was not the paper in which the column appeared, but it could be counted upon to give Jack much stronger support than the evening *Review-Journal*, which carried the column but was supporting the Republicans. Greenspun was an old-fashioned, two-fisted frontier newspaperman who wrote a front-page column entitled "Where I Stand," in which he expressed views that can best be described as frenzied. He had instantly seized on Jack's column and begun clamoring for an explanation from the Republicans. When Fike and Laxalt had tried to brush off the charges as politically motivated, Greenspun answered with an angry column, declaring, "A flippant accusation is no substitute for a plain answer." Greenspun's militance had no doubt been a factor in Laxalt's decision to accept Jack's debate challenge.

That Wednesday passed with agonizing slowness as we waited for some word from Las Vegas. The wait was made longer by the fact that there was a two-hour time difference. Finally, about eleven o'clock Eastern Time, I got impatient and put through a call to Jack's hotel room. He answered in a hurried, distracted voice.

"Hi," I said, "it's Brit. How did it go?"

"Uh, fine," he responded, still distracted. "Look, can I talk to you later? I'm in the middle of a press conference."

Well, that told me nothing at all, except that the debate was over. We had to wait until he got back the next day for the full report. When we heard it, we could hardly believe it. Jack looked weary when he came in that afternoon, but he was in high spirits. Everyone gathered in his office to hear the story. As he told it, he paused frequently to shake his head and chuckle, and his sentences were punctuated repeatedly with giggles.

"Oh," he said, "it was all very formal. They held it at a TV studio that turned out to be owned, in part, by the governor's brother. I was playing the underdog, so I made good use of that. The moderator was a local judge. The rules were that we would have ten minutes each, then five minutes each. You couldn't interrupt while the other guy was talking. Laxalt was very cordial when I met him backstage. He said, 'Well, you're the challenger, so you go first.' Well, I wasn't going to let him do that, so I said, 'No, let's be fair. We'll flip a coin.' He could hardly say no to that."

"Not in Las Vegas," Les said.

"No," said Jack, "not in Las Vegas. So we flipped. And he

27

lost. I made him go first, naturally. So he started out attacking me as an outsider and a member of the 'eastern press' and he said the charges were a political smear and an attempt by outsiders to tell the people of Nevada how to handle their affairs, and on and on like that. He really laid it on with this eastern press business. I really was surprised. He said I had aimed to smear honorable officials of the state with good reputations but that instead I had missed my target and insulted the people of Nevada."

"Is that all he said?" I asked.

"Well, he went on a lot longer than that, but that's the gist of it. When my turn came, I started off by asking, 'You may wonder why I have come all the way out here at my own expense to face the most popular and charming governor in the West on his own home ground in a television studio owned by his brother. Well, I'll tell you why. It's because I believe somebody has to stand up to the politicians.' "

Everyone roared at that. "You called him a politician right off, eh?" I said.

"That's right," said Jack, laughing. "Always call them politicians. They can't deny it and it has a negative connotation. Anyway, he had chosen to play the demagogue, so I figured I was entitled to play the same game.

"I told how I wasn't an eastern newsman at all, I explained that I was born and raised in Salt Lake City by Mormon parents. About half of Nevada is Mormon and 80 per cent of them are Republicans. He must not have known I was a Mormon, because you should have seen the look on his face. Poor bugger.

"I went on about how my mother had driven a taxicab to raise the money so that I could go on a mission for the church when I was nineteen. I said my parents had always taught me to tell the truth and to seek the truth, and obey the law. I held up the documents and said I had evidence the law had been broken. I said, 'I wrote about violations of law. Law-and-order candidates have broken the law. The violations are flagrant. The violations are easy to document.' I said that in Utah, the people take the law seriously and consider it a serious matter when anyone violates it, no matter who it is. I said I was sure the people of Nevada felt the same way."

By now, we were all whooping with laughter. Laxalt had really underestimated his opponent. Jack had done little preparation, but the governor had obviously done even less. His presentation was just an elaboration of what he had been saying to the newspapers in the days before the debate. He undoubtedly had been sure he could make Jack go first, so that he would have the last word. That was foolish enough. But the worst of it was that he had not done any checking into Jack and his background. Not knowing that Jack was a Mormon was disastrous. But if Laxalt had done any homework at all, he would also have known that Jack was an experienced public speaker, able to think quickly on his feet. The only way to trounce Jack in a debate is to lead him into deep water where he is insufficiently informed to hold his own. But Laxalt had chosen to attack Jack on the most shallow, emotional issues. In that kind of contest, Jack Anderson is a tiger.

"He just sort of rambled around in his five minutes," Jack went on. "He said Fike had been 'scrupulously clean' but he didn't answer the charges. When my turn came, I challenged him to come to an open press conference and to bring Fike, right after the debate, where anyone in the press could go over the documentation to decide for themselves who was right. Laxalt got rattled and interrupted and the judge had to tell him to be quiet.

"I held the press conference afterwards at my hotel and a lot of reporters came. But Laxalt and Fike did not show up. So I tried to put through a call to them from my room, but I couldn't get them, which was no surprise."

"Did you get any idea of the public reaction?" someone asked.

Jack produced a copy of that day's Las Vegas *Sun*. PUBLIC RULES ANDERSON WIDE WINNER IN DEBATE, screamed the front-page headline. Above that was an overline which read, GOV. LAXALT

LOSES COOL. The story said, "An informal poll taken among viewers immediately following the debate showed the public favoring Anderson's arguments over Laxalt's by an eight to one margin. The poll was augmented by approximately 60 calls to the SUN switchboard expressing a similar eight to one margin."

We later got a copy of the next day's issue of the *Sun*, in which editor Greenspun devoted his front-page column to the debate, describing Jack's triumph in biblical terms. Jack, he said, had "about as much trepidation as little David felt when he stepped forward to battle with Goliath . . . He was debating a man skilled in speech, law and the political arts with a popular following unmatched by any former governor. . . . Anderson came to the fray armed only with faith—faith in the truth of his writings and faith in the integrity of his profession. And David reached into his bag and brought forth some documents and smote the giant with the truth."

Greenspun's enthusiasm notwithstanding, any fair judgment of how badly the Republicans had been smitten would have to await the election returns. The debate had clearly been a debacle, but the effect of such things is unpredictable. Besides, O'Callaghan was so far behind that it seemed unlikely, in such a strong Republican area, that he could close the gap in the short time before the balloting. He did, however, and won the race. As Jack related it afterward, O'Callaghan called Jack to thank him and tell him that the scandal had been the deciding factor. O'Callaghan wanted to know if there was anything he could do for Jack. Never one to pass up an opportunity, Jack suggested that O'Callaghan insist that Howard Hughes come out of hiding before the State Gaming Commission would renew the licenses for the numerous gambling casinos Hughes now owned in Las Vegas. If the billionaire recluse did make himself available, naturally Jack wanted an exclusive story on it. O'Callaghan said he would try.

The Ed Fike case had been an unqualified success for Jack and the column, although it was little publicized outside Nevada. But even if he had done badly in his debate with Laxalt, Jack would still have been pleased that he plunged headlong into the fray. He operated on the same theory as many movie stars, namely, that notoriety is as good as fame. It had been an article of faith with Drew Pearson. "Drew always taught me," he would tell us, "that controversy is good for the column. If you write a column like ours, you've got to be controversial. People will read you even if they hate you."

To illustrate Pearson's affinity for controversy, Jack would often tell a story about the famous Sherman Adams–Bernard Goldfine case during the Eisenhower administration. Adams, the former governor of New Hampshire, was Eisenhower's chief of staff and therefore one of the most powerful men in Washington. But he had been accepting gifts from New England industrialist Bernard Goldfine, a friend for whom he had intervened with several federal regulatory agencies. Jack had first broken the story in the column, including the fact that Adams had accepted the now legendary vicuña coat from Goldfine. It created an uproar in Washington. Eisenhower was subsequently asked about the affair at a press conference. His answer, which no President except Eisenhower could have gotten away with, was something to the effect that, "Governor Adams was indiscreet, but I need him."

Goldfine was subsequently the object of a House of Representatives Subcommittee investigation and a House staff member took a room next to Goldfine's in the Carlton Hotel in downtown Washington to eavesdrop on his conversations. At one point, the investigator asked if Jack would like to come along and listen. Sensing a good story, Jack went. However, Goldfine's lawyer, Roger Robb, had hired a private eye who caught on to what was happening. He began banging on the door, demanding that it be opened. Jack and the House investigator waited for a while, but finally opened up. By then there was a huge crowd in the hallway. Jack was mortified. He had been caught red-handed participating in the invasion of someone's privacy. When he got back to Drew's office in Georgetown, he was most upset.

Pearson, however, was calm. In fact, he seemed to be enjoying the flap. "I could tell he was enjoying it," Jack said, "because his white mustache was twitching slightly. He always did that when he was amused. Besides, he had this gleam in his eye and a sort of mischievous look on his face. He always looked like that when we'd stirred things up. I thought it was a disaster. I was opposed to this kind of thing, eavesdropping and bugging. I'd only gone along because I thought it was a possible story. I figured any other newsman would have done the same. I kept telling Drew, but he wasn't concerned. Finally, the phone rang. It was the Associated Press. They wanted a comment from Drew about me being caught in the room next to Goldfine's. 'Well,' Drew said, 'Jack was indiscreet. But I need him.' That quote appeared all over the country. It ended the whole thing."

FOUR

How did it feel, I was often asked during my early months with Jack Anderson, to have someone else receive the credit for my work? No matter how frequently it was asked, this question never stopped surprising me. For one thing, Jack was extraordinarily generous with credit to his staff. If you wanted your name in a column you had worked on, you simply put it in. Usually, the mention went something like, "Reached at his Capitol office by my associate Brit Hume, Senator So-and-so angrily denied the charges and hung up the phone." So not only did we get credit, but we had important-sounding titles. Not mere "reporters" or "assistants," we were Jack's "associates." What's more, he continually encouraged us to write for other publications. "I think it's good for the column," he would say, "to have my staff known in their own right." When I bogged down in my book about the United Mine Workers, Jack repeatedly urged me to press on with it and finally gave me time off with pay to finish it.

As important as the recognition was the freedom we had. Jack sometimes suggested story ideas, but he rarely made formal assignments. We were at liberty to pursue whatever we wanted and our ideas about how information should be handled were the last word. "You're the reporter," Jack would say, "so I'll accept your judgment." Naturally, we had to keep him posted on what we were doing and what progress we were making so that he could plan the columns. And he always edited or, when necessary, rewrote the draft columns we submitted. But this was to get them into the idiom of the Merry-Go-Round, not to second-guess the reporter. After editing, a column always went back to the reporter who submitted it so that any errors or distortions that might have crept in could be caught.

Such reliance on the judgment of reporters is almost unheard of. In most news organizations, reporters are at the beck and call of editors who decide what should be covered and how. And once stories are written, editors feel free to hack away at them with abandon. Reporters assigned to cover regular areas or "beats" may seem to have more freedom in that they get fewer orders from their editors. But such reporters frequently find themselves so busy simply keeping track of the obvious daily happenings on their beat, that their freedom is an illusion. The problem for investigative reporters is even worse. Their work engenders controversy and, sometimes, litigation. The management of news organizations have little use for either. Even those willing to publish such reporting often lose patience with projects that take considerable time. Investigative reporters find they are shunted off on various spot assignments by editors who think that anyone not writing for the next edition is not busy. Morale among investigative reporters is even lower than among other newsmen, and that's low.

"The Washington Merry-Go-Round" published little besides investigative reporting. And any story fit. If it was a major exposé, it could be spread out over several columns. A minor item could be taken care of in a single paragraph. The kinds of stories that other news organizations were skeptical of or not interested in were virtually the only kinds Jack Anderson wanted. And he handled them the way the reporter thought best. All of us loved this atmosphere, but no one more than Les Whitten. He had been in the newspaper business for twenty years, most of them with the Washington *Post* and, later, the Washington bureau of the Hearst newspaper chain. He had been a successful reporter and enjoyed a good reputation among his colleagues. But the Hearst papers have little impact in Washington, and Les's days at the *Post* were marred by continual clashes with a legendary tyrannical city editor. In those years, he had embarked on a variety of outside writing projects, ranging from the translation of Baudelaire poems to the publication of two lurid thrillers. Now, though, he was consumed by his work for the column. I was amazed by him. He was forty-two and had covered virtually every kind of seamy Washington story imaginable. He had seen both politics and journalism at their worst. Yet he showed no trace of the cynicism which overtakes many younger newsmen after just a few years in Washington. He looked boyish and he acted boyish. It took me a while to get to know him, not because he was aloof but because he was phenomenally busy. His office, the first on the corridor past the reception room, was often jammed with people conferring with him about stories. Frequently he would be on the phone at the same time, with calls waiting and more callers waiting in the reception room. I saw him most often when he came back to my kitchen office to use the Xerox machine. But even those visits were brief. Les never walked from one room to another. He dashed, frequently in his sock feet, so that when he came down the hall to my office, he half ran, half skated, stopping just in time to make the sharp left turn into the room without crashing into the wall. He always had a cheerful greeting, but there was little opportunity for conversation, for once the Xerox machine had disgorged its last copy, Les vanished as quickly as he had arrived. The result of all this frantic activity was a vast amount of material for the column produced in an astonishingly short time. Yet all of it was so painstakingly double-checked that no Les Whitten story ever got the column into a jam. But the quality of Les's reporting could not be detected by looking at his copy. He typed as fast as he worked and could not be bothered with such details as changing the ribbon in his typewriter. The result was that his copy looked like the practice sheets of a secretarial-school novice. What's more, he never saw the need to use new sheets of paper. Instead, he used the back side of any unneeded used paper he could find. His stories appeared on Jack's desk typed on the flip sides of everything from government press releases to stray business letters.

Les Whitten wrote like no other newspaperman I have known. Of course, I have known no other newsman who also wrote thrillers and translated Baudelaire. There was a streak of incurable romanticism in him. It would sometimes show on the rare occasions when he was free for lunch. He was an authority on French food and wine and would address the waiters in French restaurants in their native tongue. Often, he would lapse into reminiscence of other, similar meals eaten long ago in the company of women he could not quite forget. But it seemed that such attacks of romanticism would also strike when he was at the typewriter. The result was prose that was ornate, flowery and high-wrought. Reporting the shelving of some consumer legislation, he once wrote that it had ended up in "Sen. John McClellan's garden of dead hopes." A routine account of waste in the poverty program was prefaced with an explanation that the job of the Office of Economic Opportunity was to free the poor from their "rusty iron cage of need." And when he caught the director of the Smithsonian Institution, S. Dillon Ripley, off on a junket in the Aegean Sea at public expense, he really outdid himself. "For two weeks," Les wrote, without apologies to Homer, "he sailed the epic, wine-dark seas . . . quaffed fine drink, sampled succulent Palaiokastritsa lobsters and viewed antiquities." And before the "idyllic cruise," there had been an evening of cocktails in Corinth overlooking the "moon-drenched Acropolis." Jack usually translated such purple passages into the blunt, racy style of the column. Thus the "garden of dead hopes" and the "iron cage of need" never made it into print. But Jack let stand Les's account of the Ripley junket. I later heard that an editor of the Washington *Star-News*, during a slow period in the afternoon, had read it aloud in front of the news room with suitable grandiloquence, while the reporters whooped with laughter.

Les's penchant for hifalutin prose was hardly a major fault, only

an idiosyncrasy that paled into insignificance beside the staggering contribution he made to the column. He was by far the most
valuable member of the staff, often contributing more than Joe
Spear and myself put together. One reason for his productivity
was that in twenty years of covering Washington he had cultivated
a broad range of news sources. Now that he was working for the
column, he found his sources more co-operative than ever. Although I had grown up in Washington, I had only worked there
as a newsman about a year. I had developed some sources but I
depended heavily upon the information that came into the office
unsolicited. It was as vast as Jack had promised when he first
interviewed me. The problem was that only a fraction of it was
worth investigating and only part of that turned out to be useful
for the column. It was therefore necessary for all of us to become
expert in spotting crackpots so that their letters could be discarded
or their phone calls terminated before too much time had been
wasted. We used several tests. Anyone who made extensive use
of the word "conspiracy" in describing his tribulations, claimed
he couldn't get an honest lawyer or insisted the FBI was in league
with his enemies was automatically regarded as a nut, letters
written or typed in varying shades of ink, or with writing in the
margins or on the envelope were either thrown out or given to Joe
Spear for his collection of crank mail. Jack loved to tell about one
such letter, which was addressed, without street, city or state, to
"Jack Anderson, liar, louse, ring-tailed rat and yellow-bellied
skunk." Although the Census Bureau estimated there were then
about 14,000 Jack Andersons in the country, the letter was delivered unerringly to Jack's door. Sometimes our screening system
for mail and calls failed. Jack once spent considerable time reading
a neatly typed, well-written, and moderately worded letter from
a woman who went on for pages about her difficulties before she
finally came to the point, which was that her husband was
obviously Hitler. Another time, I picked up the phone and soon
found myself deep in conversation with a man who identified

himself as something like "J.C. Hollins, of Hollow Creek, Kentucky, buddy." He said he was running for President on the Jehovah ticket. I hung up, but he immediately called back, apologizing for the disconnection. "Now don't you think it would be something, with all of this corruption going on, if we could get a real God-fearin', Bible-believin' man in the White House?" He then allowed that the Lord himself had told him he should run for President. Joe Spear, who was working at a desk next to mine in the kitchen, had stopped what he was doing by this time and was watching me, wondering who my caller was. Opal also happened to be in the room and she was equally curious. She had not questioned him when she answered the call, because he asked for me by name. All they could hear, of course, was my end of the conversation, but they could see by my expression that I was stuck with a clinker.

"Well," I asked, "when did you first realize that God wanted you to be his candidate for President?"

When Joe and Opal heard that, they burst into laughter, so loud I could barely hear poor Hollins as he urged me to pray for him and, more importantly, to attend the press conference in Kentucky where he would announce his candidacy. I finally struck a bargain with him. If he could get James Reston of the New York *Times* to attend, then so would I. I also gave him the names of several of my friends in the newspaper business. They later reported receiving repeated calls from him.

On another occasion, I got a call from a man who identified himself as the ringmaster of a nationally known circus. He said he was in Washington to determine whether he was now or ever had been under FBI investigation. That should have tipped me off. But he was articulate, earnest and reasonable. He said he had a story to tell that might be of interest. I agreed to see him. When he arrived later that day, he brought with him a scrapbook full of news clippings establishing his identity. He had an extraordinary tale. His ex-wife, he claimed, had been a prostitute who engaged in her profession in New York when he was on the road with the circus. He had thought she worked for a modeling agency, but it turned out to be just a front for an expensive call-girl operation, whose clientele he said, included the Kennedy family during John Kennedy's presidency. He never knew of any of this until he came home to their rented hotel suite one day and found her gone and the place cleaned out of all belongings except his clothing and a few sticks of furniture. In rummaging through a bureau drawer, he discovered a diary, partly hand-written, partly typed, which she had apparently made for her psychiatrist as part of her treatment. It contained extraordinary tales of sex at the White House and the Hyannis Port compound. In the ensuing divorce proceeding, he used the diary against her, he said, but neither she nor her lawyer denied its authenticity or even its truth. But ever since, he said, he had been hounded by the FBI. They had questioned his friends, visited his relatives, even harassed his parents. He gave a detailed account of confronting one agent in his parents' home to demand to know the purpose of the investigation. He got no satisfactory answer, but he had the agents' name. Ultimately, in desperation, he faked his own death and changed his name. At this point, my credulity all but vanished, but he produced newspaper clippings, showing photographs of himself wearing his ringmaster's costume first with one name, then a new one. He also had a clipping reporting his death in the Point Pleasant, West Virginia, bridge collapse. After that, he said, the harassment stopped for several years. But now it had apparently begun again and he was receiving reports from his superiors at the circus that the FBI was asking questions about him. Yet before he had come to my office, he said, he had gone to the FBI and was given assurances that he was not now, and never had been under investigation. He was unsure what to do now, and wanted our advice. I didn't know what advice to give him, and his tale, although partly documented with the clippings, was utterly fantastic. But I was intrigued by the diary, so I told him to send it to us, promising that we would make an investigation if it were warranted. He left, promising to send the diary. I later got a letter from him, dated the same day, thanking me for seeing him and urging me to telephone his employers to tell them he was not in hot water with the FBI. He enclosed the phone number of the person he wanted me to call, plus the name and phone number of a New York belly dancer he said had known about his wife's activities and been present on some of the visits to the Kennedys. I decided to do nothing until I had seen the diary. Weeks later, he wrote from Greece, apologizing for not sending the diary, but promising to do so. Finally, in October, it arrived. The handwritten and typed pages were filled with random excerpts from the author's life, mostly dealing with her teenage years. It was utterly routine except for three typed pages, written on a different typewriter from the rest, which contained a huge serving of pornography. It began with the suggestion that the author was sleeping with her analyst ("but even in sex, you seem to give more than you take"), proceeded quickly to an earlier affair with a man ("I wanted him so much I ached"), then one with a woman ("the first time she touched me it was like an electric shock"), then told of trips to the White House and the Kennedy compound ("We were taken to Marine terminal in what appeared to be secrecy"), complete with explicit details of all the Kennedys in action ("Jack seemed to have a foot fetish . . . always kissing the girl's feet before doing anything else."). The finale was an account of Bobby Kennedy's long-rumored romance with Marilyn Monroe, which concluded that she had not committed suicide, but had been bumped off by the CIA. The document, although worth a few laughs in the office, was useless. Even if it hadn't seemed to be such an obvious fraud, it was the word of a prostitute communicating with her psychiatrist, hardly the most credible evidence. What's more, it was a sex story and we rarely came across a sex story that seemed legitimate for the column. So I let the matter drop, although I remained curious about who was behind the incident and what its purpose was. It might have been interesting to investigate further, but the column's insistent demand for copy dictated that we stick to matters that seemed certain to produce stories. Besides, I felt a little embarrassed at having gone along with the ringmaster and his wild tale as long as I had. I wished I had stuck to our usual rule of avoiding anyone who talked in conspiratorial terms and suspected the FBI had joined forces with his enemies.

The job of screening mail, phone calls and visits from strangers fell to the staff, because Opal did a good job of protecting Jack from anyone he didn't know. But Jack had another problem—fending off those he did know. In more than twenty years as Drew Pearson's principal legman, he had made innumerable acquaintances, many of whom considered themselves far closer friends of his than Jack did. The problem was compounded by the fact that Jack was much too gentle and kind to hang up on a caller or cut off a face-to-face conversation in a way that might have seemed rude. The person who took greatest advantage of this was Irving Davidson, a lobbyist and wheeler-dealer who occupied the suite just below Jack's. Years ago, they had shared the same suite, and Opal had worked as secretary to both of them. But that was before Jack had become a famed columnist and Irv had become one of the more savvy—and shady—backroom operators in Washington. Now, of course, they were poles apart. Jack was the relentless muckraker bent on exposing corruption and deception wherever he found it. Irv was the shadowy political insider using his contacts on behalf of such illustrious clients as Jimmy Hoffa and François "Papa Doc" Duvalier. Irv looked the part. A short man, bald at the top, he kept his silver hair long and combed straight back on the sides. His face was dominated by a large nose and, usually, by a cocky, but somehow winning, grin. His wardrobe featured sleek, well-tailored suits and alligator shoes. He always seemed to be carrying large sums of cash. Yet Jack genuinely liked Irv and so did everyone else in the office. He had a certain friendly and cheerful way that made him hard to dislike. What's more, he was an excellent source. He had numerous contacts in such diverse areas as the Nixon administration, the government of Israel, and the Mafia. A few days after Bobby Baker, the former secretary to the Senate Majority, left prison, Jack got word that he was writing a book on his experiences. He called Irv, and shortly thereafter, Irv marched into the office with Bobby Baker in tow. But this relationship had its price. For one thing, Irv was in the office every day, it seemed. Sometimes, he just dropped in to pass on the latest joke that was making the rounds in town. If that was the case, he usually avoided Jack, because Irv's taste was for jokes that were either too racist or lewd to appeal to Jack. But frequently, he would bring visitors with him. They ranged from shifty-eyed, swarthy characters I took to be Mafiosi to stupefied relatives of Papa Doc who obviously had no idea who Jack Anderson was or why they were being introduced to him. Usually, all Irv wanted to do was say hello and chat briefly, apparently to prove to his associates that he and Jack Anderson really were friends. Sometimes, though, Irv would want something from Jack. He tried to arrange for a favorable story on Papa Doc, even promising the red-carpet treatment for me if Jack were willing to send me to visit the old dictator in Haiti. Jack listened politely to the idea, then instantly vetoed it once Irv had left the office. Another time, we got a minor story about dealing with one of the sons of Clint Murchison, the Texas multimillionaire, who had gotten a job with Senate Majority Leader Mike Mansfield. Murchison was one of Davidson's clients, and he got wind of the story. Irv was in our office in a flash. He darted from one room to another trying to persuade someone that the item should not be used. The story was used anyway. On another occasion, Irv arrived, seemingly just to chat. But as he and Jack were talking in Jack's office, the phone rang. It was Irv's secretary. He had an important call downstairs. Instead of leaving, however, Irv had her put the call through to Jack's office. When it came, Irv announced proudly that he was in his friend Jack Anderson's office. Then he suddenly thrust the phone into Jack's hands and said, "Say hello to my buddy so-and-so." Jack, taken aback, held the phone like a hot potato for a moment, then put it to his ear and, with a pained expression, said hello. There followed an awkward conversation between two people who didn't know each other and obviously had no desire to talk to each other. In 1972, the frequency of Irv's visits dropped sharply for a time after he was indicted in connection with a West Coast real estate deal. Ultimately, he pleaded guilty, but later the charge against him—and his plea—was quietly dropped. When I last saw him he was his old, ebullient self once more.

In an effort to avoid losing too much of his time seeing visitors like Davidson, Jack had gotten into the habit of spending his mornings at his suburban Maryland home working on the column. Although there were occasional telephone interruptions and some of his nine children might break the calm, Jack could usually hole up in his wood-paneled den on the first floor of the large fieldstone and wood house and write. The shelves of the den were packed with books about Washington and politics and I was quite impressed when I first saw them. Jack assured me, however, that he hadn't read them. They were review copies, he explained, which he had received free from the publishers and kept to use as reference books. This was characteristic of Jack. He never bothered to learn much about matters that were not of immediate concern to him. But when he turned his attention to a subject—usually something he needed to understand for the column—there was little that was beyond his grasp. It was one of his most endearing characteristics that he made no pretensions of being a great intellect. When he and his wife Olivia went to see the slow-paced, artistic film *The Go-Between*, with my wife and me, Jack slept through most of it. Afterward, he confessed that although he could tell it was a fine movie, he would have preferred to have been in the theater next door where *Dirty Harry* was playing. "I'm a cultural and intellectual dud," he said with a chuckle. Another time, he took Clare and me to a concert given by the Utah Symphony Orchestra, for which some of his Mormon friends had dragooned him into buying box seats. It was obvious from the expression on his face that it was all he could do to sit through it. But when the orchestra, in an encore, burst into a spirited rendition of "When Johnny Comes Marching Home Again," Jack beamed and turned to me. "This is just about my speed," he said.

Jack's easygoing ways and absence from the office much of the time left considerable authority in the hands of Opal, who had been with him longest and knew his affairs best. Technically, Les was in charge when Jack was out of the office, but actually, Opal was. This was mainly because Les was too busy rushing about after the news to bother with office business. Opal and Jack were a strange combination. Jack was a devout Mormon, a teetotaler who didn't smoke and rarely swore. Opal gave no evidence of ever having been to church, smoked heavily and drank and swore as robustly as any man. In fact, it was usually to Opal that Irv Davidson would first go with his crude jokes. Opal was a tall, rather hefty woman with short, reddish hair and a somewhat imperious manner. But her Georgia upbringing had given her a certain natural grace and poise. She had a ready smile and easy manner in meeting strangers, making introductions and conducting a conversation with almost anyone under almost any circumstances. The result was that she had countless friends, many her own and many who sought her out as a way to getting close to Jack. There was a continuous stream of visitors in her office at all hours of the day and the kitchen counter was used far less for the preparation of food than for the mixing of drinks, usually bloody marys, for Opal and her friends. None of this seemed to interfere with her work. She was a crack secretary who could do a day's work in a matter of hours. What's more, she was dedicated to her job and devoutly loyal to Jack. He recognized this and had come to depend upon her heavily. She planned and kept his schedule, including many of the lecture dates that occupied more and more of his time, managed his travel, handled all his correspondence, typed and sent the column each day. She also took charge of the maintenance of the office and kept the supplies in stock. In addition, she put together, from material already used, columns each week for weekly newspapers and the Italian language New York City weekly *Il Progresso*. Opal knew how important she was to Jack and she showed her feeling of job security by a totally irreverent attitude both toward him and some of his associates. One Washington public relations man, a long-time friend of Jack's, constantly tried to reach him on the phone. I never once saw Opal put the call through. She simply didn't like him. She called him "old flannelmouth" behind his back.

Nothing gave Opal more pleasure than a practical joke. When she discovered I could make a realistic farting sound by squeezing my palms together, she called upon me several times each week to demonstrate it for her friends. And when someone particularly stuffy was in her office, she would literally beg me to come and sit down and, with a straight face and my hands hidden, rip off a few loud ones. I went along with her the first few times she asked, but she could never keep from breaking up into whoops of laughter that sent tears streaming down her face, so I stopped. She did, however, get me to perform in the presence of "old flannelmouth" one day. His expression of consternation and embarrassment was memorable. Opal had to leave the room. I found her back in my office doubled over in laughter.

Another joke she particularly enjoyed came during the 1972 presidential campaign. Charles Colson, a senior aide to President Nixon, had sent a strongly worded memo to his staff demanding "maximum output" to help the President's re-election. "I am totally unconcerned with anything other than getting the job done," the memo said. "Just so you understand me, let me point out that the statement in last week's UPI story that I was once reported to have said that 'I would walk over my grandmother if necessary' is absolutely accurate."

The memo got out and was printed in the Washington *Post*. Colson and his grandmother became symbols of the supercharged effort President Nixon's associates were making to assure his reelection. During one slow afternoon in the office, with Jack out of town and most of the staff gathered in the kitchen, I put through a call to Colson's office at the White House. A secretary answered.

"This is Ted Davis with the United Press here in Washington," I said, disguising my voice with a southern drawl. "Our bureau in Milwaukee has just told us that a woman out there named Hattie Madigan has called a news conference. She says she is Charles Colson's grandmother and she's apparently going to come out for McGovern."

"What!" said the secretary, laughing.

"That's apparently what she said," I responded, keeping my speech slow and my face straight. "Do y'all have any comment?"

"Just a minute," she said, putting the call on hold.

Moments later, she was back on the line to tell me that Colson's grandparents were all dead. She said he had no comment. I hung up. We waited a few minutes, then Jim Dawson, an intern with the staff, called Colson's office. I listened on the other line.

"This is John Evans of the Associated Press," he began when the same voice answered. "We've just gotten word that a woman . . ."

"He doesn't have a grandmother," she interrupted.

Again, we waited a few minutes. Then Rachel Scott, a friend who had dropped in the office, was pressed into service. She called and identified herself as "Laura Smith of the Milwaukee *Journal*'s Washington bureau."

"He doesn't have a grandmother," said the secretary, even sooner this time.

"Well, it's very strange," said Rachel. "Apparently there's this ninety-one-year-old woman out there and she . . ."

"I'm sorry, he doesn't have a grandmother."

By this time, Opal, who had listened in on several of the conversations, was back in the kitchen and brimming with enthusiasm. She called next, identifying herself as "Susan Bryan of the Chicago *Tribune*."

"He has no living grandmothers," said the beleaguered secretary.

"He has no living grandmothers?" said Opal. "Well do you know anything about this press conference. Do you have any comment on it."

"No comment," said the secretary. "No grandmothers."

It seemed we had carried the joke as far as it could go. No one could think of a way to keep it going. Then I got an idea. I dialed the White House and asked for Colson's office. The same voice answered.

"This is Hattie Madigan in Milwaukee calling," I said in a voice approximating the one Jonathan Winters uses for his Maude Frickert routines. "And you can tell that grandson of mine that he's not going to walk all over me, because I'm for McGovern. I understand he's been telling the newspapers he's never heard of me. I think it's shocking. Here I am, ninety-one years old and he's trying to disown me."

"Who is this?" said the secretary, half laughing, half serious.

"This is Hattie Madigan. And he's not going to walk all over me."

"Just a minute," she said, putting the call on hold. I wanted to stay on the line in the hope that Colson would pick up the phone and I could really give it to him, but everyone in the room was laughing and I could no longer keep a straight face, so I hung up.

Although Jack was out of town when this incident occurred, it would probably have happened anyway if he had been there. We captured most of it on a tape recorder and he roared over it when he got back. Such office hijinks were not exactly encouraged by Jack, but he tolerated them with benign amusement, just as he tolerated Opal's ways without criticizing her. The reason for this,

I always thought, was that for all his prominence and his image as a crusading muckraker, he refused to take himself too seriously. He was, for instance, utterly oblivious to fashion. When I first began working for him, he dressed like a man who never noticed the passing of the early 1950s. He wore baggy, pleated pants that drooped over his shoe tops, faded white shirts with narrow, nondescript neckties, and brightly colored socks. He frequently padded around the office in his sock feet and sometimes he would remove his socks to rub his feet or pick at his toes. He also occasionally picked his ear with a paper clip and would emerge from even the most elegant restaurants with a toothpick in his mouth. Although he later began to update his wardrobe a bit, he never lost the manner of an easygoing country boy from the West.

FIVE

By mid-1970, Vice President Spiro Agnew had broadened his attacks on the news media to include a variety of other targets. In speeches before appreciative gatherings of the party faithful, he came down especially hard on "affluent, permissive, upper-middle-class parents who learned their Doctor Spock and threw discipline out the window when they should have done the opposite."

In September, Les Whitten got word from an acquaintance in Baltimore, Agnew's home town, that the Vice President's son Randy had left his wife and moved in with a male hairdresser. I arrived at the office on Wednesday, September 2, to find Les and Jack full of excitement about the story. They called me into Les's office where they were discussing it to ask my opinion on the best way to pin it down.

"I've got the address," Les said. "You used to work in Baltimore. You could probably find the place."

Les gave me the address. I recognized it as a street in Bolton Hill, a remodeled neighborhood of brick and brownstone townhouses at the edge of downtown, which had become quite fashionable.

"Do you want to take on this one?" Jack asked.

"I guess so," I said. "But I'm not sure it's fair. If it were the Vice President himself, that would be one thing. But the only reason we're interested in the son is because of who his father is. It doesn't seem fair to publicize his private life because of his father."

"Look," Jack said firmly, "Agnew's been flying all over the country telling people how to bring up their children. He's posing as an expert and making all these pious pronouncements. Here's a

49

story that suggests that his own son is having some troubles, that he may be a homosexual. I don't have anything against him, but I think the public's got a right to know about it."

"Besides that," Les said, "it's a hell of a story."

"Is there any reason to think that this situation is all it appears to be?" I asked. "I mean is there any other reason to think he's a fag?"

Les shot me a significant glance. "My source says he works as a weightlifting instructor in a health spa of some kind over there."

"That doesn't look good," I conceded.

The discussion was interrupted by a telephone call for Jack. But it resumed later in the afternoon in his office. This time Opal joined in. Jack sat behind his desk and listened intently to all the arguments. They lasted the better part of an hour.

"It just isn't a good story for the column," Opal said. "It looks like we're trying to get Agnew through his son. It's likely to get you in even more hot water at the Washington *Post*. I just don't like it, that's all."

"When a person makes a conscious decision to cross the line into public life," I argued, "then he should be subjected to pitiless scrutiny. But the only reason Randy Agnew's a public figure is because of who his father is. It doesn't serve the public interest in any way to delve into his private life, especially when there's no proof that he's doing anything wrong, or even that he's having any real troubles. Besides that, even if he were, we have no proof that his father is responsible."

Les, sitting in a chair in front of Jack's desk, across the room from the couch where I sat, looked at me with a knowing smile as I spoke. When I was finished, he said, "Look, the sons and daughters of Presidents and Vice Presidents have always been public figures. The press has always covered their activities. This story is news, there's no doubt about that, and I don't think we can just sit on it."

So it went, with Jack silent most of the time, until he finally sat forward in his swivel chair and interrupted. "You've got a point," he said, nodding at me and Opal, "but I think Les is right. It's news and our job is to publish the news, not to suppress it. Agnew's been lecturing the nation about child-rearing and that makes it legitimate. But we want to be fair. So, Brit, I'm assigning you to do the story. That way, I'll be sure Randy will be treated fairly because of your reservations about the story. We better move fast because someone else might be on this. Can you go over to Baltimore in the morning?"

It was about eleven o'clock the next morning when I found the street where Randy was supposed to be living and parked my car. The background material I had assembled overnight told me that his full name was James Rand Agnew, that he was twenty-four and was a veteran of the Vietnam War. His wife's name was Ann and they had one child, a daughter, Michelle Ann, after whom the Vice President had named his 1968 campaign plane. The streets in Bolton Hill were virtually deserted, except for a few women pushing baby carriages. My footsteps sounded unusually loud as I walked down the street searching for the right address. It turned out to be a red brick townhouse. Randy's friend, Buddy Hash, occupied the ground floor and the basement. I walked up the steps and pressed the doorbell. No one answered and I was about to turn and leave when I heard someone coming toward the door. It opened. A handsome, dark-haired young man in a blue and white striped shirt, open at the collar, white jeans, and bare feet stood in the doorway. From pictures I had looked at before driving over, I recognized him as young Agnew.

"Hi," I said, "I'm looking for Randy Agnew."

"I'm Randy Agnew," he said quietly.

"My name is Brit Hume. I'm with the Bell-McClure newspaper syndicate. The reason I came over is that we've been told that you were living in sort of a hippie crash pad with a lot of wild parties going on and drugs being used and we thought we'd better check it out. From the looks of this place, the report doesn't seem to be true. Can I talk to you for a minute?"

The Bell-McClure Syndicate distributed the column, and we often used its name instead of Jack's, where identification with the column might have had a chilling effect. The tale about the hippie crash pad was something I had thought up on the way over. It is a common enough technique—you persuade the person you are questioning that you have been told a truly lurid story. In eagerness to disabuse you of it, the person will frequently tell you the truth.

Agnew stepped aside and let me into the apartment. It was, like many old townhouses, rather dark. We sat down in the front room, which seemed to be the dining room, at a large, heavy wooden table which was ornately carved. Considerable care seemed to have gone into the apartment's decor, which included unusual paintings, and wall-to-wall carpeting. I questioned Agnew about how he came to be living there.

"Well," he said in his soft-spoken way, "Buddy is a friend of a friend and he was nice enough to let me stay here until I got straightened out . . . I've got my own place now, but I just stopped by here to use the bathroom, to take a shower. I've got an apartment in Towson. The plumbing isn't hooked up yet, though. I've still got some of my clothes here. I had been living here about a month."

He confirmed that he worked as a weightlifting instructor at the Holiday Health Spa in Towson, a suburb just north of the city, in Baltimore County, his father's old political base. He and his wife had been separated about six months, he said. I asked if there was a chance of a reconciliation.

"I would rather not comment about that," he said. "Anything can happen during a separation."

"How does your father feel about it?" I asked.

"Well, it's completely in my hands."

We chatted a while longer about nothing in particular. He

seemed to be a modest, pleasant, and gentle young man. If it were true, as he said, that he was no longer living with Hash, I suppose I should have felt lucky to have caught him at the house. But I didn't. This was not an enjoyable assignment and the fact that Agnew had turned out to be such a nice guy didn't make it any more so. I was relieved when I got out of the house. I hadn't produced a notebook during the interview because I didn't want to alarm him. So when I got in my car, I hastily wrote down all the quotes and other details I could remember. My next stop was the *Evening Sun,* where I had worked a couple of years before and was allowed to use the library. The clippings had only a few details of young Agnew's marriage. We had been told that Buddy Hash had a police record, but if he did, it hadn't made the newspapers. When friends who worked at the paper asked me what I was doing in town, I told them I was working on a story about the Vice President, but that they didn't have to worry about feeling scooped by the column because it wasn't their kind of story anyway.

From the *Evening Sun,* I walked a few blocks to police headquarters, which is located just a few hundred yards from Baltimore's notorious "Block," a strip of sleazy waterfront nightclubs and strip joints which had sprung up to grab the trade of sailors whose ships docked in the Baltimore harbor, but had become so gamy that it was a major tourist attraction, virtually the only such attraction the city had besides crabmeat. Its proximity to police headquarters had not stopped it from flourishing, although it was a hotbed of prostitution and B-girl activity. Now it lay in the path of an urban renewal project, but the city fathers were hardly breathing sighs of relief to be rid of the sinful spot. Instead, a group of city councilmen were trying to find a place where all the clubs and theaters could relocate, intact and en masse.

The police department's central records division revealed that Buddy (alias Glen) Hash, white-male, born 10/28/42, 5-10, 165 lbs., brown hair, blue eyes, had been arrested on January 25, 1964, for allegedly maintaining a "disorderly house" and again September 20, 1969, on a charge of marijuana possession. He had been cleared of both charges.

Buddy Hash's beauty salon, which he operated with his mother, was called La Triolet. It was located along Eastern Avenue, a major commercial thoroughfare which slices through the large, ethnic, blue-collar residential sections of East Baltimore. Hash matched the profile of the police records, except that he also had long hair, a mustache, and a goatee. I gave him the same story I had given Randy about the hippies and the wild parties.

"Randy's nowhere near the hippie type," Hash said, "he's really very, very goody-goody." He spoke of young Agnew with genuine concern. "He has a lot of debts," he said. "I guess it's because he has a wife and kid. He only paid me a little rent because he wasn't there much. Everybody thinks because his father's the Vice-President, he should have a lot of money, but it just isn't that way."

I didn't stay long talking to Hash. I had all I needed after I had spoken to Randy. The rest was just routine checking, an effort to be thorough and fair. I found a telephone booth a few doors down the street from the beauty parlor and called Jack. He was delighted I had interviewed Agnew in Hash's apartment. Les Whitten was also on the line as I gave Jack a summary of what I had done. "You may not like this story," Les said with a laugh, "but you're sure doing a hell of a good job on it."

Jack had already decided not to put the Agnew story out the same day, Thursday, because that would have meant it would be published the following Monday, which was Labor Day. Instead, it would be sent Friday for publication the following Tuesday. There was a risk it would leak out during the long weekend, but Jack felt this was better than having it appear on a day when most people aren't following the news. Besides, Jack wanted time to contact the Vice President about the story. It was one of the ironies of this episode that Jack and Agnew had once been close friends. During Agnew's race for the governorship of Maryland in 1966, he had frequently consulted Jack for advice, which was freely given, in part because Agnew was running as a moderate against a notorious reactionary Democrat who had won the party nomination by demagogic exploitation of the open-housing issue in the party primary. During Agnew's early days in Washington, after he had received what he considered to be unfairly rough treatment at the hands of the national press during the campaign, he saw few newsmen. Jack was one of them. The relationship finally came apart because Agnew got furious over stories in the column embarrassing to him and the Administration. "Ted just couldn't understand how we could be friends and yet unfriendly stories could appear in the column," Jack said. "He's strictly an amateur."

The next day, Opal and I made one last effort to dissuade Jack from using the story. But we had no new arguments and the old ones had already failed. Jack's position was hardened by the fact that the story had now been confirmed. He reiterated his view that Agnew's public preaching about parenthood had made the story legitimate. And Les repeated his undeniable argument that the story was news. I found myself becoming persuaded that going ahead with the story was the right course. If Les and Jack were right, the story might be picked up by the rest of the news media. It might cause the kind of notice we had all wanted. We all agreed, however, that the story should deal as much as possible with the Vice President's feelings about the situation, so that it would not simply be a scandal story about an important person's relative. But Jack did not want to bring up the subject of the hairdresser with Agnew, fearing that the Vice President would see what was coming and rush out a statement to blunt the column's effect. He put through a call, but Agnew was out. Presently, though, he called back. When Kay Hodges, the receptionist, answered, Agnew said, "This is the Vice President calling. Is Jack there?" Jack later said this was a sign that Agnew was learning, because many experienced politicians like to put through their own calls rather than have an aide or secretary do it. It makes them seem like regular guys. But

Jack said that if Agnew had really had the touch, he would never have identified himself as anything other than "Ted Agnew."

"Hi, Ted," Jack said, "good to hear your voice. Look, I know this is a sensitive matter and because we've been friends, although I know you're mad with me, I wanted to check with you. We understand that Randy and his wife have broken up and I just wanted . . ."

Jack scribbled notes, then questioned Agnew a bit further, seeking to draw him out, especially about his own feelings about the matter. Apparently Agnew didn't bite, because Agnew's quotes were hardly revealing. He said the marrriage had ended "amicably" and that he kept in close touch with his son, although he hadn't seen his new apartment. The two families shared custody of the daughter. Despite the bland comments, Jack said it was obvious Agnew was worried about his son.

The draft column I prepared began, "Vice President Agnew is deeply troubled about his son Randy, who has broken up with his wife and has been living for the past month with a male hairdresser in Baltimore." Putting the hairdresser in the very first paragraph, of course, only emphasized an implication we could not prove was correct. Nevertheless, I reasoned, this was by far the most newsworthy part of the story. Without it, the story would be a simple account of a marriage on the rocks. Besides, what if Agnew had been living with, say, a stripper from the "Block"? Would any newsman fail to put that fact in the lead of his story, whether or not he could prove the relationship was anything but platonic? The column made pointed mention of some of the Vice President's more pious comments about family life.

By the time I finished the draft, I was beginning to get enthusiastic over the column and to worry about whether it would hold until the designated publication date. Jack made only minor changes in the copy and it was sent to New York. By late afternoon, two newspapers, the New York *Post* and the Baltimore *News-American*, had telephoned to express their fear the story would not hold. Jack told me proudly that the editor at the *Post* who called had said he was worried because the story was so "well reported" that it would be easy for another newsman to quickly retrace our steps and break it ahead of us. Jack made a quick decision to let the column go the next day, Saturday. The syndicate was told to notify as many clients as possible by wire or phone and the Saturday column was rescheduled for Tuesday. An atmosphere of excitement began to envelop the office. From their reactions, the *News-American* and the *Post* seemed likely to give the story special treatment. On a slow vacation weekend, it could become the major story and stay in the news for days. I still had misgivings about it, but I was by now willing to let the judgment of the rest of the media determine my final outlook. The story had, after all, included the full explanations of both young Agnew and Hash, and had quoted the Vice President on the matter. It was undeniably true. No conclusions were drawn. The reader was presented the facts and could make up his own mind. By the time I left the office, I had myself persuaded that Jack and Les were right all along. When I got home, though, the bubble burst. My wife, Clare, whose judgment I value greatly, thought the column was a disgrace. I argued with her, but she was unmoved.

"I don't care if it is news," she said, "the column doesn't have to run everything it can get its hands on. You can choose the stories you think are important. And this is not an important story. It's a dirty story." The point came over with particular impact, because I had said much the same thing in arguing earlier with Jack and Les.

About ten o'clock that night, I drove downtown and pulled up next to the newsstand outside the Statler-Hilton Hotel, around the corner from the Washington *Post*; the early edition of the paper usually went on sale there about ten-thirty. The *Post's* handling of the story would be a strong indication of how it would be received. I had previously dropped off copies of the full column at the two major wire-service bureaus, so that, if they wanted to pick it up, they would not have to rely on what might be a truncated version in the Washington *Post*. There was a stack of early *Posts* on the stand when I drove up. The attendant walked over and handed one through the car window to me. I gave him a quarter. As always, he kept the change. I glanced down the front page for the index, found the comics page, where the column always ran, and turned to it. What I saw gave me a sinking feeling. Only about half the column was printed. The rest of the column's normal slot was filled with wire-service copy on other matters. The *Post* had left the account of the marriage breakup intact, but had removed all references to Buddy Hash and Randy's living with him.

I felt the *Post* was justified in editing the column, but it made me angry anyway. I hadn't wanted us to use the story, but since we had, I wanted it to succeed, to be accepted as legitimate news. I hoped the New York *Post* and the Baltimore *News-American*'s handling of the story would stir some attention. But despite the *News-American*'s worries over the story leaking out, the paper did not publish the column. Instead, it ran a considerably toned-down story of its own on page two, with a picture of Hash's house. The New York *Post* ran the column in its usual place. UPI picked it up, but gave it only brief treatment, a routine account of a marriage breakup. The UPI story appeared in the society section of the Washington *Star*. The next day the New York *Times* had a short story highlighting the end of the marriage, but including the information about Randy's friend and attributing it to the column. The story, lost in the back pages on a holiday weekend, caused no sensation.

As it turned out, only the Anderson column itself played up the hairdresser angle. Word eventually got around in Washington that there was more to the column than the Washington *Post* had printed and many people found out what the missing parts were. Information of that kind always travels fast by word of mouth. In the end, it revealed the story for what it really was—

gossip. Other newsmen I spoke to who knew of the story seemed surprised and disappointed we had published it. They considered it a cheap shot, unworthy of serious reporters. Les and Jack always maintained that the story was news, but I sensed that if we had it to do over again, they might have decided to pass it up. I could take no satisfaction from my original misgivings about the story having been proved justified. After all, I had ended up doing all the work on it and hoping it would create a sensation.

It might seem that the lesson of the Randy Agnew case was that sex stories should be shunned. But it was not that simple. The question of when the private lives of public persons become the public's business had been around for a long time and no one in the news media had ever satisfactorily answered it. The rule of thumb for most newsmen was to steer clear of sex scandals. But this did not resolve the question, it merely avoided it. After all, some sex stories are unquestionably legitimate. No one would argue, for example, that the celebrated Profumo affair, which shook the British Government of Harold Macmillan to its roots, was not an important news story. The trouble with the Randy Agnew story was that its link to the public's business was just too tenuous. If Randy's difficulties were what they appeared to be and if they were caused, at least in part, by his father's negligence— rather than, say, Randy's experiences in Vietnam—then it might be possible to conclude that the Vice President's credentials as a public spokesman on parenthood were lacking. We had no proof that Randy was a homosexual—if he had been, it would have been hard to prove it was a sign of moral turpitude—nor could we prove Randy was having serious personal problems. And we had no evidence at all that his father was in any way responsible for his present circumstances. So I thought the story was clearly out of bounds. In its aftermath, I doubted that I would ever become involved in another sex story again. But it was not long before I was deep into the investigation of another one.

Shortly after the Randy Agnew story, Kay Hodges, the unfailingly cheerful office receptionist, came back to my office and handed me a letter that had just arrived in the mail. "Here," she said, "this is for you since you're the column's sex editor."

The letter was typed, double-spaced, on both sides of a sheet of plain white paper. It was unsigned. It told of an episode involving Al Capp, the cartoonist and political commentator, which occurred a couple of years earlier when he was at the University of Alabama to deliver a lecture. "Capp told the U of A people he was doing a survey on sex on campus for NBC and advertised for volunteers to tell him their stories," the letter said. "When girls showed up at his motel, Capp asked if they fucked, sucked, etc. He got all this down on tape. Then he told the girls to take off their clothes and suggested they fuck, suck, etc. If the girls refused, Capp threatened to play the tapes for their parents, teachers, etc. One of the girls happened to be the daughter of a dean, who told her father. The father immediately checked with NBC and discovered NBC was not doing a story on sex on campus . . . The administration did not want to make a fuss so they brought no charges but had Capp and his pal escorted to the state line . . . This is no shit. It takes time, but it's a helluva story. I'm not going to sign my name as I'm now a teacher and it's not my problem."

It was, as the writer said, quite a story. But the Agnew case had left a bad taste in my mouth and I was in no humor to charge off after another sex scandal. The letter lay around on my desk for several months. In the meantime, Capp was becoming as well known for his acid political opinions as he was for "Li'l Abner." His broadcast commentaries were syndicated to some two hundred radio stations. I saw him frequently on televised talk shows. He was earning between $3,500 and $4,500 for lectures on college campuses. He had begun a syndicated column of political commentary. He also edited and wrote the introduction to a collection of *bons mots* by Vice President Agnew, of whom Capp was an ardent admirer. One of Capp's principal themes, especially in his campus talks, was the moral shortcomings of college students and faculty.

"Princeton," he said, "has sunk to a moral level that a chimpanzee can live with, but only a chimpanzee. It has become a combination playpen and pigpen because it disregards the inferiority of the college student to every other class."

"President Nixon," he once remarked, "showed angelic restraint when he called college students bums."

On another occasion, he said, "Colleges today are filled with Fagin professors who don't teach, they just corrupt."

Perhaps his most controversial remarks came after four students were killed by National Guardsmen trying to quell an antiwar demonstration at Kent State University in Ohio. "The real martyrs," said Capp, "were the Ohio National Guardsmen."

I was rummaging through the papers on my desk one day in March when I came across the letter again. This time, it struck me differently. Capp was preaching about the immorality and corruption of college students while at the same time, if the letter were correct, using his entree to the campuses as a way of getting women students into bed with him. I noted as I read the letter over that it named a former top university official as being familiar with the case. The obvious place to start checking the story was with him. It occurred to me that if I could get him to confirm the basic facts, I would know from the start that the story was true and therefore worth the painstaking effort that would be needed to pin down the details. The former official would probably not want to be quoted, I figured, but might be willing to talk if his name were kept out of the story. Anyway, it was worth a try. It took me a while to locate him, but I finally tracked him down at the Waldorf-Astoria in New York, where he was staying during a business trip. It was midafternoon, so I was pleasantly surprised when he answered the phone.

"This is Brit Hume calling," I said. "I'm with Jack Anderson, the syndicated columnist in Washington."

"Yes," he said, his voice betraying a trace of anxiety common to those who received calls from Jack and his staff.

"We've established most of the facts about an incident involving Al Capp at the University of Alabama a few years ago. I'm sure you know what I'm talking about. The reason I called you is that I know you were there then and I understand you are familiar with the case. We have enough now to go ahead with a column on it, but I'd like it to be as thorough and accurate as possible. I wondered if we kept your name out of it, if you'd be willing to co-operate, in the interests of thoroughness and accuracy."

"I recall the incident well," he replied. "Yes, I'd be willing to help you out on the basis you describe on one condition. I don't want any of the women involved to be embarrassed by this . . ."

"Oh no," I interrupted. "We would not use the names of any of the women students except in the most extreme legal circumstances."

"Fine. You know John Chancellor of NBC once checked into this and I talked to him about it, but he never used the story."

"Has anyone ever printed this story?"

"No."

"Well, our information is that when it happened, you sent letters to several hundred other universities to warn them about this. Is that correct?"

"No, that's not. I thought of doing something like that, but I never did. We just didn't want to spread this around."

By now, of course, the basic accuracy of the story had been confirmed and I had his promise of co-operation. I felt I could safely begin to go into some of the details mentioned in the letter. Even if they gave away the fact that I knew less about the episode than I had pretended, it was too late for him to reverse himself.

"I gather that Capp claimed he was doing some sort of a survey on student sex attitudes for NBC and then tried to use the taped interviews he made with women students to blackmail them into bed with him . . ."

"I don't remember that," he said. "Now I'm not sure of all the details of this, because I didn't handle this directly. So that could be. I just don't remember anything about a survey or about tape recordings. There is no doubt though that he was very forceful with at least one of the girls. The way it was reported to me, the guy apparently exposed himself to her and then took off his clothes and apparently he even took off his artificial leg—one of his legs is missing, you know—and he pursued her around like that."

"You mean he chased her naked and one-legged. Where did this happen?" I asked.

"In his hotel, as I remember. He got her to come up there for one reason or other and then this happened. She was very shaken by it. I didn't find out about it until a couple of days later and by then he'd made advances at some other students. The chief of the university police was finally sent down to ask him to leave town. He finally ended up escorting him out of Tuscaloosa."

The official went on to give me the names of several others who were familiar with the facts, including the University Police Chief, Colonel Beverly Lee, and Sarah Healy, the Dean of Women. He also gave me the name of the woman student whose harrowing experience in Capp's hotel room he had just described. He agreed to assist in getting Colonel Lee and Dean Healy's co-operation and told me where he thought the former woman student could be contacted.

Investigative reporting is, much of the time, tedious and discouraging work. An investigative reporter's job is to establish the facts that those in power want most to keep hidden. There is no way to compel answers to embarrassing questions, no subpoena power. Countless stories which a reporter may suspect strongly are true must be abandoned because there is no way to verify them. Occasionally, though, an investigative reporter finds himself on the trail of a major story he knows to be true virtually from the start. It doesn't happen often, but it makes all the dead ends and bum steers encountered on other stories seem worth it. The reporter knows that if he is thorough and careful, he will succeed in making a significant revelation that, without his efforts, might never have been made. This is the feeling I had once I had gotten basic confirmation of the Al Capp incident from the former University of Alabama official.

Before my conversation with him, I had been merely interested in the story. Now that I knew it was true and that I had a good chance of nailing it down, my interest turned to excitement. It was the kind of story every effort would be made to discredit. It would have to be flawlessly reported. It would no doubt cause great controversy.

But, if it were done right, everyone would know it. When I told Jack about it, he agreed that it would have to be handled with extreme care. He told me to take whatever time I needed to do the job. This was unusual, because the column's demand for copy was such that Jack normally wanted us to pursue major projects only in our spare time.

I had little difficulty in getting Dean Healy and Colonel Lee to confirm what they knew of the incident. The dean said she had learned of the incident when two of Capp's victims had come to her office to report it. I asked why the university didn't insist that Capp be prosecuted.

"The young women were not physically harmed and we felt that the publicity and notoriety should be avoided," she said.

Colonel Lee said he had acted under orders from the University President Dr. Frank Rose. "Capp," he said, "was asked to get out and he did get out and went to Birmingham." Lee added that he had followed Capp's car to the town line.

The information from these university officials was useful because they could be quoted and because they corroborated what I had been told by the former college official whose name I could not use in print. But I still had no firsthand information about the alleged incidents involving the women students. Persuading them to co-operate would be difficult.

The first of Capp's alleged victims I contacted was the one whose name had been given me by the former college official. I began the conversation with a lengthy explanation of who I was, what I knew so far and what I hoped to find out. I made it clear that no names would be used except "in the most extreme legal circumstances." The reason I didn't make an absolute promise not to reveal names was that I wanted to be able to produce the women as witnesses if Capp decided to sue the column for libel. The other reason was that there was obviously no way to keep the names from him. He knew them already. She agreed to co-operate and told me one of the most astonishing stories I had ever heard.

As a student leader, she had worked in the university's annual "Festival of Arts" program in which Capp's lecture was a central event. He arrived in Tuscaloosa by plane on Sunday, February 11, 1968. She was one of several students who met his plane and had lunch with him afterward at a Tuscaloosa restaurant. Afterward she and a reporter for the campus newspaper took Capp and his traveling assistant to the Hotel Stafford, where Capp was staying. Capp asked if he could have a copy of the most recent university yearbook and a student directory. He had called long distance the day before to say that he planned to tape interviews while at the university for an NBC series called "Al Capp on Campus." During the phone call, he asked her to arrange interviews with other women students. He said he had spoken mainly to men on other campuses and wanted to balance his material. The yearbook was needed to help him select those he wanted to interview and the directory, he said, would enable him to contact them. He had also requested earlier that students write out questions which would form the basis for his "Ask Al Capp" lecture to be delivered the following night.

Having left Capp and his assistant, whom Capp identified as an NBC employee, in their rooms, she went back to the campus to get the yearbook, the directory, and the questions that had been prepared. The student newsman stayed at the hotel to interview

Capp. The plan was that she would bring the materials back, then she and the student reporter would go back to the campus.

When she returned, it was late afternoon. She called upstairs from the hotel lobby to suggest that Capp and the student reporter meet her in the coffee shop. Capp said, however, that they were having coffee in his suite and invited her to come up. When she arrived, though, the student had gone, supposedly to get a fresh pot of coffee. At this point Capp told her he was impressed with her ability and her record at the university. He suggested that she might be the right person for a job traveling with him for NBC to assist in the production of the "Capp on Campus" series. At about this time, Capp's assistant left the suite, supposedly to find the student newsman. When he had left, Capp began making advances toward her. He grabbed her and tried to kiss her. She broke away and tried to leave, but he grabbed her arm. She got loose and tried to open the door, but couldn't. He then threw himself against it. By now, he had removed much of his clothing and he continued to undress until he was completely naked. He even took off his artificial left leg. Somehow, he was able to move about without it. She tried to fend him off, but he finally grabbed her, pushed her to the floor and tried to force himself upon her. She broke loose again and locked herself in the bathroom of the suite. She screamed at him for about ten minutes, warning that she was influential on the campus and close to many top school officials. She threatened to ruin him. He shouted back crude, insulting remarks. Finally, however, he agreed to let her leave. She opened the door, grabbed her coat and hurried out of the hotel.

Two days later, with the festival nearly over, she found that another student leader had had a similar experience. Together, they went to Dean Healy and told her of the incidents. Then, exhausted and distraught, she checked into the university infirmary where she remained, under sedation, for several days.

This account was not spilled out to me all at once. It took considerable coaxing and patience to get all the details. I repeatedly reassured her that we planned to use the information most carefully and were determined to avoid embarrassing those Capp had victimized. She finally acknowledged also that she had seen a psychiatrist, though not regularly, in an effort to straighten out confused sexual attitudes that had resulted directly, she said, from her experience with Capp.

There was no way of knowing, of course, how widespread such conduct on Capp's part was. But what this woman had told me made one thing plain. This man was no mere lecher or fanny pincher. What had been described to me was a sex crime, an attempted rape. Any doubts I might have had about the legitimacy of the story were gone now. I was outraged. From her, I got the names of two other women whom Capp had approached. I began trying to track them down.

The first of the two women readily agreed to tell her story. She had attended Capp's news conference on the campus the day after he arrived. Capp's assistant approached her and took her up to his room afterward, ostensibly to discuss a possible job offer. As they were approaching Capp's suite, the assistant suggested that when she went into Capp's room, she give him a kiss. She responded that she wouldn't do such a thing. The assistant said that Capp liked that sort of thing. Capp was seated at the desk in his room when they arrived. A short time later, the assistant said he had to make a phone call and left. Capp got up and came over and sat next to her on the sofa. He made some comments about oral sex, then exposed himself to her and asked her to touch him. She got up and hurried out of the hotel. Later that day, she reported the incident to a family friend who was a vice president of the university.

The third woman I reached had had only a mild experience with Capp. She had been invited back to his suite after the Monday night lecture by his assistant, who had interviewed her for what he said was a planned broadcast entitled "The Now Morality." The assistant said there would be a party in Capp's room. Instead, there was just Capp. He made a pass at her. She successfully re-sisted it and fled.

It took several days for me to locate the fourth woman, whose name I had gotten. I finally found her on the West Coast. She was bitter about Capp's having gotten away with what he had done but was at first reluctant to co-operate. I explained my pur-pose, told her all I had learned from the others. She finally agreed. She said she had been part of the group who met Capp's plane. Because it was one of her jobs in student activities to greet visiting speakers, she had later gone to his hotel to see him. She said he exposed himself to her. She got up and tried to leave the room but had difficulty getting the door open. He finally agreed to let her go when she threatened to open a window and scream for help.

So now I had the personal accounts of four different women to-ward whom Capp had made advances. I had the word of a univer-sity dean that these incidents had been reported to her and I had confirmation from the college police chief that he had ushered Capp out of town. There could no longer be the slightest doubt that the story was true. The women had not come to me with the facts, but had had to be tracked down one by one and persuaded to co-operate. The stories they had told me matched the stories they had told college officials at the time. I decided, nonetheless, to seek further insurance against legal actions by Capp. I got back in touch with the three women who had had the roughest experi-ences with him and asked them if they would be willing to testify against Capp should he decide to sue the column. I also asked if they would be willing to swear out affidavits attesting to what they had told me. All three said they would testify if it came to that, but the woman living out West said she would prefer not to make out an affidavit. That was just as well with me, because it would take considerable time to get it drafted, signed, and mailed East. I had already spent several weeks making literally dozens of phone calls to the women themselves, the college officials, to the former university official who had gotten me started. I even spoke with John Chancellor about the story, since I had been told that he had earlier looked into it. He said he had but had been forced to drop it, because "there is no way to get a story like this on the air." He agreed with me that the story was legitimate and encouraged me to go through with it.

I had worked on nothing else during this period, and Jack was becoming impatient. I drafted the two affidavits in my office, read them to the women over the telephone and made the corrections they wanted. The woman who had had the roughest experience wanted me to tone down the most lurid parts of her story in the affidavit, which I did. "It's true the way you have it," she said, "but I'd rather have the affidavit be more general." I then had them typed in the proper legal fashion and mailed them. I worried that when it came to signing their names to the documents and having them notarized, they might change their minds, but several days later, I got the affidavits back in the mail, signed and bearing notary seals. In the meantime, I had taken the final step —contacting Capp himself.

The rise to fame and wealth of Al Capp, whose real name was Alfred Gerald Caplin, was a remarkable success story. Now sixty-one years old, he had overcome poverty and the loss of his left leg in a boyhood streetcar accident. His career as a cartoonist began in the 1930s when he worked for Ham Fisher, the creator of "Joe Palooka." The hillbilly characters who eventually became the dramatis personae of "Li'l Abner" had their first incarnation in "Joe Palooka" during a six-week period in 1933, when Capp was drawing the Sunday strip. By August 1934, he had left Fisher and gotten started with the Sunday Boston *Globe* drawing the strip that would ultimately have a daily readership estimated at 60 million. His keen wit and liberal politics made him a favorite at Cambridge political gatherings. He eventually made Cambridge his home, at the urging of such Harvard friends as John Kenneth Galbraith and Arthur Schlesinger. His home on Brattle Street became a tourist landmark. But in the 1960s, Capp's politics began to change. Although he campaigned against Barry Goldwater in 1964, he found that he had little sympathy for the anti-Vietnam War movement, particularly as it was manifested in campus protests. He carried a caricature of Joan Baez in the comic strip, called Joanie Phonie. And a group of bearded, scruffy protesters also turned up in the strip, known as "Swine." He considered, but decided against, running against Senator Edward Kennedy in 1970. I had no trouble recognizing the confident, nasal voice that came over the telephone from his studio in Boston when I called him on Monday, April 12, 1971.

"This is Brit Hume," I said. "I work for Jack Anderson, the syndicated columnist."

"Yah," he said.

"I've developed a detailed account of an episode involving you that happened at the University of Alabama in 1968. If you recall, you were down there to appear in their Festival of Arts Program, between the eleventh and the thirteenth of February. You stayed at the Hotel Stafford, as I understand it, and you had an assistant with you whom you identified as an NBC employee . . ."

"Right," he said, sounding a bit apprehensive. I went on to explain in as much detail as I could the version of the first, and most serious, of the incidents in his hotel room. I used the woman's name and made it clear that I had her word of this. When I got to the part about him pursuing her naked and without his leg, he interrupted.

"I pursued her without my limb?" he asked incredulously. Then he laughed in his confident way. "Ha, that's a great picture."

I was trying to get as much of what I knew said before he blurted out a denial. I hoped that if he realized that I had all the facts, he might not deny them, although I knew this was a longshot. He interrupted again.

"I'm getting . . . Gee whiz . . . That is the most sickening thing for me to listen to."

"Well, I can assure you," I said, "I have checked this very carefully, not only with the young women, but with the university administration and they have all confirmed it. In fact, Colonel Beverly Lee, the chief of the university police has told me that he personally went to your room and asked you to leave town and that you did."

"I never saw the man in question," he said, still sounding surprised, but not terribly shaken. "There is nothing about that that sounds familiar to me."

I continued to press home the details, repeating some I had already mentioned, naming the women's names, and trying to impress upon Capp how sure we were of the facts. Suddenly his voice dropped to almost a hoarse whisper.

"I may be quite ill right at the moment," he said. "Could I call you back?"

"Of course," I said.

"If you were me and you got such a call, you might find it difficult . . . Give me an hour to pull myself together." He said he wanted to talk to his former traveling assistant and his lawyer. "I don't feel very good . . . What are you out to do? . . . Has anyone made any complaint? . . . I need more than an hour really . . . This is important enough to me to come to Washington."

As he was making these rambling, somewhat incoherent comments, I kept pointing out that he had neither confirmed, nor denied the facts I had cited.

"Don't be too rough on me, will you?" he finally said. "Give me some time just to recover my equilibrium. Where is Anderson reachable?"

My answer was that Jack did not allow anyone to go over the head of one of his reporters to deal with him on a story.

"I'll deal wholly with you," Capp said hastily.

It was now about quarter to noon. I suggested Capp call me back at one o'clock, which would give him time to confer with his lawyer. He agreed and hung up. But at noon, the phone rang again. It was Capp. He had been unable to reach either his ex-assistant or his lawyer. He wanted to know if he could see Jack and me if he flew to Washington that day. This was something I hadn't expected, but there was no choice but to say yes. Anytime an investigative reporter is on the verge of publishing a damaging story, he must make every effort to accommodate the subject of the story in giving his side of it. Capp was badly shaken. "I don't care if I don't make another speech in my life," he said. "I just can't hit my kids this way. I'm going to see you without anyone with me." I told him to feel free to bring along anyone he wanted, especially his lawyer, if he saw fit. A short time later, Capp called back to say he was booked on the next plane and would call me from the Washington airport when he arrived.

Now I had to act quickly. Jack was still at home working on the column. I called him to tell him Capp was on his way, but Jack had left. Soon, though, he arrived at the office. I told him what had happened. He immediately canceled his lunch date and made arrangements to postpone his plans for the rest of the afternoon. It had been some time since I had talked to Jack about the story and he knew only the outline of it. I filled him in as quickly as I could and he thought a few minutes, then decided how we would handle Capp. We were to use an old interrogation technique familiar to policemen. One questioner plays the relentless prosecutor, the other the understanding friend. The idea is to get the person being questioned so intimidated by the first interrogator that he will open up to his more friendly partner.

"I'll take the position that I don't know the facts of the matter and can't make any judgment until I've heard them," Jack said. "Then you start reviewing them. Maybe Capp will think he's better off telling the truth and hoping that I'll be nice enough to overrule doing the story."

It was shortly after 2 P.M. when Capp arrived. I was sitting at my desk and watched him come down the hall and go into Jack's office. I had seen him make his way across the stage to take his seat on television talk shows and had noticed his limp. But I never

72

saw him limp in as pronounced a manner as he did walking down the hall. He was practically dragging his artificial leg behind him. He was wearing a snappy brown pinstripe suit with a matching vest which had a shawl collar, and a brown-and-white shirt and brown tie. He was carrying a broad-brimmed brown hat in his hand. His face, though, was ashen and he looked worried. The jaunty self-confidence which he normally displayed was gone. I didn't know whether he was really as upset as he looked, or whether he was trying to play upon our sympathy.

I heard Jack greet him cordially, and a few minutes later, Jack called me in. I walked into the office and introduced myself to Capp. He barely looked at me as we shook hands, but he gave me a strong handshake. He was seated in one of the chairs in front of Jack's desk. I sat down on the sofa adjacent to the desk.

Jack played his part to perfection. He wore a serious but sympathetic expression. He treated me politely, but as if I were a somewhat zealous junior member of the staff who needed reining in from time to time. He treated Capp with the greatest courtesy, repeatedly expressing his admiration for him and calling him "Al" as if they were old friends. Capp responded in kind. The air was thick with mutual admiration. Capp obviously had made this trip without consulting his lawyer, or against his lawyer's advice. He must have thought that since he and Jack were both syndicated newspapermen and public figures he could establish a rapport that would lead to Jack's dropping the story. He got off to a terrible start.

"Jack," he said, "you speak on college campuses, don't you?"

"Yes," said Jack, "I'm on the campuses almost every week."

Capp leaned forward in his chair, dropped his voice slightly and with a knowing leer, said, "Well, you know how these young babes come up to you and . . ."

Jack, the devout Mormon, father of nine children, including a daughter in college, gave Capp an icy, indignant stare that cut him off in midsentence. He slumped back in his chair.

73

I tried repeatedly to question Capp about the specifics of the story, but every time I raised the subject, saying that I needed to fill Jack in on what I knew, Capp would stop me.

"Please," he said, looking pained. "I don't want to hear that again. It makes me sick. Suppose I leave the room while you fill him in."

Between my efforts to steer the conversation onto course, Capp made various plays for Jack's sympathy.

"I'm old enough and rich enough now," he said at one point, "so that I don't give a damn about what anybody says about me. It's my grandchildren I'm concerned about. They're going to school in this country now and they're with us on weekends. I couldn't bear to have something come out that would be an embarrassment to them."

Jack nodded sympathetically and said, "My personal inclination is to let this matter drop. But I have a rule around here that I never let my personal feelings for an individual interfere with the integrity of the column. So it's a difficult decision. As I say, I like you and have always admired your work, so I'm inclined to let this one go. But I have to listen to my staff."

Jack swiveled in his chair toward me. "What about these girls who have told you this," he said sternly. "Are they credible?"

I stared straight back and nodded slowly. Jack turned back to Capp. "Well, I've got to know what the facts are to make a decision. I think we should go over this."

"I have never," Capp said, shaking his head and gesticulating in his characteristic manner, "become involved with any student."

That, of course, didn't mean anything. I insisted he be more specific. "Please understand," I said. "This is an effort to get your side of the story. It's hard to be fair if we don't know your position on these things." I then began repeating the detailed allegations. Capp averted his gaze from me and looked most uncomfortable. Jack knitted his brow in an expression of concern, even shock. When I got to the details of his naked pursuit of the first victim around his hotel suite, I said, "Now she has told me in great detail of this episode. Is it true?"

"Of course not," Capp said.

I reviewed the other incidents briefly. His response each time was a stricken look and "Of course not."

Now, there was nothing more to say. Jack stood up. Capp was still making rambling conversation about his grandchildren, still trying to find the combination that might win mercy from Jack Anderson. Jack looked upon him with an expression of pity that looked real. Jack had not heard the vivid recollections of these four women himself. He had merely heard my summaries of them. But he had seen Capp make his pathetic entreaties not to print the story. Jack, evidently, was moved. But it seemed to me a little late for Capp to be worrying about his grandchildren. Jack again repeated that he was inclined not to use the story and promised to notify Capp of his decision.

After Capp had left the office, Jack looked at me with a worried expression and asked, "Do you think maybe we should forget this one? I think the poor guy's sick."

"Hell no," I said. "This guy's a goddam sex criminal. He just came down here to try to weasel out of this. He doesn't give a damn about his grandchildren. If he did, he wouldn't have gotten mixed up in something like this. And besides, he didn't admit anything. If he had come down here and told us that it was all true and that he was sick and would take treatment, if he really leveled with us that would be one thing. Instead, he gave us a bunch of bullshit about his grandchildren, denied the whole thing, and left. Besides, this is an important story. I'm not even sure if he had come down and told us the truth, we should have withheld it. We're not the police, or the courts, we're reporters and our job is to publish the news, not to sit in judgment on people."

"You're right," Jack said. "Let's see. This is Monday. You'll have the affidavits later this week. I guess we should move ahead with this as quickly as possible."

75

After talking to Capp, I phoned Len Appel, a lawyer with the firm which had represented Jack for many years. Len, a mild-mannered, scholarly man with a strong devotion to the First Amendment, had handled a libel suit against Jack and me filed several months earlier by a United Mine Workers official. The suit had led to a court order against me to reveal the source of the story. Since it was a confidential, inside source, we were resisting. If the order were to stand, and I still refused to name the source, the judge might enter a judgment against me for default, throw me in jail for contempt of court, or both. It was a tough spot. In working to get out of it, I had come to know Len well and respect his advice. Now I went over the steps we had taken in the investigation of the Capp story. Len felt we had been thorough enough to defend successfully against any suit Capp might file. He agreed that the affidavits would help but said they would be less effective in court than as a deterrent to Capp in deciding whether to sue us.

Although I knew we would ultimately win any lawsuit, my experience in the one involving the mine union official had not been pleasant. I didn't want to be sued again if I could avoid it. This was one of the reasons I had qualified my promise to keep the victims' names secret and sought the affidavits. Len talked it over with the other two members of the firm who worked closely with Jack. They all agreed that we were on solid ground legally, but one of the partners, Betty Murphy, said she thought it was a sleazy story that we should avoid.

"I like to think of you and Jack pursuing stories like the Dodd case and the mine workers. But this is different," she said.

It bothered me a little, because I respected Betty's judgment. But I believed strongly in the story and felt that, unlike the Randy Agnew affair, it would be a credit to the column.

The next step was to draft a column which would at once make clear that Capp's advances to the women had been brutal and indecent without being so graphic as to be unpublishable in most newspapers. If we said too little, the incident might be dismissed as trivial. If we said too much, the column might be spiked for being obscene. It would also be necessary to make clear in the column how thoroughly the story had been checked, to show that Capp had been fully consulted and also to make the case for the column, based upon Capp's public criticism of campus morality.

The column I drafted for Jack's approval began as follows: "Al Capp, the famed cartoonist and caustic critic of college students, was shown out of town by University of Alabama police a few years ago after he allegedly made indecent advances toward several co-eds." The early mention of the police was deliberate. Most newspapers, whatever their policy about sex stories, will report incidents where the police are called. The column went on to call the episode "both ironic and significant. For Capp's scathing denunciations of college students and their morals have made him one of the most controversial commentators of the day." It cited his syndicated newspaper column and broadcast commentaries. Then it quoted from his more biting comments about campus morality, noted that he had denied the charges against him, but cited all those who had confirmed them and told of the four interviews with the victims and of their affidavits. Then it summarized the incidents, telling how Capp made "forceful advances" and "exposed himself," but went no further. Capp's explanation followed, then ours:

"It gives us no pleasure to make these revelations about a man whose legendary 'Li'l Abner' cartoon creations have amused millions of Americans for generations.

"But Al Capp today is much more than a gifted cartoonist and brilliant humorist. He is a major public figure whose views reach and influence millions. He even seriously considered running against Sen. Edward Kennedy (D-Mass.).

"Therefore, we believe the public has a right to any information which may bear upon his qualifications to speak, particularly when the incident involved is so obviously relevant to the self-same subjects on which he has been holding forth."

The column, virtually unchanged by Jack, was sent out Monday, April 19, for publication the following Thursday. I thought a compelling case for publishing it had been made, but I had no idea how editors around the country would react. The next day, we got word from the Washington *Post* that it would not publish the Capp column. When Jack asked why, he was told that the newspaper had a policy against publishing any sex stories on prominent persons unless there was official action involved such as an arrest. I was bitterly disappointed. The *Post*'s policy, if there really was such a policy, seemed to be to abdicate the paper's news judgment to the police.

I remembered an earlier instance when Peter Yarrow of the Peter, Paul and Mary folk group had been charged with a morals offense on the say-so of a young teen-aged girl who had gone to visit him in his room on her own. The *Post* splashed the story all over the lower part of the front page, with a large photograph of Yarrow. Despite the suspicious circumstances, the *Post* spared no details. There was no appeal from the *Post*'s decision, however. We could only hope other newspapers would not be as timid. (I later had a conversation with Benjamin Bradlee, the *Post*'s executive editor, following an appearance with him on the Dick Cavett Show. Cavett mentioned the Capp column and said how glad he had been that someone had blown the whistle on Capp. I reminded Bradlee that his newspaper had refused to print it. He remembered it, but couldn't recall why. I told him it was because of the paper's policy on the subject of sex. He couldn't remember what the policy was. So I explained it to him.)

Two other newspapers also called about the column before publication date. Claude Sitton, editor of the Raleigh, N.C., *News and Observer* wanted to find out how thorough our documentation was. "It's a hell of a story," he said. I explained all that we had done in checking it. He seemed satisfied. I also got a call from a reporter from the Boston *Globe*, one paper we strongly hoped would publish the column. The *Globe*, it seemed, was agonizing over it. Editor Thomas Winship, one of the nicest men in the newspaper business, wanted to know the full details of our documentation. I spent about an hour on the phone with the *Globe*'s man, during which I dictated the two affidavits to him. The *Globe*, however, did not publish the story. And, except for the New York *Post*, neither did any other major newspaper in the Northeast, including the Philadelphia *Bulletin*, the Hartford *Times* and the Baltimore *News-American*. The Chicago *Daily News* also killed it and so did the Atlanta *Constitution*. From what we could tell, the column was suppressed by at least half of our subscribers and a majority of the major ones. Aside from New York, the only major cities where the column appeared were Miami and San Francisco. But the episode was far from over.

Sitton's *News and Observer* did publish the column after calling Capp and getting his reaction. He blamed the whole affair on an effort by the "radical left-wing underground to shut me up." "The allegations are wholly and ludicrously faked and untrue," he said. "For the past three years, I've been warned to cut it out or they'd get me. My fear was that it would be a bomb or shooting me. I have had one or two physical threats recently, but I have lived in fear of a bomb at my home. I have feared getting into my car—afraid there'd be a bomb in my car. But I've gone on.

"You ever see the sheet they pass out giving instructions on how to get people? It's a sheet they pass out on all campuses . . . This is a classic example of what is in the underground textbooks on how to get someone.

"I had one leg amputated at the hip when I was nine years old. And I have a bad ankle on my one remaining leg. I am usually met at the airport with a wheelchair. I frequently have to use crutches to stand. So you see, I'm not physically able, in any physical condition to pursue or restrain anyone. For the past ten years or so, I find walking difficult . . . While I was there in Tuscaloosa, they were very nice to me. While I was there I had with me an assistant, someone to run out and get coffee for me . . . An assistant is always there. My man is always with me. It's a part of the new left-wing manual. If I was a bad character, it looks like they would have let me know in less than three years. Since then I have spoken at hundreds of colleges. That is the statement I want to make about it."

On the day the column was sent out to the newspapers, Jack had written a letter to Capp notifying him, as he promised he would, of his decision. I took it home with me and dropped it in a mailbox in suburban Maryland, near my home. We didn't want Capp to know about the column too soon before it appeared because we feared that he might threaten to sue before the column came out. We thought a threatened lawsuit might intimidate many of our editors into killing the column. As it turned out, they didn't need any intimidating. Capp's response to Jack's letter arrived the day the column appeared. It was a telegram, which read as follows:

DEAR JACK, THANK YOU FOR YOUR OFFER TO MAKE A RESPONSE TO THE COLUMN. MY FEELING IS THAT RESPONSE TO ANYTHING LIKE THIS SERVES ONLY TO GIVE IT GREATER SPREAD. YOU DID WHAT YOU THINK BEST. I'M DOING WHAT I THINK BEST AND I AM SURE WE WILL BOTH SURVIVE IT. BEST, AL CAPP.

We later received word that when the daily shipment of New York *Posts* arrived at one major downtown Boston newsstand, someone was waiting for them and bought them all. We never learned whether this was done at Capp's instigation or not, or whether any effort was made to buy the other copies of the *Post* that might have made their way into Boston that day. But gradually, we got bits of information that gave us an idea of his reaction to the column. The day it appeared he had been scheduled to speak to the Young Americans for Freedom chapter at the University of Missouri. But he canceled the appearance, giving bronchitis as the reason.

Although many papers killed the column, the mail from readers poured in. Most letters supported Capp and blasted us. Carl Ruby of North Miami wrote: "What possible satisfaction can one derive from being a raker of muck, a keyhole peeper, a searcher through waste baskets and a character wrecker. What a loathsome way to make a living." Graham Foster of New York agreed, "Your column today about Al Capp was really sickening. Who appointed you God?" A reader from Brooklyn, whose name was undecipherable, called the column "a disgusting display of old type yellow journalism." In a postscript to the letter, which was addressed to the New York *Post*, he urged Jack, "Please show this to your city editor." Another correspondent, identified only as "Reader," wrote, "True or not—and it's probably true—I would have thought twice about telling the world. It seems to me it was less than Christian." My favorite among Capp's defenders was Maurice Knobbe of the Bronx, whose letter appeared on stationery which bore a drawing of a baby in diapers holding up an American flag. "I read your article concerning the virility of Al Capp, in the New York Post. Until then I never realized that Capp in his appearances on the college campus, was speaking out against *seduction*."

There were some letters of support, too. Raymond Haber of New York, sent a note scribbled on Merrill Lynch, Pierce, Fenner & Smith paper, saying, "Your article concerning Al Capp was the finest display of courageous journalism I have ever encountered." And Colin Miller of Berkeley, California, wrote, "Releasing the Al Capp column took guts. Capp can be a vindictive man. I'm sure you had your facts and I was relieved that you possess affidavits." More important than these, however, were two other letters. A woman from Berry Creek, California, wrote, "I had a similar experience with him which if you are interested, I could describe in more detail. I met him in New York City in the summer of 1967." And another woman from Modesto, California, wrote, "I feel it is my duty to society and other young ladies who have endured what I endured from Al Capp to report to you. I was asked

to be 'secretary' to Mr. Capp when he appeared on our campus
. . . The head of the Arts and Humanities division asked me to
fulfill the wishes of Mr. Capp's letter asking for a young attractive, reasonable, intelligent girl to type for him before the appearance. I met him at the airport and accompanied him to his room,
where he had dinner sent up and began on his notes. However,
he then began this Capp on Campus bit with me and called his
cohort in and spoke with him about hiring me. The rest goes just
as' your Alabama girls tell it . . . My husband and I, along with
my aunt, sought our lawyer's advice. When I had written an
affidavit describing everything I could remember, my lawyer indicated that he wouldn't suggest my tying my name up with the
horrible things I had said Capp did, and that he very easily could
turn the tables on me, with his influence and it could be an un-
pleasant experience for me . . ."

In addition to these letters, I also got several phone calls from
women who reported similar experiences with Capp. I had suspected from the start that the Alabama episode was not an isolated
instance. The letters and the calls were evidence, if not proof, that
it had been one of many, and that fear of scandal had prevented
college officials and victims in a number of places from blowing
the whistle.

Still, I felt the story had not succeeded, largely because so many
papers had refused to print it. I was more convinced than ever
that it was legitimate and that we had reported it as thoroughly
and fairly as possible. This made my disappointment even greater.
What I did not know at this point was that three weeks to the
day before the column appeared and only days before Jack and
I had talked with him, Capp had been involved in another incident with a woman student.

It occurred in Eau Claire, Wisconsin, site of a branch of the
University of Wisconsin. Capp had used his purported need for
a secretary to lure a young woman to his room, and the rest followed Capp's familiar pattern. The full story was later related to

me by Lawrence Durning, the prosecuting attorney in Eau Claire, who happened to be a staunch political conservative. The victim, a young married woman, had wanted to press charges but had faced the same dilemma as others in the same circumstances. Did she want to face a trial in which she would have to reveal her ordeal in open court? And Durning also faced a difficult choice. If he decided to bring charges, Capp would first have to be extradited to face them. And in the end, it would be Capp's word against the young woman's. Would the jury believe her or Capp?

No decision had been reached by April 22, when our column appeared in the local Eau Claire paper. Durning told me later that the column convinced the victim that she was not alone and stiffened her determination to press charges. So Durning filed charges against Capp for indecent exposure, attempted sodomy, and attempted adultery. He moved to have Capp extradited from Massachusetts to face the accusations. Now there was no way the story could be avoided, because the authorities had acted. The wire-service stories from Wisconsin noted that the charges against Capp came three weeks after Jack's column had made similar allegations. So, many papers that had refused to print the column originally ended up publishing the charges it had made. Capp finally returned to Wisconsin to face the charges. A trial was averted, however, when he agreed to plead guilty to the attempted adultery charge in exchange for the dismissal of the other charges. The judge placed him on probation.

I never viewed the purpose of "The Washington Merry-Go-Round" as "getting" people we deemed to be enemies of the public interest. The column had a long history of exposing the corrupt and destroying their careers. But its impact on individuals seemed to me secondary to its more important function of constantly reminding the public of a part of the truth about government and politics that was hidden from view in much of the news that came out of Washington. The Capp story was different, however. His antics were not representative of any general hypocrisy and depravity that I could perceive among others equally famous or influential. He was an isolated case. But he was a fraud and a menace. Responsible officials of at least one university, and apparently numerous others (prosecutor Durning said he was contacted by about fifteen other women around the country who said they had also been Capp's victims), had refused to act against him. So, apparently, had a number of prosecuting attorneys. Thus Capp had gotten away with what he had done and might have continued to. I hoped the column put a stop to it. Apparently, it did. When last I heard, Capp was living in London.

SIX

One reason Jack Anderson had proved to be such a resourceful reporter was his brazen willingness to ask for even the most sensitive information and to act as if he fully expected to get it. Drew Pearson had been a master at behind-the-scenes reporting of Washington. His columns often carried detailed accounts of the private meetings of top government officials, which sounded as if Pearson had eavesdropped on them himself. In fact, they were usually pieced together from fragmentary reports obtained from the participants. Not long after Jack joined Drew in 1947, he found what he thought was a better way to get such inside information. Transcripts are made of many closed-door government meetings, especially on Capitol Hill, so why not get them? It mattered not to Jack that such transcripts were closely held, that many were never made public and that even those dealing with budgetary requests were only released months later, after being sanitized of any "classified" information. Jack had found that members of Congress were generally eager to befriend him as he made his way about the Capitol hallways in search of information for Drew. He began to watch the bulletin boards in the press galleries of both the House and Senate for notices of executive sessions held by the various committees. The next day, he would check the newspapers to see if the press had been told of what had occurred in the closed hearings. If not, he would seek out friendly committee members to find out what he could. If a hearing sounded interesting, he would then go to one of his more pliant sources on the committee in question and request a copy of the transcript. As often as not, he got it.

Indeed, one of his more co-operative sources in the Senate for a while was the ambitious young John Kennedy of Massachusetts. Jack liked dealing with Kennedy because he found him decisive. "If he was going to go along," Jack told me, "he'd say, 'Stop by my office about three o'clock this afternoon.' If he wasn't, he'd say, 'No, I don't think it's in the public interest.' That would be the end of it."

The publication of excerpts from the transcripts of the Senate Foreign Relations and Armed Services Committees by Jack and Drew ultimately led both committees to place additional restrictions on access to the documents. Nevertheless, other committee transcripts remained available to the column and they frequently contained much newsworthy information about defense and foreign policy. There was also the drama of confrontations between miserly appropriations-subcommittee chairmen and executive-department potentates insisting on the validity of their budget requests. Such hearing records, embellished with imaginary descriptions of how the congressmen "stormed" or "demanded" or "snorted," while the witnesses "squirmed," "admitted sheepishly" and "insisted angrily," were the stuff of many "ready-made" Merry-Go-Round columns, so-called because they could usually be written from the documents themselves with little other reporting. Once when Les Whitten wrote a column based on a transcript, he made reference to a "dignified Negro serving coffee" to the senators in the closed hearing. A few days later, one of his friends in the news business called him on the phone and said, in an Amos 'n Andy voice that he was "Rastus." "Who?" said Les. "This is the dignified Negro who was serving the coffee at that hearing," was the reply.

Not long after I started with Jack, he called me in to explain how such transcripts were gotten and to encourage me to start making rounds on Capitol Hill and elsewhere to obtain transcripts and other restricted material.

"Now a lot of these guys want to co-operate," he explained. "But they're nervous about it. You've got to put them at ease by letting them know that we get this kind of stuff all the time. I've always had a little better luck in the Senate. You go down to the President's room—that's the little reception room off the floor—and send one of the pages in to get whichever senator you want. You'll find they'll come out to talk to you, even if they don't like the column. They can't resist. Their curiosity makes them come. Then you've got to con them a little. Pretend you know all about whatever they're doing, even if you don't. A lot of these guys don't have any news judgment and they don't know what's a story and what's not. So if you just get them talking, they'll sometimes mention things that are of great significance without realizing it. Then you press for all the details. If it's something that happened in a hearing, go for the transcript. There are a million stories on the Hill. Those guys are hungry for publicity. It's the richest vein in town. All you have to do is go up there and mine it."

Jack made it sound easy, which, for him, it was. He had long since mastered the backslapping and mutual flattery so common among politicians. He knew how to talk to them and he knew how to make the most extravagant requests of them in a way that made it all seem routine. And he was persistent, even relentless, in the pursuit of news and cultivation of news sources. His style of reporting had been developed in twenty-two years of making the rounds for Drew Pearson. He probably had the broadest range of sources of anyone in town. He dealt directly with members of Congress. He got information from cabinet officers. He lacked the entree to the Oval Office in the White House which Pearson often had enjoyed, but he always was in close touch with influential men around the President. And he had found other officials in nearly every government department, not always at the very top, but in important jobs where they knew what was going on, and recruited them carefully and patiently as sources. The result was that he knew someone who could give him authoritative inside information on virtually any area of the government. No matter how co-operative his sources were, he never ceased trying to persuade them to tell him a little more or to give him access to even more sensitive documents than he was already being allowed to see. He regarded his sources as his most precious asset and he went to extraordinary lengths to protect them. The staff, for instance, was rarely told the name of any of them. He met them in out-of-the-way places where necessary, and would deal with them through intermediaries if it was required. He frequently wrote his columns in such a way as to make it extremely difficult for the information to be traced to a source, even if doing so meant withholding newsworthy information.

Jack's care in not exposing his sources helped most of all in prying information out of the Pentagon, the most secrecy-prone of all the government departments except the Central Intelligence Agency. Jack always covered the Pentagon for Drew, leaving the State Department to Pearson himself. He trekked its endless hallways nearly every day and over the years developed a huge network of highly placed generals and admirals, who trusted him with classified information. Jack knew how to play upon the interservice rivalries, to persuade his contacts that publication of the information he wanted would help their cause. There is nothing unusual about such strategic leaks of defense information, but Jack was able to open the leaks on his initiative, instead of simply receiving the leaked material. For years, he had access to the daily digest of intelligence information that circulates at the highest levels of the military. Much of the information in these documents can be found in the newspapers, but each week, there is usually some fresh material turned up by the U.S. intelligence community that is news. When there was, Jack always got it first. In addition, his military sources often sat at their desks with classified documents before them and told him some or all of their contents without actually showing him the papers. Jack, of course, constantly pushed to be shown the documents and to be allowed to copy them. Sometimes, he was.

Pearson's column frequently embarrassed the Pentagon, often

with stories written by Jack. He would then put on his most per-
plexed expression and explain to his military sources that he had
tried to talk the boss out of the story, but Drew wouldn't budge.
Drew would similarly blame Jack for stories that angered his
sources.

When the Gulf of Tonkin incident occurred in 1964, and President Johnson went on television to tell the nation that two of
its ships had been attacked twice without provocation by the
North Vietnamese, Jack got a different version from his Pentagon
sources. They told him the cable traffic from the U.S. ships indicated that the first time the North Vietnamese PT boats fired on
a U.S. destroyer, it could have been the result of confusion about
the purpose of the American ship's mission. What's more, the second "attack" might have been just a radar foul-up that made it
seem the ship had been fired upon. But with the public aroused
over what the President had portrayed as a mini-Pearl Harbor,
Johnson had no trouble getting approval for the air attacks he ordered as retaliation and for the congressional resolution he used
thereafter as his constitutional license for prosecution of the Vietnam War. There was, however, one brief flurry of controversy and
doubt about the incident. It was caused by a Pearson-Anderson
column reporting that top military men were worried that President Johnson had been "trigger-happy" in his reaction to the
Tonkin incident. The column contained a general account of the
version of the Tonkin episode which Jack's sources had given him.
But it was the word of newspapermen quoting anonymous sources
against the word of the President of the United States. Johnson,
naturally, prevailed, and the massive escalation of the Vietnam
War ensued. "I wonder," Jack would say, "if we had had those
documents, if we had had the proof, could we have stopped it?
I bet we could."

Late in 1971, war broke out between India and Pakistan. Although India attacked, it did so only after thousands of refugees
from East Pakistan had streamed across its border in the aftermath

of the Pakistani dictatorship's suppression of the civil rebellion in East Pakistan. In public and in conferences with congressional leaders, the Nixon administration gave repeated assurances of its neutrality in the conflict, depite some public criticism of India for launching the attack. Henry Kissinger, the President's foreign-policy adviser, insisted in an early December briefing for newsmen that the administration was not "anti-India." Meanwhile, part of the U.S. fleet moved into the Bay of Bengal, off India's coast. Russia was aligned with India in the conflict, and Communist China was siding with Pakistan. Soviet ships were already deployed in the bay. Secret Intelligence reports from New Delhi said India Prime Minister Indira Gandhi was worried about the American ships, but had been assured by Soviet Ambassador Nikolai Pegov that Russia would take care of any American naval intervention. The State Department, trying to balance its initial remarks critical of India, made conciliatory statements. But despite the protestations of neutrality, the Administration had secretly decided to help Pakistan. The State Department's soothing words were greeted with anger by Henry Kissinger. At White House meetings of the top-secret Washington Special Action Group, a top-level strategy council, Kissinger said India was trying to turn Pakistan into a "vassal state." Kissinger said he was "getting hell every half-hour from the President" because of the failure of the State Department to make the "tilt" toward Pakistan the President wanted. There were discussions of ways to sneak military assistance to Pakistan through Arab nations, so as to disguise their origins.

India, of course, had long been an ally of the United States. What's more, it was the largest democracy on earth. It was locked in a war with a military dictatorship whose internal problems had stemmed, in part, from its forceful suppression of the results of a democratic election in East Pakistan. The Nixon administration was saying one thing and doing the opposite. There was a clear possibility of a naval conflict between the U.S. and Russia in the Bay of Bengal. And the public knew nothing of any of it. Little by little, Jack was finding out about it from his sources, several of whom felt that what the Administration was doing was not only wrong but dangerous, even reckless. Soon, Jack had the broad outlines of what was happening. "It was just like what happened seven years before," he said later. "The Bay of Bengal looked like it was going to be the next Gulf of Tonkin. There was only one way to get the truth out. I had to get the documents. I had to get the proof."

In this instance, Jack had more to go on than the usual desire of sources to co-operate with him or to promote some particular project. There were highly placed officials in the government who thought the nation might be on the verge of war with Russia. It still took some persuading, but Jack finally succeeded. His sources gave him copies of virtually every current document dealing with the India-Pakistan conflict, including intelligence reports, cables and, most important of all, the minutes of the secret White House meetings where Henry Kissinger had issued his orders to "tilt" toward Pakistan. In addition, his sources also turned over a number of documents revealing duplicity in the Administration's conduct of foreign policy in Cambodia and the Mideast. At first, his sources gave him only a few papers. But Jack insisted that he had to have a full set, or his stories could be challenged as being only a partial glimpse of the picture, out of context. All of the material bore the highest security classification. It was an astonishing haul.

The material Jack now had was at least as remarkable as the Pentagon Papers on Vietnam, whose publication the previous June had touched off a historic confrontation between the government and the press. The Pentagon Papers were a historical study of the origins of the Vietnam War. But they only covered the years up to 1967. So everything in the papers was at least four years old. Still, the publication of the documents provoked an extreme reaction from the Nixon administration, which went all the way to the Supreme Court seeking an injunction to stop the press

from printing them. If the Administration would do this to suppress years-old material which did not even cover its own activities, what might it do to prevent publication of highly damaging
material that was only a few days old and contained proof of the
baldest sort of duplicity? Understandably, Jack said little around
the office about what he had. After he had written the first column
quoting from the documents, he told me that he was about to give
one of his sources a "baptism of fire" by publishing excerpts from
highly confidential material.

The column, scheduled for publication December 13, began
quietly enough. It was Drew Pearson's birthday and Jack paid
him tribute as a man who never lost hope that there could be peace
in the world. Near the end, he got around to current events. "In
the backrooms of the White House, foreign policymaker Henry
Kissinger has been downright hostile toward India. He has contended that India seeks to turn East Pakistan into a 'vassal state,'
that we cannot permit Pakistan to be overwhelmed while the Russians supply aid to India, that our other allies will lose faith in us
if we don't honor our commitment to Pakistan, that our whole security structure could be jeopardized if we let Pakistan down." The
column mentioned Kissinger's anger over State Department remarks conciliatory to India. "Finally," the column said, "Kissinger
passed the word that President Nixon would like to see Pakistan
throw back the Indian attack."

Becoming more specific, Jack mentioned that top Indian military officials had complained to U.S. military attaché Colonel
William King that there had been a recent shipment of military
cargo which arrived in Karachi, November 29 at 10:30 P.M. Then
Jack quoted briefly from the U.S. ambassador to India Kenneth
Keating's "urgent, classified message to the State Department on
the matter." Jack knew that the column would cause great consternation inside the White House. No one privy to the India-
Pakistan discussions could read it without knowing that Jack's
information was coming from the highest levels and that he had

obtained at least portions of classified documents. He assumed that knowledgeable newsmen would immediately reach the same conclusions. His information was simply too detailed, too specific to have sprung full-grown from his head. There was, however, no reaction whatever from the news media, although Warren Unna, a longtime Washington foreign affairs reporter, later told me that he knew Jack was on to something the minute he read the first column, and he began sending it and the succeeding columns to *The New Statesman of India,* for which he was acting as Washington correspondent.

The next day's column began, "A dangerous confrontation is developing between Soviet and American Naval forces in the Bay of Bengal." The column went on to quote directly from the minutes of the White House strategy meetings which had occurred December 3 and 4. Kissinger's remark that he was "getting hell every half-hour from the President" was included. Although Jack's sources reported that there was no doubt at the White House that a major breach of secrecy had occurred, the press still didn't catch on. Two days later, Jack returned to the subject, disputing Kissinger's background briefing to reporters in which he had insisted the U.S. was not "anti-India."

"Behind guarded doors of the White House Situation Room, however, Kissinger sang a different tune," Jack wrote. He told top planners, who met on December 3 to map strategy, "I'm getting hell every half-hour from the President . . ." Jack quoted at length from the secret sessions, still without saying that he had obtained the minutes. Jack also mentioned a cable from Washington to the American embassy in Jordan with instructions to "keep open the possibility of authorizing King Hussein to rush several U.S.-supplied P-104 fighter planes to Pakistan." Still, no reaction from the press.

There were two further columns, the first quoting the cables back and forth between Washington and New Delhi and Islamabad and the second quoting intelligence reports describing the ominous assurances given India by Soviet Ambassador Nikolai Pegov. When the last column on the subject appeared December 21, there had been five in a nine-day period. Still, not one newsman paid the slightest attention.

Of course, this was hardly the first time Jack had seen his work ignored or discounted by his colleagues. The Washington *Post*, for example, had refused to publish the first of the series of columns which led to the censure of Senator Thomas J. Dodd (D-Conn.), for misuse of campaign funds. It took a personal assurance from Drew Pearson that the material was solid to get the *Post* to publish the other Dodd columns, and even then, the *Post* occasionally lopped off a chunk that made the editors nervous. One of the *Post*'s star reporters, Richard Harwood, went to Connecticut during the exposé and wrote a story the general theme of which was that the charges by the column were unlikely to be of much political consequence. *Newsweek* reached similar conclusions. It was not until Dodd formally denied the charges and asked the Senate to make an investigation that the press got moving on the story.

Almost a year before the India-Pakistan columns, Jack had published a series revealing that the CIA had made six attempts to assassinate Fidel Castro during the Kennedy administration. The columns were loaded with details—times, places, methods used, and the names of individuals who had been hired by the agency to do the job. John McCone, who had been CIA director at the time, denied the story, which is what a CIA official must do when questioned about clandestine operations. The column was barely recognizable when it appeared in the Washington *Post*. The details of all the assassination attempts except the first had simply been cut out. McCone's denial, which had been reported near the end of the column because it was automatic, was moved to the second paragraph. The *Post* made no discernible effort to determine independently if the story were true, nor did any of the rest of the media. The story simply died.

The five columns Jack wrote about India-Pakistan did not specify that they were based upon a batch of secret papers. They were written in the column's familiar style, as racy and colorful as possible, but also easy to understand. I had thought as I read them that he had done a good job of making a complicated issue clear. The quotes he used from the documents seemed especially vivid. After Christmas, Jack made a most unusual move. He decided to write the India-Pakistan story all over again, only this time he would announce that he had a stash of classified material and would quote at length from the documents. It would probably bore the Kansas City milkman, but it might stir some interest from Jack's colleagues. The first column in the second series ran on Thursday, December 30. After a characteristic "Merry-Go-Round" beginning, it was given over to generous slices of direct quotation from the documents.

It worked. The column caught the eye of Benjamin Welles, a veteran diplomatic reporter in the Washington bureau of the New York *Times*, who called Jack to ask him about the material. Jack assured him of its authenticity. Welles also got similar confirmation from sources inside the government. The result was a story about Jack's column on the front page of the New York *Times* the next day. The column that day carried another long excerpt from the India-Pakistan documents and again Welles followed up in the next morning's *Times*. The second story ended with a quote from an unnamed top government official, who said that Jack "has gotten ahold of something and nobody seems to know how to stop him." We all loved that.

Two days later, Monday, January 3, Jack called Henry Kissinger a liar in the column, basing the accusation on the obvious discrepancy between Kissinger's "We're not anti-India" remark to reporters and his behind the scenes insistence on a "tilt" toward Pakistan. By now, the *Times*'s stories had attracted the attention of other news organizations. The Associated Press had carried a story saying an investigation was under way to trace the source of the leaked material. The NBC nightly news Monday edition carried a summary of Jack's reporting based on the documents, which by now Jack had dubbed "The White House Papers" in an effort to put them in the same league with the Pentagon Papers. The next morning's *Times* contained another report on the column by Welles and, more importantly, a column by Tom Wicker entitled "The Anderson Papers." It praised Jack generously for his "public service" in publishing the "remarkable series of documentary excerpts" on the India-Pakistan war.

Wicker's column seemed to have a decisive effect. That morning, Marvin Kalb of CBS News arrived with a camera crew to interview Jack in his office. During a break, I heard Kalb, his voice filled with something approaching wonder, say, "I've seen some security leaks before, but I can't remember one that was this close to the events themselves, can you?" Jack, naturally, allowed that he couldn't either. The BBC trooped in after Kalb left, and ABC was next. That afternoon, the Washington *Post*, evidently a little embarrassed that the media was making such a fuss over something it had been publishing on the comics page, sent over a reporter. By now, Kissinger, in reaction to Jack's accusation that he had lied about U.S. policy had made a terrible blunder. He claimed that Jack had quoted him out of context. This gave Jack the opening he needed to release the minutes of the meetings themselves, to make public, in effect, the context. It would have been unseemly for him to do so without provocation. He chose to give the documents to the *Post* exclusively. It seemed a shrewd maneuver. The papers would give the *Post* a story of its own and allow the newspaper to recover from the embarrassment the story had caused it. The *Post* would probably be grateful for that. It would probably also give the story generous play, which might generate requests from the rest of the media to copy the material, which, in turn would lead to more stories.

Late in the day, Jack accepted invitations to appear the next morning both on NBC's "Today" program and the CBS morning

news. Millions would see those broadcasts. Jack would undoubtedly be questioned closely on whether he was justified in
making public material that authorized government officials had
decided should be kept secret. Wasn't he arrogating to himself
power better left with duly elected and appointed public servants?
It was a question I had been thinking about for many months.

When a federal judge had ordered the New York *Times* to
cease publication of the Pentagon Papers study of Vietnam the
previous summer, it had ruined the last days of a week's vacation
I had taken. Although the judge's ruling was merely a temporary
restraining order designed to freeze the issue until a full hearing
could be held, it still stopped the presses and the government had
never been able to do that before. Although the judge ruled several days later that the papers could be published, he was quickly
overruled by an Appeals Court and the issue headed for the Supreme Court. Meanwhile the Nixon administration had moved
against the Washington *Post* and the Boston *Globe,* which had
also begun publication of stories based on the documents. Never
had such a basic liberty seemed to me to be in such danger. If freedom of the press meant anything, I thought, it meant that the
news media could publish the contents of government documents,
no matter whether an official had chosen to stamp them secret or
not. If the government were allowed to suppress information by
simply putting a label on it, the power to control what the public
knew of its activities would be firmly in its grasp forever. The ideal
of an informed, sovereign people governing the republic would be
lost.

There was no doubt, of course, that a system which made it
possible for newspapermen to expose the secrets of state was a
risky one. If the government couldn't count, at least for a while,
on the confidentiality of current diplomatic contacts or keep the
lid on its weapons technology, its ability to conduct foreign relations and defend the nation would be impaired. But the risks in
allowing the government to make an inviolable state secret of any-

thing it wished seemed to me infinitely greater. After all, the entire purpose of national defense and foreign policy was to protect the liberties that set America apart from all the nations of the world. If the freedom of the press were to be suspended whenever some government official thought it would be a good idea to keep information from the public, democracy would be destroyed in the name of protecting it. Far better, I thought, to accept the risks of freedom than to pervert the Constitution and subvert democracy by allowing government the power to control what the people know.

Besides, the security classification system was based not on law but on an executive order of the President, binding legally only on employees of the executive branch of government. And even if it had been rooted in law, the First Amendment to the Constitution said, "Congress shall make no law . . . abridging the freedom of speech, or of the press . . ." So any such law would have been invalid.

What's more, the authority to classify documents had been so misused and overused that the entire system had been reduced to a farce. There were at least 20 million classified documents, some of them dating back to World War II. At least 30,000 military officials had the power to use the secrecy stamps. No one could say how many officials in the government as a whole had such power, but the estimates ranged into the hundreds of thousands. Defense Secretary Melvin Laird had been forced to issue a special directive to keep the Navy from putting secrecy stamps on newspaper clippings. Departing government officials routinely helped themselves to classified material for use in memoirs and other writings.

When Lyndon Johnson left Washington for Texas, he took truckloads of documents, many of them classified, for use in the preparation of a history of his administration. He was paid $1.2 million in advance for his book, *The Vantage Point*, and when it appeared it turned out to contain many of the same secrets the Nixon administration had been so intent on suppressing in the

Pentagon Papers. In particular, it contained an account of "Operation Marigold," a 1966 communications channel the Johnson administration opened with Hanoi through a foreign diplomat. In trying to stop publication of the Pentagon Papers by the Washington *Post*, the Justice Department had argued in secret before Judge Gerhard Gesell that this was the single most sacrosanct piece of information.

Ultimately, of course, the newspapers' right to publish the Pentagon Papers was upheld by the Supreme Court. But three Justices dissented from the decision and two others indicated that, had the circumstances been different, they might well have voted to suppress the material. During the fifteen-day period in which the court battle over the papers was fought, I did nothing for the column. I was totally absorbed by the case. My feeling was that, if the government prevailed, it was a new ball game in America as far as the press was concerned and I wasn't sure I wanted to play. I attended all the court hearings in Washington, including the Supreme Court arguments, and read every line of information I could find on the subject. It seemed to me when it was over that the press had won an important battle, but could easily lose the long-term conflict over secrecy. Opinion polls had shown public sentiment against the publication of the Pentagon Papers and, paradoxically, against the Administration's attempt to stop it. Jack Anderson seemed to be in the midst of what might become a major new battle in the war over secrecy. If he handled it well, he might swing public opinion a long way toward the view that secrecy is dangerous. If he handled it poorly, the public might become persuaded that the news media posed the greater danger. I caught Jack alone in his office for a moment late in the afternoon of Tuesday, January 4. He was in a buoyant humor.

"I had a couple of thoughts on arguments you might want to stress," I said. He nodded for me to go ahead. He was stuffing some of the secret documents into his briefcase, which he apparently intended to take to New York for his television appearances there the next morning.

"Well," I said, "it seems to me you want to stay on the offensive as much as you can."

"Oh, by all means," Jack said. "You've got to stay on the attack. If they get you on the defensive, then you look bad. I'm going to keep pounding away at the fact that these documents show that the government has been lying. They can't use secrecy stamps to cover up their lies."

"Yes," I said, "and you can also say that the government itself, not the press, has made a shambles of the security classification system. There's no use saying there should be no secrets. But if you blame the government for debasing and cheapening the security labels by using them for everything in sight, then you're in a stronger position. It's an argument people won't be expecting and besides, it's true beyond doubt."

"You're right," he said. "That's a good idea. I'll use that."

"You'll undoubtedly be asked at some point, 'Who elected you to decide what should be kept secret and what shouldn't?' One answer might be that the people who wrote the Constitution did."

By now, Jack was on his way out the door. He had to stop at WTTG, Metromedia's Washington television station for whom he had been doing regular commentaries, to tape an additional broadcast on the India-Pakistan documents. After that, he would go home and get ready to go to New York.

"Look," he said, "can you put all these ideas and any others you have in a memo and drop it by my house? That way, I'll have time to study them and can take the memo with me."

I missed Jack's appearance on the CBS morning news the next day, but I saw the "Today" show. The previous summer, while Jack was on vacation in his home town of Salt Lake City, one of his friends had taken him to a clothing store and insisted he update his baggy, dowdy wardrobe. The best-looking of his new clothes was a light gray suit whose tailoring disguised Jack's pot belly and was becoming to his slightly pallid coloring. He wore it on the "Today" program, and he never looked better. In an interview with Frank McGee, Jack was ready with answers to all questions. His background as a lay preacher and a platform speaker, as well as his years with Drew Pearson on radio, had given Jack a public speaking style that usually seemed bombastic and overbearing on television. But in the interview with McGee, he was earnest, soft-spoken, and persuasive. He held up several of the documents and the camera moved in for titillating close-ups that showed the black security markings they bore. Jack made good use of some of the arguments I had suggested in my memo the day before, particularly mentioning the little-known fact that Herb Klein, the Administration's communications director, had said back in 1969 during an appearance at the National Press Club that under no circumstances did the government have the right to lie. The India-Pakistan story was Jack's from beginning to end and it was an extraordinary job. But it was exciting for me to be a part of it, if only to the extent of suggesting a few ways he could defend what he had done.

Meanwhile, the Washington *Post* led its Wednesday morning editions with a story on the documents Jack had given it the day before. The *Post* called Jack's release of the papers "a major challenge to the Administration's secrecy" on the India-Pakistan war. By the time Jack got back to Washington, the office was in a virtual state of siege. Other major clients of the column, such as the Chicago *Daily News*, were incensed that Jack had made an exclusive release to the *Post*. Every major news organization in town now wanted its own set of the papers. The phones rang continuously the entire day. At one point, there were thirty-one messages piled up on Jack's desk and that was after he had returned all the more important calls. Some radio stations and newspapers were willing to interview anyone in the office. I went on a live radio show in Cleveland by telephone and held forth with abandon for fifteen minutes. Others in the office performed similar tasks.

Inside Story

The Xerox machine never stopped that day, as Jack made public the documents he had given the *Post* and also had copied other, related papers for release. He went over each one himself, giving explicit instructions on what should be removed from them by painting them with "Wite-Out," a liquid substance used to cover typographical errors. All markings that might have indicated from whom he obtained the material were removed. So was any information contained in intelligence reports that might have given away the identity of the nation's intelligence sources. After the papers were painted with "Wite-Out," they were then recopied.

The release of the documents proved an even bigger story than his publication of their contents originally. Now the rest of the media had their own sets of the secret papers, which seemed to double their enthusiasm. In every story, of course, Jack was mentioned as the source of the material. There were also a rash of feature stories on Jack himself. The New York *Times* published a flattering "Man in the News" profile of him. Robert Walters, an investigative reporter for the Washington *Star* whom Jack had once tried to hire, wrote that the India-Pakistan affair signaled Jack's emergence from the shadow of Drew Pearson. Even the Washington *Post* praised Jack in an editorial for a "contribution to the public's right to know."

There were, to be sure, some contrasting opinions. The redoubtable Joseph Alsop argued in his widely syndicated column against the conclusions Jack had drawn from the documents, but spoke nonetheless of how "able" Jack had been in obtaining them. Alsop's fellow Georgetowner, Joseph Kraft, complained in his column that Jack had done his country a "disservice" because the revelations would only make a secretive administration more secretive. Kraft also contended that the leak must have been the result of some personal grudge by an administration insider because no serious official attempting to influence policy would have chosen Jack Anderson as his vehicle. That infuriated me and I told Jack so. He just chuckled and said all that mattered to him was the headline on Kraft's column in the Washington *Post.* I looked at it again. It read, "The Anderson Papers."

The documents stayed on the front pages for a week. They were released gradually and in a fashion carefully orchestrated to keep the story alive and to keep the column's clients satisfied they were being treated fairly.

All of us wondered during those happy, hectic days what the Nixon administration might do to stop Jack. The papers were a terrible embarrassment, a far greater one than the Pentagon Papers, which covered only the years before the Nixon presidency. We knew that an investigation had been launched into the leak, and there were reports that senior officials were being given lie-detector tests. Privately, though, several administration officials told reporters that the papers had caused no important breach of security, just some diplomatic and political embarrassment. No effort would be made, these officials said, to halt their publication.

When these reports appeared in print, they caused sighs of relief in the office. It was impossible to know the reason behind the decision, but I suspected that it was because the publication of the documents had caught the Administration by surprise. After all, two weeks earlier, he had published excerpts from them and nothing had happened, at least in the press. There had been no scandal. This had probably led to the conclusion that Jack had merely been given some excerpts from the documents instead of the papers themselves. Then, suddenly, he was doing it all over again, this time with huge chunks of direct quotation. And Kissinger's defense that he had been quoted out of context was greeted by release of the context itself, and more. During all this, Jack himself was seen and heard constantly, repeatedly emphasizing his charge that the secrecy stamps had been used to "cover up lies." The Nixon administration had the largest public relations apparatus of any White House in history. No one was more sophisticated in the selling of policies and the men who make them. And the President could pre-empt network programing at his pleasure to address the nation on television. Every word spoken from the White House was treated as major news. In such circumstances, it is not easy to overwhelm the Administration with a media blitzkrieg. But Jack seemed to have done it.

The more important question, of course, was what good did the publication of the material accomplish? Jack believed strongly that the leak of the material could well have prevented the Nixon administration from taking some further reckless action in defense of the Pakistani dictatorship. He felt the situation that had developed in the Bay of Bengal was terribly dangerous. Even an accidental clash of U.S. and Soviet warships during the night could have risked a nuclear holocaust. What's more, he believed that the deception practiced by the Administration had to be exposed. Joseph Kraft had dismissed this as a justification for publishing the documents because, he said, everyone knows that the government lies. But the press has more than an obligation to reveal that the government lies. It must also reveal the truth which the government won't tell. Jack thought he had done both. So, apparently, did the committee which confers the highest honor in American journalism when it voted several months later to award Jack the 1971 Pulitzer Prize for national reporting for his India-Pakistan disclosures.

The "Anderson Papers" were the breakthrough we had all been awaiting. They gave Jack an instant and significant boost in standing both with the press and the public. The United Feature Syndicate, which took over distribution of the column when it bought out the old Bell-McClure Syndicate, reported that dozens of new subscribers were lining up to buy the "Merry-Go-Round." Jack signed a contract with Random House for a book entitled *The Anderson Papers*. The advance: $100,000. Jack's lecture fees increased sharply and so did his bookings.

Yet Jack was philosophical about all the acclaim. "Don't worry," he told me cheerfully, "pretty soon they'll be giving us hell again. All of this was nice while it lasted, but the column has always been Peck's Bad Boy and sooner or later we're bound to do something they think is outrageous."

I hoped he was wrong. I didn't think we should imitate the rest of the Washington press. But the India-Pakistan affair showed that muckraking, if accurate, will attract both the attention and praise of the rest of the media. And this, of course, multiplies its impact. I thought it would be a long time before another story of comparable importance came along. But I hoped that when it did, it would receive the kind of treatment the India-Pakistan documents had finally gotten. I had no way of knowing then that, in a matter of weeks, I would find myself caught up in a furious political controversy caused by a story far more explosive than the Anderson Papers.

SEVEN

I was at my typewriter busy with a story the morning of Tuesday, February 22, 1972, when I heard Opal Ginn get up from her desk and walk the few steps down the corridor to my kitchen office. She handed me a document and told me I was to check it out. "This is a good one," she said.

I was too preoccupied to do more than note that it was on the stationery of the International Telephone and Telegraph Corporation. I had previously written several stories about the giant corporation's influence in Washington, including one which disclosed that ITT, after making a donation to the John F. Kennedy Center for the Performing Arts, had ended up with contracts to handle the center's parking, food, and maintenance. My earlier reporting about the company made it natural that I would receive any leads about ITT that came into the office.

When I read the document later, I realized it was the single most incriminating piece of paper I had ever seen. It was the original of a two-page memo, dated June 25, 1971, addressed to W. R. Merriam, head of ITT's Washington office. It was from "D. D. Beard" and the initial "D" was penciled in next to the author's name. The subject of the memo was given as "San Diego Convention." Here is what it said:

> I just had a long talk with EJG. I'm so sorry that we got that call from the White House. I thought you and I had agreed very thoroughly that under no circumstances would anyone in this office discuss with anyone our participation in the Convention, including me. Other than permitting John Mitchell, Ed Reinecke, Bob Haldeman and Nixon (besides Wilson, of course) *no one* has known from whom that 400

thousand committment [sic] had come. You can't imagine how many queries I've had from "friends" about this situation and I have in each and every case denied knowledge of any kind. It would be wise for all of us here to continue to do that, regardless of from whom any questions come, White House or whoever. John Mitchell has certainly kept it on the higher level only, we should be able to do the same.

I was afraid the discussion about the three hundred/four hundred thousand committement [sic] would come up soon. If you remember, I suggested we all stay out of that, other than the fact that I told you I had heard Hal up the original amount.

Now I understand from Ned that both he and you are upset about the decision to make it four hundred in *services*. Believe me, this is not what Hal said. Just after I talked with Ned, Wilson called me, to report on his meeting with Hal. Hal at no time told Wilson that our donation would be in services *only*. In fact, quite the contrary. There would be very little cash involved, but certainly some. I am convinced, because of several conversations with Louie re Mitchell, that our noble committment has gone a long way toward our negotiations on the mergers eventually coming out as Hal wants them. Certainly the President has told Mitchell to see that things are worked out fairly. It is still only McLaren's mickey-mouse we are suffering.

We all know Hal and his big mouth! But this is one time he cannot tell you and Ned one thing and Wilson (and me) another!

I hope, dear Bill, that all of this can be reconciled—between Hal and Wilson—if all of us in this office remain totally ignorant of any committment ITT has made to anyone. If it gets too much publicity, you can believe our negotiations with Justice will wind up shot down. Mitchell is definitely helping us, but cannot let it be known. Please destroy this, huh?

I couldn't identify some of the persons mentioned in the document, but I didn't need to, to grasp its implications. The author was telling the Washington vice president of the company to keep mum about a huge contribution to the Republican National Convention because the money was helping the company in its anti-trust difficulties with the Justice Department. I got up and walked into Opal's office.

"Do you think this could be real?" I asked.

"It certainly sounds like Dita Beard," she replied, letting me know for the first time that the author of the memo was a woman.

"Do you know her?"

"I don't really know her, but I've met her. She's ITT's top lobbyist. The time I met her, practically the first thing she said to me was, 'Your boss is a son of a bitch and I wouldn't touch him with a ten-foot pole.' She has a foul mouth. She's powerful, though. You should see the way Irv Davidson fawns over her."

I walked back to my desk and read the document again. I had no idea who "EJG," "Louie" and "Hal" were, but I knew, of course, that John Mitchell was the outgoing Attorney General. And I knew that Richard McLaren had been the respected head of the Justice Department's antitrust division, which had filed three major antitrust suits against ITT during the Nixon adminis-tration. The cases had seemed bound for the Supreme Court until they were suddenly settled the previous July.

While the settlement required ITT to make a massive divesti-ture, it had come as a surprise for two reasons. The first was that it had allowed the company to keep the vast Hartford Fire Insur-ance Co., thus ratifying what by many estimates was the largest merger in corporate history—and one which the Justice Depart-ment had firmly warned ITT against in advance. The second was that McLaren had repeatedly expressed determination to take just such a case to the Supreme Court, where he believed that existing antitrust laws would be found applicable to conglomerates like ITT. The history of antitrust law seemed to bear him out; the government had rarely won a case in the lower courts and virtu-ally never lost one in the Supreme Court. Although there was some doubt the pattern would hold in the ITT cases, McLaren was not one of the doubters. Moreover, by the time of the settlement, the ITT cases were the only major anti-conglomerate suits left. All the others had been settled. When the ITT case was settled, McLaren lost any chance he had of making good on his principal objective.

Soon after the abrupt settlement, McLaren was just as abruptly appointed to the federal bench in Chicago and confirmed by the Senate in a single day, without hearings. The entire sequence had raised eyebrows all over Washington, but nowhere was there more skepticism than in a modestly furnished office above a downtown art supply store, where a plump, bespectacled young lawyer named Reuben Robertson III kept an eye on ITT's activities for Ralph Nader.

I had known Reuben since well before I began working for Jack. He has a relaxed, easygoing personality that contrasted with the supercharged atmosphere of the Nader operation. We saw each other often, both on business and socially, and he had often told me of his and Nader's efforts to stop the ITT-Hartford Fire merger in the Connecticut courts. He had told me of his suspicions about the settlement of the antitrust cases and urged me to look into it. The last time we had discussed the subject, he had called my attention to a story written from San Diego by one of the most resourceful reporters in town, Robert Walters of the Washington *Star*. The story raised questions about the coincidence of the settlement and ITT's cash pledge for the Republican convention. My reaction was that there might be a connection, but that it would be extremely difficult to prove because the fixing of cases in Washington is rarely as overt and crude as a simple bribe. Yet I now had a memorandum which suggested strongly that the antitrust settlement was directly linked to the pledge of money for the Republican convention. I picked up the phone and called Reuben.

"I've got a document here I think you'll be interested in," I said.

"I don't know if it's real, but you might be able to help me. It's on ITT paper and it's marked 'Personal and Confidential.'"

"That's one of their terms," Reuben said.

I began reading the document. Before I was halfway through, he interrupted in a voice that was almost hoarse with excitement. "Can you come over here right now?"

The walk to Reuben's office about eight blocks away took me past ITT's Washington headquarters, on L Street just off Connecticut Avenue, around the corner from the Mayflower Hotel. The display windows on the ground floor of the large concrete-and-glass building were filled with exhibits promoting the company's telecommunications service around the world. But ITT was now much more than a telephone and telegraph company. By the time the Justice Department moved to stop the merger with the Hartford Fire Insurance Co., ITT had become the eleventh largest industrial concern in the nation. This growth was achieved by a series of mergers that had given ITT control over a staggering variety of smaller companies, but also over some of the larger corporations in America. It owned the Sheraton hotel chain, the Avis Rent-A-Car System, the Continental Baking Co., largest in the nation, the huge Levitt & Sons home construction company, and Rayonier, Inc., a leading producer of chemical cellulose. Its tentacles reached into insurance, food vending, parking, and even building maintenance. ITT was everywhere.

Reuben identified all the ITT officials whose names were unfamiliar to me. "EJG" and "Ned," for instance both referred to Edward J. Gerrity, ITT's vice president for public relations. And "Hal" was evidently Harold S. Geneen, the brilliant, aggressive, and, according to his critics, ruthless president of ITT, who had directed its phenomenal growth by merger. Both of us knew that Ed Reinecke was the lieutenant governor of California, and that Bob Haldeman was President Nixon's right-hand assistant. And we assumed that "Wilson" referred to Representative Bob Wilson, the Republican congressman from San Diego, who was also chairman of the party's congressional campaign fund committee. Neither of us, though, could identify "Louie," whose conversations with John Mitchell had persuaded Dita Beard the money promised for the convention was helping in the antitrust battle.

Reuben was more excited than I had ever seen him, which was understandable, since he had long suspected something improper about the merger settlement. For me, excitement would have to await certainty that the document was not a fake. We discussed ways of establishing its authenticity. I had pretty well decided there was only one way, and that was to confront Dita Beard and hope that, if the memo was real, I could get her to admit it. Reuben had reservations. He was afraid she would simply deny it and, after that, there would be no hope of confirming it through any other ITT source because everyone in the company would immediately be alerted. My concern was that if I spoke to anyone else at ITT about it first, Mrs. Beard would learn we had the memo. With time to think, she would undoubtedly deny writing it. Then, no matter what anyone else said, it would be extremely difficult to establish the memo's authenticity.

I called Mrs. Beard's office on Reuben's phone. She wasn't in, so I left my name with her secretary, telling her I worked for Jack Anderson but not what my call was about. I let Reuben copy the memo and walked back to my office. He later told me he showed the memo to Nader after I left. He said Nader also questioned the wisdom of a direct approach to Mrs. Beard, but said of the document, "If this is real, it's curtains for those guys."

There had been no opportunity to discuss the story with Jack. All I knew was the document had been made available to him by a confidential source, but I had no idea who the source was. At the time, I was facing a court order to name the source of a story about the United Mine Workers. We had always been careful about naming our sources of information, even to each other. Now, though, thanks to that court order, we had all adopted the habit of keeping our sources to ourselves except in the rarest cases. The feeling was that the fewer people who know about such things the better.

I thought Jack would certainly approve of my direct approach to Mrs. Beard as the best way of establishing the memo's authenticity, or lack of it. But it was going to be extremely tricky. My plan was this: I would tell her I had a document from her office files which interested me as a possible story. Actually, of course, the document was more likely from Merriam's files, since he was the addressee. But I didn't want to give her any idea in advance of what I had. I would tell her I was worried the document might be misleading if taken out of the context of other correspondence on the same subject. I would decline to discuss it on the phone and ask to see her. Then I would make a copy, stash it in my desk, and take the original to show to her. I ruled out asking her directly if the memo were real. This would make it clear that I didn't know. I also decided against saying I knew it was real, because this might seem an obvious bluff. After all, if I knew it was real, I would have no reason to say so. I didn't want to raise the question of authenticity at all. I knew that if the memo was a fake, she would immediately say so, no matter what I said, and that would probably be the end of it. If it was real, however, I hoped that seeing the original in my hands would cause her to jump to conclusions about my sources inside ITT. Then a denial might seem futile, or even risky. After all, no one wants to add lying to whatever else he may be guilty of.

Dita Beard did not return my call Tuesday. I wasn't surprised. Most lobbyists have no reason to want to talk to anyone working for Jack Anderson. When I called her again the following morning, I decided to tell her secretary I had a document from Mrs. Beard's files that I wanted to discuss with her. Mrs. Beard was out, but my message did the trick. She returned my call within forty-five minutes. I was casual and cheerful, trying to avoid betraying my growing excitement. I wanted this to sound like a routine matter. She said she was "dying of curiosity" and accepted my suggestion that I come right over.

It was shortly before noon when I arrived in the bland, carpeted reception room of the executive offices on the second floor of the ITT building. I was first met, not by Mrs. Beard, but by a pleasant-looking, dark-haired man in his forties who identified himself as Bernie Goodrich, manager of ITT's Washington press relations. He showed me into an adjacent conference room and took a seat across from me at the long table. Moments later, we were joined by Jack Horner, another, older ITT public relations man whom I had never met but had talked with by phone in connection with other stories. He greeted me as if we were great pals. This was not the kind of interview I had hoped for, but there was nothing I could do about it now. In a few minutes, Dita Beard bustled in through a door behind me.

She was an astonishing sight. A large woman in her mid-fifties, she had gray hair that showed traces of having once been red or blond or dyed one of those colors. Her skin was leathery and puffy and she wore no make-up. A paper clip held her horn-rim eyeglasses together where one of the hinges had broken. She had on a chartreuse, short-sleeved sweatshirt and a pair of soiled yellow cotton slacks. Her flat, slip-on shoes were battered and dirty. Her voice had a raspiness that might have been the result of the Chesterfield Kings she chain-smoked. The impression she gave, though, was not of a broken-down woman but of a middle-aged tomboy. She moved and spoke with self-assurance, and it occurred to me as we shook hands that she must have had considerable influence in that office to get away with being dressed as she was in the middle of the week. She reminded me of Tugboat Annie. I liked her.

She sat down a couple of seats from me at the table. I explained once more my concern that the document might be misleading "although we have confidence in our sources." I said I wanted her to have a chance to check it against other correspondence on the subject so that it could be seen in its proper context. I tried to speak calmly and seem at ease. I didn't want her to know that this was the crucial moment in what could be the biggest story I had ever had.

I reached into my inside coat pocket, took out the memo, unfolded it, and slid it down the table in front of her. My heart was pounding, but I sat back in my chair and tried not to stare at her.

There was a period of silence that seemed long to me but probably wasn't. Then she began shaking her head. "It didn't work out at all," she said, apparently referring to the company's role in the convention. "We weren't involved at all. We *aren't* involved at all. You see, it all happened so goddamn fast. We were trying to help get it into San Diego. We offered to do anything we could, which isn't much . . ."

She went on this way for a while, reading a bit, then shaking her head, repeating her disclaimers, not of the document but of its implications. So far, so good, I thought. She was terribly flustered, denying things I was almost certain were true. But she was not denying she wrote the memo. At one point, she noted in passing that the penciled initial at the top of the first page was "my own little 'D.'" I felt I had it then. She continued her rambling and somewhat contradictory comments.

"I had nothing to do with the settlement . . . I had been asked to see what we could do about the settlement . . . The timing was stinking. I was doing this [the convention plans] without having any idea what was happening in the Justice Department. All we ever did was offer to help raise that money. We were going to help Sheraton raise that money . . ."

I interrupted to ask her if she wanted to check her files. She accepted and left the room with Goodrich, taking the document with her. Horner and I conversed aimlessly for several minutes. When they still had not returned, I asked him, a little impatiently, if they were coming back. He assured me they were. Shortly, they did. She was carrying a file folder filled with pink carbons.

"My files are a mess," she said. "I can't find anything. There's nothing in my chronological file." She sat down and looked at me, her face filled with apprehension. "All right," she said with a sigh of resignation, "what do you want to know about it?"

I suspected any explanation she gave me under these circumstances would be of little use, but I wanted to find out who "Louie" was. My questions were gentle and general and I avoided pressing her about the most incriminating passages. With help from Goodrich and Horner, she spelled out the company's official story on the Sheraton contribution to the Republican convention. Goodrich, who Mrs. Beard later told me had been kicking her under the table repeatedly during the meeting, gave me a copy of a Sheraton press release explaining the matter. "Louie" turned out to be Louie Nunn, a former Republican governor of Kentucky who she said was an old personal friend.

I offered to let them make a copy of the memo and followed Goodrich into an adjoining room where the Xerox machine was. He put the first page on the machine and pushed the button. When the bright green light went out, I reached down and picked up the original. I did the same with the second page. He seemed a little surprised, but said nothing. I put the document back in my coat pocket and prepared to leave. I told them I was leaving town overnight to appear on a television show and was uncertain I could get back before late the next day, Thursday, February 24. I explained I had a busy Friday planned and it might be the following week, therefore, before I could meet with them again. I stressed again my concern that the document might be misleading and told them they would have plenty of time to search their files and discuss the matter with company officials before we went any further. The purpose of these final assurances was to keep alive their hopes that we might not write a story after all. I didn't want them to panic and release the document themselves, together with a self-serving explanation that would blunt the impact of the column.

As I headed back to the office, I felt the surge of elation and excitement that always came when I had established that there was substance to an important story. I nearly broke into a run as I turned the corner, out of sight of the ITT building. Once back at my desk, I called Reuben to tell him the news. He was surprised the direct approach had worked.

My next call was to Judge Richard McLaren in Chicago. I caught him in his chambers. I read the memo to him. He laughed at the part about "McLaren's mickey-mouse." When I was finished, he turned serious. He called the memo an "amazing document."

"Mitchell had absolutely nothing to do with the negotiation and settlement of that case," he said. "I never discussed it with him. It was completely my operation. I made the decision as to what was the proper basis for a settlement."

McLaren explained that he and his staff had drafted a proposed settlement, which was taken to Richard Kleindienst, then Deputy Attorney General, for approval. Mitchell had officially disqualified himself from the case because his old law firm had links to ITT. McLaren said Kleindienst had approved the proposal without change. He insisted emphatically he had felt no pressure from above in negotiating the agreement. McLaren had an excellent reputation. He had been most persuasive on the phone. Suddenly, I was beginning to have doubts about whether the memo, real or not, was correct in its implications.

Jack was still out of the office, so I left a note in his typewriter relating what had happened. I caught a 4 P.M. flight for Dayton, Ohio, where I was to appear on Phil Donahue's syndicated talk show the next morning. A late afternoon snowstorm closed the airport before the plane left. The flight was held over for several hours. As I waited and sipped the complimentary cocktails airlines often provide to placate passengers on delayed flights, it suddenly dawned on me that I had neglected to ask McLaren a crucial question. He said there was no pressure on him in drafting the settlement proposal and in the negotiations over it that followed. But what about the decision to settle the cases in the first place? In view of McLaren's avowed desire for a Supreme Court test of his conglomerate policy, the turning point was in persuading him to discontinue the litigation, not the bargaining over details that followed. I later tried to reach McLaren to ask if there had been any pressure to settle the cases. He was not available, so I left the question with an assistant. No one ever called back with the answer.

Phil Donahue's staff had a taxi waiting when the show ended at eleven-thirty the next morning, and the driver rushed me to the airport just in time to catch a noon flight back to Washington. I was in the office by one-thirty, hours earlier than I had anticipated. I called Dita Beard's office, but she was out, so I left word for her to call me back. By the time I left at five-thirty, she had not called. I had to go directly to a Cub Scout dinner with my nine-year-old son that night and I didn't get home until after 9 P.M. A short time later, I got a call from Joe Spear. He told me Dita Beard had called the office soon after I left. "Les and I picked up the phone at the same time," he said. "She sounded like she'd been crying. She said she wanted to talk to you immediately. She practically begged Les to find you. She kept saying, 'I want to tell him the truth.' " I took the number she had left and called her immediately.

"I didn't expect to hear from you until next week," she said, in a voice that was weary and slightly hoarse.

"Well, I got an earlier flight back from Dayton than I expected to, so I called you," I said.

"I was out all day, but I tried to reach you. I want to tell you the truth about all this, I've never done anything that was wrong or crooked in my life and I just want you to believe that. I'd like to talk to you."

"I've got a busy day tomorrow," I said, "but I'm free at the moment."

"Where do you live?"

"In Maryland, just over the city line."

"Oh, that's too far. I'm way over in Virginia, in South Arlington."

If she was in a confessional mood, I wasn't going to let a little distance keep me from seeing her. "Oh, I don't mind," I said. "Besides, it's not that far. How do I get there?" She gave me directions.

Just before leaving, I called Jack at home. He agreed that I should go right over. "When somebody's ready to talk," he said, "you've got to move fast before they change their mind."

It was a raw night, and rain was coming down hard as I drove across Key Bridge into Virginia. I found Mrs. Beard's home without difficulty, however. It was a modest, red-brick house in an old residential section. A large collie lay on the front stoop as I walked up and rang the bell. The front door was open, and I could see through the glass in the storm door that several people were in the living room, just inside. Mrs. Beard approached the door, peered at me, then retreated. A young man then let me in. The atmosphere was tense and gloomy, as if there had been a death in the family.

Mrs. Beard was standing in the middle of the living room. She gazed at me balefully, almost fearfully. I tried to strike a cheerful note, introducing myself to the others with a friendly smile. The boy who opened the door was Mrs. Beard's teen-age son, Bull. The others were Beverely Sincavage, her secretary, and Walter Benning, a paunchy, balding middle-aged man I later learned was an ITT employee from Fort Wayne, Indiana. They made no move to leave the living room and I didn't want to talk with them present. I asked Mrs. Beard where we might talk alone. She suggested the kitchen.

We sat on wooden slat stools that were most uncomfortable.

I was at the end of the counter with my back to the door leading into the other rooms. She sat at my left. Mrs. Beard was wearing the same clothes as when I had seen her at her office the day before, but her brassy self-assurance was missing. It was evident from the redness and swelling around her eyes that she had been crying. A trace of thickness in her voice indicated she had also been drinking. She nursed a highball as we talked and smoked one Chesterfield after another. I wanted her to open up, but it was going to be difficult, because she was so overwrought. I had a notebook in my hip pocket, but I decided not to produce it. A notebook would only be a constant reminder that I was a reporter on a story, not just a polite young man fresh from a Cub Scout dinner.

Our conversation lasted about two hours. In her desperation to persuade me of her—and ITT's—innocence, she veered erratically from one subject to another, showing first one aspect of her personality, then another. At times, she was cocky and cynical—the tough woman lobbyist. Then she would become pathetic and emotional, fighting back tears and not always succeeding. At other times, she was bitter and assertive, calling upon an extensive vocabulary of four-letter words.

She began by offering me a drink, which I declined. She apologized for the two PR men's having been present at the first meeting, implying that she could have explained things more satisfactorily alone. She spoke of them contemptuously. She had not summoned them, she said, but they had been alerted before she could do anything about it. Then she accused a Washington public relations consultant and former White House assistant named Jack Gleason of having leaked us the memo. ITT was one of Gleason's accounts, she said, and he worked closely with Bill Merriam, who must have given him the memo. I replied that I had never heard of Jack Gleason, which I hadn't. She shot me a suspicious glance. I wanted to steer the conversation toward the memo, but she embarked on a lengthy autobiography. There was no choice but to listen patiently.

Dita Beard made her debut in Washington in 1939, worked for a while on Capitol Hill, and married twice. With her second husband, Randy Beard, she had lived for a time in Alabama, where she said they had a beautiful home filled with antiques. Eventually, the family fell upon hard times, and she was forced to sell her home, leave Beard, and return with her five children to Washington. For a while, she worked as a secretary and moonlighted driving used cars from a Washington distribution center to various points in the East. Eventually, she got a job as a secretary at ITT, when the company opened a Washington office in the early 1960s. Her earlier experience on Capitol Hill proved useful, and she soon began doing political chores. She was now ITT's only registered Washington lobbyist.

She broke off her story several times to ask, pleadingly, if we were going to destroy her. I said that our only intention was to find the truth about her memo. At one point, she remarked that there was no point in trying to fool me about the document. "I wrote it," she said. "Of course I wrote it."

I knew this already, of course. It was the whole basis of our meeting. But I was glad nevertheless to hear her reaffirm it so explicitly. Mrs. Beard said some ITT officials had advised her to tell me she made up the most damaging portions of the memo, while others recommended that she leave town and stop talking to me. That afternoon, she said, Edward J. (Ned) Gerrity, the senior ITT vice president for public relations, had told her to give me a sob story in the hope of persuading me not to write a story. She said she had rejected all this advice in favor of telling me the full truth. There was no doubt, however, that I was getting a sob story along with whatever truth she was telling.

Finally, we began to discuss the memo. I had brought a copy, which I opened on the counter in front of us. She said she wrote it in an effort to "put some sense into the head of that stupid shit Merriam." One of her repeated themes was that Merriam was politically naïve and that she had worded the memo strongly to be sure he got the point. She never quite said that she had embellished the facts to make the necessary impression, but this was the obvious implication.

She explained that the idea of helping bring the GOP convention to San Diego grew out of a conversation she had early in 1971 with Ed Reinecke, California's Republican lieutenant governor, who she said was an old friend. Reinecke had been assigned to help get the convention into his state and had mentioned this to her during a visit to Washington. Reinecke had said he thought San Diego could accommodate the convention. Mrs. Beard said she went out to San Diego several times in the next few months, casing the city for hotel space and trying to determine if ITT's new Sheraton Hotel under construction there would be finished in time. This would give Sheraton three hotels in operation during the convention and mean a lot of free publicity for the company. Finally, she said, she raised the subject with Geneen during the company's annual meeting in San Diego in May. He reacted enthusiastically, she said, and expressed willingness to underwrite the convention for several hundred thousand dollars. She insisted neither Geneen nor anyone else in the company believed ITT would have to put up the full sum. They were only making a commitment so that San Diego would have something to fall back on if local fund-raising efforts fell short. She said John Mitchell was informed of the ITT promise by Reinecke when he visited the Attorney General during one of his trips to Washington. But she insisted repeatedly that the convention pledge was totally unrelated to the antitrust suits.

If they were unrelated, I asked again and again, then what did she mean by her memo? I never got a useful answer until I expressed my theory that any deal on the cases must have come while there was still the danger they would go to the Supreme Court—still the danger of ITT's losing them all and losing the precious

Hartford Fire Insurance Co. She gave me a startled glance, as if I had hit on something. I decided this was the time to press her. I asked if there had been such a deal. "If I tell you," she said, "will you destroy me?"

I said I was less interested in the memo than the truth and would be glad to keep her out of the story if it could be written without mentioning her. Could it? I asked. She shook her head, biting her lip. Again, I asked if there had been an agreement between ITT and the Administration along the lines I mentioned. She nodded. She was weeping now, with her head in her hands. Was it negotiated by her? Again, a yes nod. With Mitchell? Again, yes, nodding. Where? She got up and went into the bathroom behind where I was sitting. I paced the floor during the few minutes she was gone. It was eleven o'clock.

When she came out, she had composed herself enough to relate this story: She was invited to be Governor Nunn's guest at the Kentucky Derby in May 1971, as she had been each year during his term. He told her John Mitchell was expected to be there. She mentioned this in a memo to Gerrity, who subsequently gave her instructions as to what to say to Mitchell if she got a chance to discuss the antitrust cases. At a buffet dinner at the governor's mansion after the race, she was introduced to Mitchell for the first time. Later, as dinner was being served, he took her aside with Nunn and scolded her harshly for the lobbying she had done in Congress on the antitrust cases. She said he cited with remarkable accuracy speeches she had arranged to have delivered in both Houses. He was angry that she had chosen this approach rather than coming to him directly. He told her he had heard of her before coming to Washington and that she was known as the "politician" in the company. Mitchell said he had even been told by the President to "lay off" ITT. When I questioned this, Mrs. Beard changed her version of what the President told Mitchell to "make a reasonable settlement." She said she was badly shaken by Mitchell's scolding, which seemed to last for an hour. But she retained enough composure to ask him after he finished if he was willing to discuss the cases.

"What do you want?" he asked.

"We want Hartford Fire and part of Grinnell [a manufacturing concern whose acquisition by ITT was challenged in one of the antitrust cases]," she recalled saying.

At first, he snapped, "You can't have part of Grinnell," she said, but subsequently, he relented. That was that, she said, just an informal agreement covering two of the principal issues in the cases. She insisted, however, that Geneen knew nothing about it when he pledged the money for the convention. Indeed, she said, he still knew nothing about it because she and Gerrity had never told him.

I thought it strange that Geneen would not have been informed of this triumph of lobbying and questioned Mrs. Beard closely about it. She stuck to it. She also insisted under repeated questioning that there was no connection between the settlement and the convention pledge. As we were going back over the main points, she mentioned almost as an afterthought that when she had arrived in the office that morning, security officials from New York had been present and a decision had been made to destroy a large number of documents from her files by putting them through a shredding machine. The episode upset her, she said, because a number of her personal papers went through the shredder also. She said the documents were destroyed to prevent their being subpoenaed when her memo became public.

By this time, her doctor, Victor Liszka, had arrived and was standing over us as we talked. He was a dark, rather mysterious-looking man. I kept thinking that he would interrupt the interview on the grounds that Mrs. Beard was too upset. She had told me she had a heart condition. He just stood there silently, however, breaking in only to ask me for my telephone number. I expected he would call me with a plea to drop the story for the sake of his patient's health. He never called, but it was not the last I was to see of Dr. Liszka.

As I prepared to leave, I promised Mrs. Beard that I would let her know what we decided to do. By now, it was about midnight and I felt I had learned all I could. She was still questioning me closely about my intentions, even offering at one point to answer any questions Jack might have if that were necessary to satisfy us of her and the company's innocence. She was fishing for some indication that her story had convinced me, that we might not write a column about the memo after all. I was noncommittal.

At the door, to my surprise, she embraced me. She acted as if she expected me to kiss her good-by, as a son would his mother. I disengaged as gracefully as possible and headed for home to type up everything I could remember about the interview. I paused only to telephone Jack from a gasoline station to tell him what had occurred. He told me he was leaving town the next morning, Friday. I was to draft a column to be sent out that afternoon for publication the following Tuesday. He would edit it over the phone from wherever he was.

Early the next afternoon, I called the Justice Department to get Attorney General Mitchell's side of the story. His press assistant, Jack Hushen, insisted I ask my questions through him. I told him briefly that I had been informed the Attorney General made a deal with an ITT lobbyist at the Kentucky Derby to settle the company's antitrust cases. He immediately declared there was "no truth" to it. Another newsman had come up with the same report two months earlier and he had determined then that it was false.

I explained that I was operating on more than an idle tip, that I had the word of the lobbyist herself and, moreover, I had a memo she had written that painted an even worse picture. I read Hushen the memo, and went back over the parts dealing with Mitchell slowly so that he could write them down. He said he would take the matter up with the Attorney General immediately. I asked him to pose two questions: Did Mitchell and Mrs. Beard discuss the ITT case, however briefly, at Governor Nunn's party, and did they discuss the convention, even momentarily? After I hung up, I gave a progress report to Les Whitten, who was in charge in Jack's absence. He suggested a third question: Did they talk at all?

I called Hushen back. He was in Mitchell's office by then and the call was transferred there. I posed the third question. "Oh," said Hushen, "we'd never deny that."

"So they did have a conversation?" I said.

"Yes, but it was like 'hello-good-by.' "

Hushen promised he would be back in touch later with more details. I stressed that we were on deadline. Several hours passed. I finished drafting a column, which included Hushen's denial at the very end. It began as follows:

> We now have evidence that the settlement of the Nixon Administration's biggest anti-trust case was privately arranged between Attorney General John Mitchell and the top lobbyist for the company involved.
>
> We have this on the word of the lobbyist herself, crusty, capable Dita Beard of the International Telephone and Telegraph Co. She acknowledged the secret deal after we obtained a highly incriminating memo, written by her, from ITT's files.
>
> The memo, which was intended to be destroyed after it was read, not only indicates that the anti-trust case had been fixed, but that the fix was a payoff for ITT's pledge of up to $400,000 for the upcoming Republican convention in San Diego.
>
> Confronted with the memo, Mrs. Beard acknowledged its authenticity. The next night, badly shaken, and acting against the wishes of ITT officials who wanted her to leave town, she met with my associate Brit Hume at her home to try to explain the document.
>
> By this time, she said, ITT security officers from company headquarters in New York had put most of her office files through a shredding machine to prevent their being subpoenaed after disclosure of the memo.
>
> Although the memo suggests otherwise, Mrs. Beard insisted

that her deal with Mitchell was unrelated to her company's pledge of cash for the GOP convention.

The column went on to elaborate Mrs. Beard's account of the Kentucky Derby episode and then to quote at length from the memo. I read it to Jack, who telephoned from Minnesota, where he was giving a lecture. He approved it with minor changes. It was then sent to New York, where the syndicate would mimeograph it and mail it to the approximately 700 newspapers that now subscribed to the column.

I remained in the office after sending the story, because if the Justice Department called back with something important, there was still time to send out the new information. Hushen finally did call, shortly after six o'clock. He had no answers to my questions. Instead, he simply reiterated his earlier denial, adding that Mitchell could "prove" the falsity of Mrs. Beard's memo. In tones so officious that I had difficulty restraining my temper, he demanded that we hold up the story until, as he put it, "we can get all our ducks in a row." My reply was that Mrs. Beard was of sufficient standing that what she said about ITT's affairs was newsworthy and that we couldn't hold up the news after giving all sides a reasonable opportunity to be heard. I didn't tell Hushen that a column was already in the pipeline, but I gave him no assurance that we would await word from the Attorney General before going ahead. I said I was ready to see Mitchell at any time— day, night, or weekend—to hear his side, and that if he could indeed disprove what we had been told, we would gladly say so in the column.

I had spoken to Louie Nunn the day before, prior to my conversation with Mrs. Beard at her home. He denied any knowledge of the convention cash promise or the antitrust case. Now I had much more to ask him about, but I was unable to reach him and he did not return my calls.

Finally, I called Dita Beard because she had told me she would look up the date of Ed Reinecke's meeting with John Mitchell at which the Attorney General was supposedly informed of ITT's commitment for the convention. I thought it could be significant if Mitchell knew about the convention commitment prior to the settlement of the antitrust cases. She said she was still uncertain of the date. I mentioned that her account of the Kentucky Derby party was being denied at the Justice Department. She replied, "Oh, can't you just tell them that old Dita has told you the truth so they won't lie to protect me?"

The column that went out that Friday was the biggest story I had ever had, but I sensed that only part of the truth had been uncovered. Mrs. Beard's seeming confession of the night before had still managed to protect her company and its president. She had denied the worst implications of the memo and had claimed that Geneen never knew about the secret deal with Mitchell. Mitchell's behavior also seemed puzzling. I had told Hushen what information we had. If it had been the whole truth, the Attorney General could easily have figured out some alibi to counter it. Perhaps he was keeping silent until he could find out exactly how much we knew. I decided then I would have to follow up the first column quickly.

I spent the better part of Saturday and Sunday in my office telephoning anyone who might have been able to tell me anything about the way ITT won its antitrust settlement. The principal source of names was, of course, my friend Reuben Robertson, who had an intimate knowledge of the company, in addition to an extensive file of press clippings on the case. We sat together in the kitchen, with me on the phone and him at the next desk, poring over his documents looking for any clue that might lead us further. Most of what I found out was just useful background, important, but not enough for another column. Then, late Sunday afternoon, I called a highly regarded former ITT executive who agreed to talk to me if I kept his name confidential. When I read him the Beard memo, he chuckled, but didn't sound surprised.

"Not only is this approach probably true," he said, "this is probably only one of several approaches. ITT is almost famous for this. The over-all theory of management is that if one approach can do it, seven approaches can do it seven times better.

"One of the other approaches to the same little target," he said, "was from Geneen through Felix Rohatyn of Lazard Freres to [Deputy Attorney General Richard] Kleindienst. That would stand a little looking into . . . I'm laboring under the general impression that out of one or more talks between Rohatyn and Kleindienst, things began to move. I haven't got any doubt that there's something there if you can trace it down."

Felix Rohatyn, Reuben explained, was a partner in the investment banking firm of Lazard Freres, an ITT director, and one of the most influential men on Wall Street. This new lead could be significant, we agreed, because it involved Kleindienst, who had not previously been linked to the case and who had been nominated to succeed Mitchell as Attorney General. My next call was to Felix Rohatyn's apartment, listed in the Manhattan telephone directory on Park Avenue. His wife told me he was on his way to catch a plane from Kennedy Airport to London. I cursed under my breath. But she said she expected him to call her before leaving. I gave her my name, but not my occupation, and asked her to give her husband a message to call me collect, if he had time. I told her it was urgent. Just then I heard a phone ringing in the background. Mrs. Rohatyn said she thought it was her husband. We said good-by. I sat at my desk, hoping.

A few minutes later, the phone rang. "Mr. Hume," said a confident voice, "this is Felix Rohatyn." I thanked him for calling, explained who I was, and told him I was looking for help in determining the significance of an ITT memo I had gotten hold of. I began reading the key passages to him. Before I was finished, he interrupted.

"That's absolute bullshit," he said.

"Well," I said, "I understand that it might be. In fact, I understand you know something about this because you had some meetings with Mr. Kleindienst about the case."

"That's right," he said emphatically, eager to persuade me of the memo's falsity. "I, as a director of ITT and an investment banker, handled some of the negotiations and presentations to Kleindienst and McLaren."

He went on to explain that he had about six meetings with Kleindienst after being assigned by Geneen to "make the case on the economic side." While he met with Kleindienst, he said, there were "parallel meetings" between McLaren and ITT's lawyers.

What Rohatyn told me did not contradict what Mrs. Beard had said, but it strongly suggested that her initiatives and the convention contribution were just part of an over-all assault on the problem. It was increasingly evident that ITT had simply pulled out all the stops to win a settlement of the cases and somewhere along the way one of its moves—or perhaps a combination of them— had worked.

I felt that the Rohatyn-Kleindienst meetings were significant but I was unsure at first how to handle them as news for the column. Later, as Reuben and I were having dinner at a Cuban restaurant near the office, I leafed through some of the documents from his ITT file and came across a letter Kleindienst had written to Democratic National Chairman Lawrence O'Brien the previous December. O'Brien had raised questions about the coincidence of the antitrust settlement and the convention cash pledge. In reply, Kleindienst wrote that the settlement was "handled and negotiated exclusively" by McLaren and his staff. What Rohatyn told me made it obvious this was not true and gave me the news angle I needed.

The column I drafted on Monday morning accused Richard Kleindienst of an "outright lie" about the ITT case. It was sent out for Thursday publication. I was unable to get much more reporting done that day because, by afternoon, everyone in Washington seemed to know that we had a big story coming out the next day, based in part on a secret document from ITT's files. It hadn't been long since Jack had stirred up the town with his India-Pakistan revelations and brought the rest of the press into the action by releasing the documents. Reporters who were hoping we might repeat the same procedure began calling me.

Naturally, I was eager to co-operate, and I knew Jack would be also. Making the document available could result in far wider play for the story. Equally important, however, was my feeling that this was the kind of story that might develop into a major issue. It dramatized one of the most sordid aspects of American politics: the special-interest financing of elections and the influence that money buys. Even if Mrs. Beard's calculation that the $400,000 had turned the Justice Department around proved inaccurate, the very fact that she would believe such a thing was revealing. And so was the fact that she would cite it with apparent pride in a memo to a vice president of the company. The problem of money and influence in Washington had been talked about for years, throughout the reigns of both parties, but little had been done. A new campaign-finance law might force the big spenders out in the open, but it seemed unlikely to diminish their influence.

This story seemed certain to embarrass Mrs. Beard and ITT and to damage the careers of those in government whom the company had influenced. It might also make it harder for companies to swing similar deals in the future. But I was less interested in these results than in the possibility of stamping the whole episode indelibly on the public consciousness as an example of the way things are in Washington. This, I thought, would have a far more lasting and positive effect.

When requests for the document first began coming in, I turned them all aside until I had a chance to offer it to the Washington *Post*. But the *Post* seemed skeptical of it, and it was late in the day, so I didn't have much hope the *Post* editors would decide to publish a story on the document in addition to the column. We also made the memo available to our other major morning subscribers. Afterward, I gave a copy to Bob Walters, the Washington *Star* reporter whose story months earlier had first called attention to the coincidence of the settlement and the convention pledge. Since the memo supported his suspicions, I thought there was a good chance it would be played up in the next afternoon's *Star*, particularly since the *Post* seemed uninterested. I also gave a copy of the document to the St. Louis *Post-Dispatch*, which had reported extensively on the ITT case, and the Louisville *Courier-Journal*, whose Washington bureau chief, Ward Sinclair, was a good friend and a superior reporter. Louie Nunn's involvement gave the *Courier-Journal* an obvious news angle.

Sometime after 6 P.M., Monday, I got a call from Jack Hushen at the Justice Department. "Thanks a lot," he said bitterly, "You've written exactly the kind of story I didn't want you to write." He accused me of violating an understanding with him about holding off until the Attorney General was ready to speak. I told him angrily that there was no such agreement and that I was surprised he would think there was. He then read me a statement from Mitchell denying any deals with ITT and saying he "was not involved in any way with the Republican National Committee convention negotiations and had no knowledge of anyone from the committee or elsewhere dealing with International Telephone and Telegraph." ITT also put out a statement later that evening, denying a deal and adding, "Neither Mrs. Beard nor anyone else except legal counsel was authorized to carry on such negotiations." This, of course, flatly contradicted what Rohatyn had told me. Obviously, he had gone on to London and the company was still unaware of his conversation with me.

I also suspected that Mitchell's plea of ignorance about the convention was false, since he had been calling the Administration's political shots from the Justice Department for a long time before stepping down to run the President's re-election campaign. The next morning, I got a call from Ed Gillenwaters, an aide to California Lieutenant Governor Reinecke, whom I had tried to reach unsuccessfully over the weekend. I was disappointed at not getting Reinecke himself on the phone but decided to put my questions to Gillenwaters. When, I asked, was the meeting between Reinecke and the Attorney General at which Mitchell was told of the convention commitment from ITT?

Gillenwaters apparently hadn't seen the Attorney General's statement, because he readily gave an answer that would be of no help to John Mitchell. He had been at the meeting himself, he said, and it had occurred on May 17 in Washington. Mitchell had been dubious about the chances of getting the convention into San Diego but was in favor of it nonetheless, he said. And had Gillenwaters and Reinecke told Mitchell about Sheraton's commitment of $400,000? "You bet," said Gillenwaters.

So now I had two more lies, one from ITT and one from the Attorney General. I prepared a column for publication Friday, charging that the company and the Justice Department were "trying to lie their way out of a scandal" over the antitrust cases.

I had lunch with friends that day at a small, busy German restaurant on Connecticut Avenue. While there, I called the office from a coin telephone on the wall in a crowded hallway. Jack Hushen had called me, so I returned the call right away. The ITT story was on the front page of the *Star*, and Hushen had gotten word we were coming out with a column on Kleindienst. He demanded to know if this were true. I told him it was. He was furious. He told me that since Kleindienst was "an officer of the Department of Justice," that I had an obligation to contact the department before writing a damaging story about him. He wanted to know the substance of the column. I refused to tell him. We shouted at each other a bit, and customers turned in their seats to stare at me.

The Kleindienst column wasn't due to come out until Thursday, two days away, but I was afraid the Justice Department would try to queer it with a statement or a threat. When I got back to the office, I suggested to Jack that we move the release date ahead a day. He agreed. We telephoned the Washington *Post* to inform the editors of the change. The syndicate was instructed to reach all other major clients by wire and to contact as many others as possible.

Jack was talking on the telephone with his feet on his desk when I walked in the next morning. He had left town overnight for a speaking date and had come directly downtown from the airport after his return flight. The final edition of the Washington *Post* was on the desk before him. The front page carried a brief, last-minute story that Kleindienst had asked for a special hearing of the Senate Judiciary Committee, which had recently unanimously approved his nomination to succeed Mitchell. Indeed, the nomination had been scheduled for a vote in the full Senate on Thursday. Now Kleindienst wanted it put off so that he could rebut the charges in the column.

"Well, now, Senator," Jack was saying, "I know you'll want to be fair. I know you don't want to have a one-sided hearing. So I hope you'll let us come and give our side." He looked up at me, smiled and waved. "I know you will, Senator," he went on. "I understand your position. I appreciate it. Thank you. Good-by." He hung up and turned to me. "That was Eastland," he said, chuckling and shaking his head. "The last thing he wants is me on the stand. But he knows we could go up there and raise hell about not being allowed to speak, so he finally said he'd try to get me on. I'll need a statement to read. You'll have to write it because I haven't got the time, and you'll have to come with me because there will probably be questions only you can answer."

I had never testified before a congressional committee and wasn't sure I wanted to. The Senate Judiciary Committee, although technically controlled by the Democrats, was dominated by a combination of Republicans and conservative southern Democrats led by Chairman James Eastland of Mississippi. The majority would be squarely in Kleindienst's corner. Several of them, particularly Roman Hruska of Nebraska, the ranking Republican, had been roasted time and again by the column and would like nothing more than a chance for revenge. Nevertheless, Jack had no doubt about the wisdom of crowding the reluctant Eastland into allowing us to appear.

Such scrapes, of course, were nothing new to Jack. Once, after he had enraged the House of Representatives with an article in *Parade* entitled "Congressmen Who Cheat," he was summoned before an investigating committee. He arrived, armed with documentation and prepared to name names. The committee, however, refused to hear his specifics and insisted instead upon trying to learn his sources. Jack defied them and the hearing ended in an uproar, which made the congressmen look foolish but left Jack and his allegations unrefuted, and further publicized. During the Senate's investigation of the charges by Jack and Drew Pearson against the late Senator Thomas Dodd, neither Jack nor Drew was called to testify. Indeed, Eastland's Mississippi colleague, John Stennis, who headed the investigation, repeatedly cut short witnesses who even implied criticism of the two columnists. He had no intention of giving them grounds for demanding the right to reply. He knew that any appearance by Drew and Jack would have been a chance to demand that the committee delve into their most serious charges, which the Senate had chosen deliberately to ignore.

Jack had often told me that the newspaper-column business was a combination of reporting and showmanship. In this case, I had provided the reporting and he was delighted to find a forum to add the showmanship. I didn't doubt his ability to perform effectively. He was the veteran of several lawsuits and a noted public speaker. But Kleindienst and his allies on the committee would be ready to seize upon any weakness in the ITT columns. It would not be Jack, but I who would have to answer them. I didn't relish the prospect.

On Thursday morning Jack and I caught a taxi for Capitol Hill. Jack was in good spirits, but calm. I was carrying a stack of copies of the statement I had written for Jack to read. I was as tense as I had ever been. I believed the columns we had done would withstand scrutiny, and the press was playing up the story. It had led the St. Louis *Post-Dispatch* the previous afternoon and was on the front page of the New York *Times*. But I couldn't get over the idea that Kleindienst wouldn't have asked for the hearing if he didn't have an ace up his sleeve. I remembered how Secretary of the Treasury John Connally, on the verge of confirmation by the Senate a few months earlier, had been revealed by the New York *Times* to have accepted income while governor of Texas under circumstances that made it appear illegal. He instantly reconvened the Senate Finance Committee, explained the matter to everyone's satisfaction and came out of it looking better than ever. The *Times* was left with egg on its face. I mentioned my concern to Jack.

"No," he said blandly. "This is the stupidest thing Kleindienst could have done. It's the best thing that could have happened to us."

There was a long line of spectators standing in the hallway outside the cramped Judiciary hearing room when Jack and I arrived. Chairman Eastland did not allow cameras inside, so the television crews had set up behind a battery of microphones in the hall. We were shown to front-row seats by the Capitol police who were tending the door. The room was packed. All four press tables were full, and reporters were standing against the wall. Kleindienst was seated at the witness table directly in front of the semicircular dais where the senators sat. He was flanked by a man I recognized from a photograph as Felix Rohatyn and by Judge Richard McLaren. My stomach felt tight and there was a sinking feeling that wouldn't go away.

As Kleindienst began his statement, however, my fears eased. He denied that he "influenced the settlement of government antitrust litigation for partisan political reasons." But he did not deny his meetings with Rohatyn. Instead, he acknowledged them and described them in detail. McLaren then outlined the reasons for settling the cases and insisted they were compelling. Rohatyn did not have a statement; he was there to answer questions. He soon got one from Senator Philip Hart, the gentlemanly Democrat from Michigan. "You thought you were negotiating a settlement, did you not?" he asked of the meetings with Kleindienst.

"I did not think I was negotiating a settlement, sir," Rohatyn responded in a voice that was higher and meeker than the one that had come over the phone from Kennedy Airport a few nights earlier.

"What did you think you were doing," said Hart, "giving an economics course?"

"I was trying to make an economic case, sir, of hardship."

It was evident by the lunch break that this would be no quick hearing. The liberal Democrats on the committee—Hart, Edward Kennedy, Birch Bayh, and John Tunney—were loaded with questions, and it would be some time before they would be finished. As Jack and I stepped into the hallway, the TV reporters, who had found Kleindienst unavailable, asked Jack for an interview. Smiling as if in wonder, Jack said, "Kleindienst has denied charges that have not been made and has admitted all the charges that have been made." I knew that would get on the air that night.

During the afternoon session, I whispered to Jack that things seemed to be going well. He said, "It doesn't matter what happens in here. What matters is what these reporters say about it." I didn't think the press could help but stress what Kleindienst had admitted rather than what he denied.

When the hearing ended late that afternoon, the liberal Democrats were still going strong with questions and it was obvious that these three witnesses would be back for at least one and possibly several more days. The huge press corps on hand assured wide coverage. But there was still the chance the press would stress Kleindienst's denials. That would have a dampening effect, making the affair seem a mere dispute rather than the scandal I believed it was.

As Jack and I walked out of the building that afternoon, I paused to look at a *Star* late edition on sale in a coin box. It told me a lot. KLEINDIENST TELLS OF ITT MEETINGS, said a bold headline across page one. Next to it was a picture of Kleindienst, looking uncomfortable and nervous, with smoke from his cigarette curling about his face. Leaning toward him, as if to whisper some confidence, was Felix Rohatyn, his dark hair and eyes making him appear somehow sinister. I never saw such a guilty-looking pair. I knew then that the story was launched.

EIGHT

Richard Kleindienst's hasty decision to reopen his confirmation hearings was, as Jack Anderson had calculated, a terrible blunder. He had expected to extricate himself from the ITT embarrassment in a single day. But at the end of that day, he had wandered far deeper into what the Washington *Post* came to call the "dismal swamp" of scandal than our columns could ever have put him. More than anything, it was the patient, persistent questioning of Senator Edward Kennedy that first led Kleindienst into difficulty. Kennedy is not fast on his feet. Nor was he especially well prepared for the hearing. But he has possibly the most able staff in Congress, an advantage afforded by the Kennedy name and fortune. The minute the special hearing was announced, four young lawyers on the senator's staff went to work, led by the self-confident and politically astute James Flug. By the time the hearing began Thursday morning, they had prepared a long list of carefully drafted questions. Flug sat right behind Kennedy. After he asked a question, the senator leaned back in his chair. As the answer was given, Flug would whisper a follow-up question in the senator's ear. The Kennedy interrogation of Kleindienst and his fellow witness had the effect of a dragnet. It combed the circumstances of the ITT settlement for any clues of irregularity. It snared two on the first day.

About midway in the morning session, Kennedy asked Kleindienst if he had known anyone else at ITT before Felix Rohatyn telephoned him for an appointment. Kleindienst replied that there was only one person, a Mr. Ryan who was a neighbor in the suburb of McLean, Virginia.

"Could you describe that relationship?" asked the senator. "Is it purely social, or is it a relationship . . ."

"It is a very casual social relationship," Kleindienst responded quickly. "Once or twice a year the neighborhood has a Christmas party or neighborhood party, and then I see Mr. Ryan."

"But there has never been a professional relationship between you?"

"None at all, sir."

"Had you ever heard of Mr. Rohatyn before his call?"

"No, sir."

"He was not introduced to you by anyone?"

"No, sir."

"Did he refer to anyone in calling you?"

"No, sir."

"He just called you out of the blue, and you took the call?"

"Well, he identified himself as a representative of the company. I think he knew who I was, my responsibilities in the department."

"And you took his call, without knowing what he was calling about, just because he was a director of ITT?"

"Yes, sir, I did."

That was damaging enough in itself. It is not easy to get an appointment with the Deputy Attorney General. But Rohatyn's mere association with ITT enabled him to do so, although he was a perfect stranger. Kennedy shortly moved on to question Judge McLaren. As he did, Rohatyn began whispering in Kleindienst's ear. Moments later, Kleindienst interrupted.

"Senator Kennedy," he said nervously, "you might have noticed that I have been talking to Mr. Rohatyn and I have had my recollection refreshed as to why he called me in the first place. I believe that Mr. Ryan, who lives out in my neighborhood, might have said at one of those parties that there would be an economic problem to ITT, and would I be willing to talk to somebody from the company and I said yes, I would. And that precipitated Mr. Rohatyn to call."

Thus the "casual" relationship which Kleindienst had with a neighbor he knew only as "Mr. Ryan" turned out to be the very contact through which ITT got the persuasive Rohatyn in the door. And Kleindienst left no doubt that Rohatyn was persuasive. "Well," he said at one point, "I was quite impressed by the assertions made by Mr. Rohatyn in my office, you know, that if they were true, then those consequences would follow from a divestiture of Hartford, and I was quite impressed by it, by those arguments."

The heart of Rohatyn's argument was that the loss of the Hartford Fire Insurance Co., which would result from a government victory in the antitrust cases, would prove disastrous both to ITT and to the entire economy. The conglomerate depended on Hartford for cash flow to meet its far-flung obligations; its divestiture could topple the entire corporate structure, creating damaging "ripple effects" throughout the economy and seriously affecting the nation's balance of payments.

It was, to say the least, a bold and remarkable position. The question of ITT's use of Hartford Fire's vast cash flow had been raised while the merger was still pending before the Connecticut insurance commissioner. At the time, ITT had given assurances that it planned no raid on the cash flow, that it intended to put more into the company than it would take out. Now it was telling the government, which had warned sternly against the merger in the first place, that to undo it would be disastrous because it desperately needed the very cash it had claimed it didn't need and wouldn't use. The underlying theme of this argument was that what was good for ITT was good for America and vice versa. Finally, it was telling the government that a victory by the government would not be in the public interest.

In the afternoon, Kennedy pressed McLaren to explain how he was finally won over by Rohatyn's presentations. McLaren said he had called upon an outside consultant to evaluate ITT's position. Why couldn't the Justice Department's own analysts do the job? Because, said McLaren, the Antitrust Division has experts in economics, but this was a financial matter and therefore required a different kind of expertise. The distinction between "economic" and "financial" was subtle, if not artificial, and it made McLaren look foolish, since both Rohatyn and Kleindienst had been using the word "economic" to describe ITT's contentions. McLaren said he had retained a man named Richard Ramsden to make a report on the matter and this report had been an important element in his decision to agree to a settlement leaving Hartford Fire in the ITT fold. Ramsden, he said, had been chosen because he had performed similar tasks before, particularly in an earlier merger case involving Ling-Temco-Vought.

"How," asked Kennedy, "did you learn about him for that case, or in that case?"

"Either the Treasury or the White House recommended him. I do not recall," said McLaren.

"The Treasury or *the White House?*" said Kennedy, a little incredulous. "Who in the White House?"

"Probably Peter Flanigan," McLaren replied blandly.

The answer was greeted with gasps from the press table. Nina Totenberg, a savvy reporter for the *National Observer*, clapped her hand over her mouth to suppress a squeal. Peter Flanigan, a presidential aide, was a millionaire former investment banker who was the White House's principal contact with the business community. He was notoriously pro-business, so much so that Ralph Nader had once called him "the most evil man in Washington."

"I had a number of matters with Mr. Flanigan of one sort or another, primarily legislation," McLaren went on. "But I knew of him as somebody knowledgeable in financial matters, and I respected his opinion. But I may have gotten the suggestion of Mr. Ramsden from Mr. MacLaury, who is the Treasury (Department) fellow. He was also on LTV (Ling-Temco-Vought)."

McLaren had quickly backed off a bit, but the mention of Flanigan's name had aroused Kennedy's curiosity. He followed with a series of questions which ended as follows:

"At any time did you talk about the ITT case with Mr. Flanigan or anyone in the White House?"

"I do not believe so."

"So you did not have any communication with anyone in the White House in any way about the ITT case?"

"Not that I recall at this time, and I think I would recall if I had."

Throughout the day, Kleindienst stuck to his assertion that he had not taken part in the "negotiations" on the ITT cases. McLaren and Rohatyn supported him, although Rohatyn had earlier told me that he had participated in "negotiations" with both McLaren and Kleindienst. But while Kleindienst might persuade the committee that he had not actually negotiated, he was still confronted with his flat statement in the letter to Larry O'Brien that the settlement had been "handled and negotiated exclusively" by McLaren and his staff. Kleindienst simply could not get around the fact that he had a role in "handling" the matter. As he finally conceded under questioning from Birch Bayh, a Democratic senator from Indiana:

"Yes, I guess I set in motion a series of events by which Mr. McLaren became persuaded that, for the reasons heretofore discussed, he ought to come off his position with respect to a divestiture of Hartford by ITT."

The questioning ranged far beyond Kleindienst's actions during the settlement negotiations themselves. This, of course, was one of the dangers of the move he had made. Having volunteered his testimony, he could not confine the questioning to the points he wanted to make. The Justice Department's—and his own—handling of the entire ITT matter was thoroughly explored. Like McLaren, Kleindienst was questioned closely as to whether the White House had intervened in the case at any point.

Asked by Senator Bayh if there had been any "suggestions" from the White House as to how the cases should be treated, Kleindienst replied firmly, "No, sir."

Later, he made this statement: "As I have testified fully, in the discharge of my responsibilities as the acting Attorney General in these cases, I was not interfered with by anybody at the White House. I was not importuned; I was not pressured; I was not directed."

At another point, he repeated the same point even more emphatically. "I would have had a vivid recollection if someone at the White House had called me up and said, 'Look, Kleindienst, this is the way we are going to handle that case.' People who know me I don't think would talk to me that way, but if anybody did, it would be a very sharp impact on my mind because I believe I know how I would have responded. No such conversation took place."

These statements were as false as they were emphatic, although we had no way of knowing it at the time. In fact, Kleindienst had gotten a call from the White House on April 19, 1973, just as the deadline for appealing the Grinnell case to the Supreme Court was approaching. The caller was John Ehrlichman. He told Kleindienst to drop the appeal. The Deputy Attorney General argued and said that the decision had already been made to make the appeal. A few minutes later, Kleindienst got another call. This one was from Richard M. Nixon, who bluntly inquired, according to later reports, about Kleindienst's ability to understand the English language. The President then ordered him to forget the appeal. Kleindienst has since said that he threatened to resign and this forced the President to change his mind. Whatever the reason, Nixon did reverse himself and the appeal went forward, only to be dropped when the cases were settled.

Throughout the day, old Jim Eastland slouched deep in his chair at the center of the dais. At times, only the crest of his nearly bald head and the end of the cigar that always stuck out of one side of his mouth were visible. Now and then, he would lean forward and, in an almost inaudible Mississippi drawl, ask one of the witnesses to speak up. Occasionally, he interrupted a fellow senator who was pressing his interrogation. "Let him answer the question," Eastland would say. Jack had told me several times that Eastland was "the most unflappable man I ever met." He might have added, the most inscrutable as well. There was no doubt he was sympathetic to Kleindienst, who was, like him, a conservative with no record of enthusiasm for civil rights. Even before the hearing started, Eastland had said Kleindienst was "guilty of nothing." The first day had not gone well for Kleindienst, but there was little Eastland could do to help him. Kleindienst had turned the hearing on and the chairman could not turn it off until his colleagues had finished their questioning. Of course, Eastland would do Jack Anderson no favors.

It seemed certain now that Jack would be allowed to testify. But there was no telling when, because Eastland wasn't saying. Kleindienst and the other two might finish at any time and Jack could be called on a moment's notice. He had to be present and ready. The result was that I had to keep his statement updated to take into account the revelations of each day's hearing. I worked until late the night after the first hearing rewriting the statement I had drafted the night before. The next morning, Opal retyped it, and we Xeroxed as many copies as time would allow, and Jack and I headed once again for Capitol Hill. That morning, the column revealing Reinecke's meeting with Mitchell appeared, adding further momentum to a situation that was becoming increasingly difficult to predict, let alone control.

There were signs when the hearing opened that the Republicans sensed the danger. Senate Minority Leader Hugh Scott, a ranking member of the committee who did not ordinarily attend its hearings because of his floor duties, was present. He was the first to speak:

"I hope that the hearings will be confined within the parameters of the framework of the confirmation, rather than develop into a broad fishing expedition on the entire functions of the office of the Justice Department. I would like to see those questions explored at some later hearing . . . But so far as the confirmation is concerned, I think the statements you [Kleindienst] have made are complete, candid and supported by testimony of other witnesses, and ought to be a complete answer to the charges and to the reason for this hearing."

Scott's statement was instantly endorsed by Senator Edward Gurney, a rangy, handsome Florida Republican who always looked to me as if he belonged on the first tee somewhere. He spoke in the broad-A tones of an Eastern aristocrat. "I sat through most of the testimony yesterday, not all of it, but certainly about nine-tenths of it," he said, "and I think that the whole matter was fully explored. As a matter of fact, it was not only explored, but re-explored again and again, and some points were covered many times. I am satisfied in my mind that there was certainly no case here of a deal with I.T.&.T. [sic] in return for any contribution to the Republican meeting in San Diego this summer. Moreover, it seems to me that Mr. McLaren, or Judge McLaren, who handled the details of the settlement, performed a rather unique and fine service here and ought to be commended for handling a very difficult situation."

Senator Eastland had left the room and the chair had been temporarily assumed by the third-ranking Democrat, Sam Ervin of North Carolina. One of the most powerful and politically canny of the old southern bulls who had for so long dominated the Senate, Ervin was fascinating to watch. He had a jowly, Santa Claus face and a nervous tic that kept his eyebrows in constant up-and-down motion. While Eastland tended to be taciturn and dour, Ervin was genial, even jovial. He loved to illustrate points by telling folksy tales he said were drawn from his experiences as a country lawyer in North Carolina. He made much of this country-lawyer pose, but it was a sham, for he was an honors graduate of

Harvard Law School, a former judge, a constitutional scholar, and as keen and sophisticated as any big-city prosecutor.

When Gurney had finished, Ervin asked McLaren and Rohatyn a couple of questions, then, with a smile, turned on the pompous Hugh Scott, who was still in his chair.

"Being a somewhat weak mortal who constantly succumbs to temptations, I cannot resist the temptation to observe that my good friend, the distinguished senator from Pennsylvania, is invoking Lidford law in reverse:

> *I oft have heard of Lidford law,*
> *How in the morn they hang and draw,*
> *And sit in judgment after.*

Now the distinguished gentleman from Pennsylvania has asked me to reverse that, that we sit in judgment first and then hear the evidence after, and it seems to me that would be very inappropriate; because I think I have been very much impressed by the candidness of Mr. Kleindienst, but I think it would be unfortunate to him if we sat in judgment first and then heard the evidence thereafter."

Scott removed the pipe from his mouth, unsmiling, and replied. "If the distinguished senator from North Carolina will yield, I do not make the same pretension toward expertise on constitutional law, but having tried some 10,000 cases in my time I have learned that unfortunately at times the court is deaf, and I am afraid that deafness has stricken the senator from North Carolina. I did not argue that we should make a judgment first and hear the evidence later.

"I specifically said that we should act on the evidence pertaining to the confirmation, that we should continue our examination on those points, but with more restricted limits, and not have a more general type fishing expedition, up a dry creek, I might add, which would serve no purpose."

Jack had sat back in his chair, relaxed and semi-attentive

147

throughout most of the testimony, but now he was sitting up straight and peering over the press tables at the two senators. He leaned over to me. "This is going to be good," he whispered. "These two guys are good and you won't see them go at it very often."

"Well," Ervin replied, still smiling genially, "justice is supposed to be blind, but it is not supposed to be deaf to testimony, and the senator from North Carolina is not willing to reach a conclusion that the creek is dry unless the senator from North Carolina first goes and takes a look at the creek and, if there is any water there, takes a wade in it a little bit."

"All I can say," responded Scott dryly, "is the senator has a very long pole." The audience chuckled appreciatively. But Ervin had a twinkle in his eye.

"My experience," he said, "has been that it takes a long pole to reach some things." The chuckling turned to a roar of laughter. Scott knew he was beaten.

"That is entirely too dangerous to pursue further," he said.

"Yes," said Ervin, ruddy with delight, "because we may get drowned in the dry creek."

Senator Edward Kennedy produced two documents during the Friday hearing which challenged Kleindienst's insistence the previous day that he had been unaware of ITT's pledge of cash for the Republican convention until October or November of the previous year. The first was a letter to Kleindienst from my friend Reuben Robertson, dated September 22, which raised questions about the coincidence of the antitrust settlement and the cash pledge. The other was a reply to the letter from McLaren a short time later. Kleindienst said he had been unaware of either document, that his staff handled such correspondence. It might have been true, but his answer did nothing to improve his image as a witness. The hearing ended early, and the three witnesses were told to return for more on Tuesday.

The Friday afternoon Washington *Star* carried a front-page

story by Robert Walters quoting California Lieutenant Governor Ed Reinecke as confirming our report that he had discussed with John Mitchell ITT's convention offer in May 1971. (Reinecke had also given the same information to several California newsmen and, more importantly, to Senator John Tunney, a California Democrat who was a member of the Judiciary Committee.) His statement, of course, conflicted with John Mitchell's insistence that he had no knowledge of the convention plans until much later. At midday Friday, however, Reinecke suddenly changed his story. He issued a statement purporting to "clarify" his earlier ones. It said he had not discussed the convention financing with Mitchell until September. This was greeted by the newsmen covering the hearing with a combination of disbelief and cynical laughter.

While the Friday hearing was in progress, Robert M. Smith, an investigative reporter in the Washington bureau of the New York *Times*, was making a phone call that would add still more embarrassment to the next morning's headlines. He contacted Richard Ramsden, the man who prepared the financial analysis on which McLaren had relied in accepting ITT's arguments, and asked how he was recruited for the job. "Peter Flanigan contacted me," Ramsden said, "and I returned the report to him. Flanigan relayed the questions to me that I was supposed to focus on." He never spoke to McLaren about the case, he said. This, of course, contradicted McLaren's testimony that he had never discussed the ITT case with the White House and provided the first clear evidence of White House involvement in the case, aside from that contained in Dita Beard's memo.

Contributing further to the unsavory appearance of things was the disappearance of Dita Beard. I had half expected her to show up the first day to dispute our column, but she was nowhere around either Thursday or Friday, despite a subpoena issued for her by Eastland. Finally, late Friday, she was traced to the Denver area by the FBI. The next day, she was found in an osteopathic hospital. No one seemed to know why she had gone there, but her doctors said her heart ailment necessitated her hospitalization. "We are trying to prevent a heart attack right now," said Dr. Dave Garland to newsmen.

At the weekend, everything I had reported stood either confirmed or undisputed. I was in high spirits. Eastland had cut short Friday's hearing, obviously to get McLaren and Kleindienst off the hot seat before further damage was done. No more testimony was slated before Tuesday. Republican senators conceded privately that they had asked for the delay to give their side a chance to regroup. Things were going well for Jack and me, but not nearly as well as I thought.

We didn't find out about it until much later, but Dita Beard's disappearance was not exactly voluntary. According to later sworn testimony, she had been hustled out of town by an ex-FBI agent named George Gordon Liddy, who worked for the White House and was later to become famous in another scandal. He had been part of a team of undercover men called the "plumbers" whose job supposedly was to track down the sources of unauthorized news leaks involving national security. Now he worked for the Nixon re-election committee. Dita Beard had left for Denver on Thursday, before anyone could have known the outcome of Kleindienst's ill-fated effort to quickly clear himself of the ITT charges. At that point, all that had come out were two columns which revealed the contents of Dita Beard's memo and some duplicity on Kleindienst's part. The fact that a White House undercover man had helped—or forced—Mrs. Beard to flee, ducking a congressional subpoena and trying to elude the FBI, meant that her memo and what she had told me in my two interviews with her were considered extremely explosive.

And this was not the last bit of skulduggery that would be used to end the scandal. Indeed, by now, although I had no way of knowing it, a group of senior presidential aides were gathering each morning in the old gray Executive Office Building adjacent to the White House for what one of them later described as "panic sessions" on the ITT case. The participants included Counsel to the President John W. Dean III, special presidential aides Charles Colson and Richard Moore, White House lobbyist Wally Johnson and various lower-ranking staff members. They were joined frequently by Robert Mardian, chief of the Internal Security Division of the Justice Department and a man widely regarded as a rightwing zealot with a natural enthusiasm for governmental surveillance. These were men, I soon found out, who played rough.

Now that Dita Beard had been located, I wondered what she would do. In an interview with the San Diego *Union,* Representative Bob Wilson, her close friend, said she had told him, "Where I'm going they won't be able to find me, and I won't be able to talk to them." The company was insisting it was co-operating in the search for her, but Wilson quoted her as saying she was being placed on leave and, in effect, told to disappear. Obviously, her conversations with me were not appreciated at ITT. What's more, Les Whitten had heard from an ITT source that the company was planning to cast doubt on the memo by discrediting Mrs. Beard. I talked this over with Jack by phone over the weekend. He suggested I go to Denver to try to get through to her. "I've been through this before," he said, "sometimes when someone opens up to you the way she did, a sort of confessor relationship develops and the person will continue to talk to you. If you went out there and came back with an affidavit from her on this, it would sew this thing up." It was the longest of longshots, I thought, but worth a try. I telephoned her doctors in Denver and told them we had information that she was about to be thrown to the wolves. I sent my good wishes and urged them to pass along my warning. They said she was taking no visitors and receiving no phone calls. I did learn, though, that Dr. Liszka was out there. I reached him at the hospital and asked him what Mrs. Beard had told him about her meetings with company officials in New York.

"They were mean to her," he said. "They never let her talk to

President Geneen. Mr. Gerrity made her talk to two lawyers. He lied to her. Mr. Geneen wanted to talk to her and he told him she had already gone. She was sitting right there. She could hear Mr. Geneen's voice on the telephone." Liszka added that "the company told her to go, to get lost. I think this was part of a plan to discredit her." He said the FBI had posted two guards outside her hospital room, as if she would try to flee. "She's not that kind of person," he said, adding, "You seldom see such a good-hearted person."

I asked if she might be willing to talk to me. "I don't think she's in any condition," he said. "Her lips and mucous membranes are blue . . . She's fairly confused, now." He said he was returning to Washington the next day and suggested I contact him then. Since Liszka also seemed to think an effort would be made to discredit her, I thought I might have a chance of getting his co-operation in an effort to get in to see her. When I reached him the next afternoon, he suggested I meet him that evening at Doctors Hospital in downtown Washington. At the hospital, I told him Jack and I stood ready to stick up for Mrs. Beard if an effort were made to malign her. Was she angry with me? I asked. He didn't think so. Might she be willing to talk to me? He didn't know. He was noncommittal on helping me get through to her. I left the hospital that night with no plans to go to Denver and a strongly renewed impression of what a strange man Dr. Liszka was.

The next morning, I slept late and was awakened by a call from one of Senator Kennedy's staff members. He told me the Judiciary Committee had suddenly been summoned back into session a day early to hear testimony—from Dr. Liszka. Senator Eastland had earlier promised that there would be several "surprise" witnesses and I assumed that Liszka was the first. I dressed hurriedly and rushed down to the Senate. Liszka was already in the witness seat when I arrived. His testimony was being billed as a report on Mrs. Beard's health and availability for testimony. That struck me as odd. There was no need for testimony on that. He could easily have supplied the necessary information in writing. Something was up, I suspected, and unfortunately, I was right.

After Dr. Liszka had told the committee Mrs. Beard might be able to testify in a couple of weeks and had given a general description of her heart ailment, Senator Philip Hart began asking about her visit with ITT officials in New York prior to going to Denver. Senator Marlow Cook, a burly Kentucky Republican and pal of Kleindienst, broke in to make sure Liszka was authorized to discuss matters beyond his patient's health. This might have tipped off the Democrats that the Republicans were eager for Liszka's testimony on her condition and nothing else. But it didn't. Soon, Senator Edward Kennedy started a line of questioning that his Republican colleagues would pursue with glee.

"And what," said Kennedy, "can you tell us as to your general conclusion as to her physical and mental health other than her heart condition?"

"Well," said Dr. Liszka, "recently it has been extremely poor."

"Could you elaborate . . . ?"

"I have met her under conditions when she was emotionally very disturbed, physically in poor shape, having signs of heart failure and it is a combination of both physically and mentally poor condition."

Before long, Liszka had testified that Mrs. Beard had a problem with "excessive drinking," that at times she was so wacky she would not have been legally capable of executing a will and that she had told him she wrote her memo when she was "mad and disturbed." Furthermore, he said, she popped tranquilizers in addition to boozing and she had been doing both the night I met her at her home. "I have never seen her mentally in a worse condition," he said. Liszka also told the committee that his patient had reported getting a severe scolding from Attorney General Mitchell after the Kentucky Derby the previous year. But, according to Liszka, she gave no indication the scolding preceded agreement on an antitrust settlement. He quoted her as saying, "I tried to talk to the Attorney General about a merger and antitrust matters and he told me that I should proceed through proper channels."

The effort to discredit Dita Beard was under way. And whether he intended it or not, it had been started by the same man who two days before had been telling me how "good-hearted" she was. Such damaging testimony, coming from Mrs. Beard's own personal physician, was so extraordinary that it was certain to make news. But I was not without ways to counteract it. Throughout the hearings, Kleindienst and his co-witnesses had refused to make themselves available for television and radio interviews. Since Eastland did not allow cameras or tape recorders inside the hearing room, the broadcast media's only chance to get filmed or taped material was in the hallway outside. Since the first day, Jack and I had gone before the cameras and microphones whenever asked. The result was nightly television news reports—to which the Nixon administration was acutely sensitive—in which the testimony of Kleindienst and his fellow witnesses was quickly summarized by a correspondent, followed by the appearance of Jack and myself, and sometimes others, to comment on it. While Kleindienst and company labored to make their case to the committee, Jack and I spoke uncontested to the public over television. After Liszka was through, I was again invited—Jack was not with me—to comment.

Liszka had generally confirmed my account of the meeting in Mrs. Beard's home, but I went over it, making clear that he was there only part of the time and reiterating the version of the Kentucky Derby party which Mrs. Beard had given me. During the hearing, Liszka had acknowledged under questioning from Senator Kennedy that he had, on his own initiative, met twice with aides to Kleindienst prior to his testimony and had given them the same information he had given the committee. Liszka had also told Senator Kennedy that Mrs. Beard had told him nothing in Denver about her meeting with ITT officials in New York. I told the assembled newsmen in the corridor what Liszka had told me she had said and pointed out the discrepancy between it and his testimony. I also noted pointedly that he had conferred with the Kleindienst aides, but stopped short of saying his testimony had been rigged. I felt afterward that part of the damage of Liszka's testimony might be offset if my comments were carried on the evening news. They were. And the next day, the committee got a letter from the head of the Criminal Division of the Justice Department. It said that Dr. Liszka and his wife, who had a joint medical practice, had been under investigation for Medicare fraud and that, while Liszka had been cleared, his wife's activities were still being examined by a grand jury. (She was ultimately exonerated also.) That seemed to explain his eagerness to co-operate with the Justice Department and finished off what was left of his credibility.

On Tuesday, McLaren changed his testimony and acknowledged that Richard Ramsden had been secured through Peter Flanigan, but insisted that Flanigan was "simply a conduit." By now, though, a more important embarrassment had developed. Kleindienst acknowledged that on April 16, 1971, four days before Felix Rohatyn first telephoned him, he had gotten a letter from Lawrence Walsh, a former president of the American Bar Association, a member of the elite New York law firm of Davis, Polk and Wardwell which had long represented ITT, and a former judge. The letter, accompanied by a legal brief to support its arguments, urged Kleindienst to delay the government's appeal to the Supreme Court in the first of the three ITT antitrust cases which had been decided by the lower courts. The letter, which began "Dear Dick," had been preceded by a telephone call to Kleindienst and was delivered by hand the same day by an employee of the firm. It began as follows:

As I told you over the telephone, our firm has represented ITT as outside counsel ever since its incorporation over fifty years ago. A few weeks ago, Mr. Harold S. Geneen, Chairman and President of ITT, asked me to prepare a presentation to you as Acting Attorney General and, through you, to the National Administration on the question of whether diversification mergers should be barred and, more specifically, urging that the Department of Justice not advocate any position before the Supreme Court which would be tantamount to barring such mergers without a full study of the economic consequences of such a step.

To us this is not a question of the conduct of litigation in the narrow sense. Looking back at the results of government antitrust cases in the Supreme Court, one must realize that *if the government urges an expanded interpretation of the vague language of the Clayton Act, there is a high probability that it will succeed. Indeed, the court has at times adopted a position more extreme than that urged by the Department . . .* It is our understanding that *the Secretary of the Treasury, the Secretary of Commerce, and the Chairman of the President's Council on Economic Advisers all have some views with respect to the question* under consideration.

Ordinarily, I would have first seen Dick McLaren, but *I understand that you, as Acting Attorney General, have already been consulted with respect to the ITT problem . . .* (emphasis added).

The letter, which was signed "Sincerely, Ed," was an extraordinary document. The lawyer for ITT was telling the top officer of the Justice Department that its antitrust case against his client would probably succeed, that the objective sought so diligently by McLaren would be reached. Thus the lawyers on both sides agreed that the government was going to win the case in the Supreme Court. Equally significant, however, was that the letter and the phone conversation mentioned in it suggested that Kleindienst had lied in his opening statement to the committee five days earlier. At that time, after explaining his contacts with Felix Rohatyn, Kleindienst had said "I had no discussions with any other officer or attorney or agent on behalf of ITT." Later that day, of course, Rohatyn had "refreshed" Kleindienst's recollection about his conversation with John Ryan of ITT. Now, Kleindienst was saying, he and McLaren "have had an opportunity to refresh our recollection" again and had remembered the Walsh letter and also subsequent conversations about it with Solicitor General Erwin Griswold, the man responsible for presenting government cases to the Supreme Court. This was another contradiction. Kleindienst had also said on his first day of testimony that he had never discussed the ITT cases with anyone in the Justice Department except McLaren. And this wasn't all. Now, it seemed, Kleindienst also remembered taking part in a meeting held back in 1969, when ITT representatives came to see him to urge that one of the antitrust cases not be filed at all.

As to the views Walsh suggested were held by the Secretaries of Commerce and Treasury and the head of the President's Council of Economic Advisers, Kleindienst said he didn't know what Walsh's letter meant. And he was equally baffled, he claimed, by Walsh's statement that "I understand that you . . . have already been consulted with respect to the ITT problem." He attributed the chummy tone of Walsh's letter to the fact that "I talk to Judge Walsh maybe two or three times a week and this because he is chairman of the standing committee on the judiciary of the American Bar Association through whom we process the recommendations for Federal District and Court of Appeals judges."

Kleindienst's opening statement had now been mostly dismantled, laying open a picture of high-level approaches to the Nixon administration on a broad front which succeeded in persuading the government to drop a case both sides agreed it would probably win. What's more, two of McLaren's principal economic advisers, Kenneth Elzinga and Willard Mueller, had now acknowledged to the press that they were never consulted about the ITT settlement. Both said they thought it was a "sham." Under questioning about this, McLaren, who had been increasingly impatient and testy, finally blew his top. His voice quavering with anger, he said, "I think it is significant that they [the two advisers] filed nothing, published nothing, and for all I know, they said nothing about this settlement before. Certainly if they knew or even had reason to suspect any wrongdoing, they had a duty to come forward. But they didn't." He seemed particularly bitter over the criticism from Elzinga, noting that he had received a congratulatory note from him after his appointment to the bench. "If he felt I was a crook, he had a peculiar way of expressing it." McLaren said he had been told that Elzinga had been reached over the weekend by Tom Susman, a young lawyer on Senator Kennedy's staff. "It is pretty plain that he did not tell him what I had testified. . . . I can only assume that he was somewhat poisoned over the weekend against me and I resent it very much." Kennedy denied there was any "poisoning."

As the affair went on, I could see that Jack was right when he had said earlier that it didn't matter what happened in the hearing room, that what mattered was what the press said about it. If the headlines and news reports stressed information damaging to the Administration and Kleindienst, it gave momentum to the scandal. But if the other side dominated the news, there was a dampening effect. Scandal, by definition, is not wrongdoing itself but, as Webster puts it, "opprobrium, ignominy or disgrace." Once Kleindienst had reconvened the hearings to respond to our columns, a battle for credibility was on. If the ITT affair were quickly cleared up, Jack and I would appear squelched and our accusations, whatever their merit, would seem to lack substance. If however, the affair refused to go away, Jack and I would appear vindicated. This was a political public relations contest in which Jack and I had no choice but to compete. Each side struggled to come out ahead in the daily tally provided by the morning headlines. But, as has often been observed, news and truth are not the same. The subtle and significant can always be chased off the front pages by the sensational and irrelevant.

No one understood all this better than old Jim Eastland, who made clever use of the special prerogatives of the committee chairmanship to help his friend Kleindienst. The sudden appearance of

Dr. Liszka was one example. Another was his imposition on Tuesday of the so-called ten-minute rule. The exhaustive interrogation by Senator Kennedy had uncovered much of the information that kept Kleindienst and his fellow witnesses on the defensive. Under the new rule, the floor shifted back and forth from the Republicans to the Democrats every ten minutes, thus breaking the continuity of questioning by Kennedy and others and allowing friendly members to throw a few home-run pitches at the beleaguered witnesses when the going got rough. It also seemed that Eastland called several recesses just in time to end a potentially damaging line of questioning. On Tuesday afternoon, with things going badly for Kleindienst, Eastland suddenly produced the second of his "surprise witnesses." It was Louie Nunn, the former Kentucky governor who was mentioned in Dita Beard's memo as the source of her knowledge that Mitchell was aiding ITT in the antitrust cases. Kleindienst and the others had not finished their testimony, but they were asked to stand aside for Nunn.

A tall, hefty man with dark hair and what seemed to me a sinister look, Nunn gave testimony that can best be described as the opposite of chivalry. He told how Mrs. Beard had repeatedly approached Mitchell at his dinner party at the governor's mansion after the Kentucky Derby the previous year, only to be repeatedly rebuffed. Finally, he said, "the Attorney General became very disturbed about it. He said that he was sick and tired of hearing this about what . . . she was trying to do in regard to it and he didn't want to hear any more about it. She moved on and the next thing that I recall was that someone came to me—we were still in the dining area and about finished eating—and said that Mrs. Beard was ill, that they had gotten a vehicle and taken her back to the motel where she was staying. I later discovered that she either had a light heart attack or she was exhausted or maybe a combination of both, together with drinks, I think. They had laid her out on the floor there for a few moments and tried to revive her somewhat and then she was removed from there. And that was the extent of what occurred there at the governor's mansion with Mrs. Beard and the Attorney General."

"Do you know," drawled Eastland, "whether or not she is a heavy drinker?"

"Well, I have observed her on occasions where she was drinking quite heavily; yes sir."

Nunn would later say under questioning that he considered Mrs. Beard a friend, but it didn't stop his dissertation on her alleged problems. "I don't recall her ever talking to me specifically about the ITT in a manner where she asked me to get information or to furnish any information or to exert any influence in any manner. But when she was drinking, when she was around a group, it was not unusual for her to go into something about the people that she worked for and who was trying to do what to her."

"What," asked Senator Hart, "did she say in those sessions?"

"Well, she would say that certain people, or they, or some of them in Washington were trying to get her job. She seemed to be obsessed about it. And I don't know why or what."

Nunn recounted a number of occasions when he had met Mrs. Beard. On all of them, he said, she was drinking. "Sometimes she was drinking more than she was others, sometimes she was drinking less," he said.

I was outraged by Nunn's testimony, the more so because once he had completed his elaborate descriptions of her job insecurity and non-stop drinking his memory seemed to go blank. He became the most intractable witness I had ever heard. He claimed, for example, that he had come to testify after being contacted by a representative of the Judiciary Committee, but he couldn't recall who it was, although the call had come the day before. He said Dita Beard had called him to warn him our column was coming out and to apologize for any embarrassment it might cause him, but he couldn't remember when. He acknowledged that his brother, Lee Nunn, worked for the Republican National Committee, but insisted he didn't know what his job was. His testimony caused repeated snickering and continual head-shaking at the press tables, but there could be no doubt it would steal the morning headlines from the earlier, damaging, but far less colorful testimony of Kleindienst and McLaren.

Inevitably, Dita Beard and her extraordinary memo had become the center of the controversy, although considerable new evidence of irregularity in the antitrust settlement had spilled onto the record. It was natural, of course, that public attention in such a scandal would focus on a missing witness, particularly a salty lady lobbyist, and an incriminating secret memorandum rather than the dry technicalities of an antitrust settlement. Thus if the credibility of Dita Beard or her memo could be destroyed, the scandal might be deflated, regardless of the other evidence. So Dr. Liszka and Louie Nunn, it seemed clear, had been wheeled in to make Mrs. Beard appear a broken-down, half-crazy drunkard on the verge of losing her job. The damaging version of the Kentucky Derby party which she had given me had been contradicted by both witnesses, whose testimony pictured John Mitchell as indignantly fending off her improper advances with such force that she was, literally, floored. But Liszka and Nunn were supposed to be Mrs. Beard's friends and their testimony therefore seemed indecent, which undermined its credibility.

On Wednesday, Kleindienst, McLaren, and Rohatyn were back at the witness table for their fourth and what proved to be their final day. McLaren was pressed hard for an explanation of why he dropped a case he seemed likely to win on the strength of a report from a young financier procured by the White House who never discussed the case with anyone in the Justice Department. The questioning caused what I thought were two subtle but important shifts in McLaren's testimony. Now he was emphasizing that the Ramsden report was only one factor in his decision and that he relied far more heavily on his own judgment as an experienced antitrust lawyer. And the idea that the divestiture of Hartford Fire from ITT would cause "ripple" effects that would threaten the entire national economy was played down by McLaren in favor of the proposition that it would "have a rather drastic effect not only on ITT, but on the stockholders and *possibly* on the economy." (Emphasis added.) The fact that McLaren seemed more worried about the impact on stockholders was important because the job of the antitrust division is to preserve competition by enforcing the law, not to protect corporate stockholders. Clearly, McLaren was defending an increasingly weak position. There is an old maxim in the legal profession that says, "When you're weak on the law, argue the facts. When you're weak on the facts, argue the law. When you're weak on both, pound the table." Before long, Mc-Laren was pounding the table.

"This is not an inquiry into Kleindienst's qualifications," he charged angrily. "Some commentator said there was no moral indignation here. I think that it is an absolute outrage the way this committee is inquiring into this matter . . . You know how the decision was made and there was no hanky panky about it, either."

So Richard McLaren, who had enjoyed probably the best reputation of all the Nixon Justice Department appointees, was now reduced to shouting his innocence. As the days had passed, it had seemed to me that the committee members addressed him less frequently as "Judge" McLaren and more often as "Mr." McLaren. Ralph Nader was sitting behind Jack and myself in the audience when McLaren concluded his outburst. I turned to him.

"His halo has certainly slipped," I said, nodding toward Mc-Laren.

"Yeah," Ralph said, "and his was the only halo they had."

At this point, the biggest hole in McLaren's defense of the antitrust settlement was the fact that ITT's lawyer had agreed in writing that the government would have won it. But before the day was out, Eastland produced another previously unscheduled witness to repair the hole. He was Erwin Griswold, a roly-poly yet ceremonious little man who once had been Dean of the Harvard Law School and was now Solicitor General of the United States, the government's Supreme Court lawyer. Griswold said he was no expert on antitrust and he couldn't remember the last time a Supreme Court majority had ruled against the government in an antitrust case. But he testified nevertheless that the government would have lost all three ITT antitrust cases in the Supreme Court and that the settlement decree, which he hadn't read, was "extremely favorable" to the government.

Griswold's testimony ended five days of hearings in which not a single witness against Kleindienst had been heard. After declaring Kleindienst innocent the first day, Eastland had run the hearings in such a manner as to help prove it. Each day as Jack and I sat waiting our turn, an Eastland aide, usually the committee's chief counsel John Holloman, left the dais and came around and entered the room from the main door at the rear. He waded through the crowd to where Jack and I sat in the front row and, with elaborate courtesy, asked Jack to step outside with him. Jack was then shown into a committee anteroom, where Eastland was waiting. The chairman always grinned, greeted Jack affably, and said apologetically that he couldn't fit Jack in that day, but perhaps the next. Jack always replied that he understood and that he appreciated Eastland's efforts. Eastland was obviously being dilatory and I asked Jack at one point why, instead of going along with the charade, he didn't blast him.

"No," he said in that bland way that always signified certainty, "that would be a mistake. I know Eastland. He's promised Kleindienst to help get him out of this and he's under a lot of pressure to do what the Administration wants. But he's promised to put us on and he will. If we blast him now, it will just turn him against us. If we play along, he probably won't give us any trouble on the stand. There are only a couple of guys on that committee I'm afraid of and Eastland's one of them. He's just as sharp as he can be, and he's mean."

Before Griswold took the witness seat late Wednesday, Jack and I were informed that we would be the lead-off witnesses the next morning. We left immediately and went back to the office. I wanted to give Jack's statement some polishing and updating, then distribute it to the press before the end of the day, with the stipulation that it not be used until the next morning. There was a reason for this beyond the desire to convenience the press. If we didn't hand out the statement until the next morning, the early editions of all the afternoon newspapers would carry stories still rehashing the testimony of the day before. The morning and midday radio broadcasts would carry the same information. But if the press had the statement the night before, stories for the next day could be readied in advance—in time to make the early editions of evening papers and the morning and midday newscasts. The fresh story about Jack's statement would push aside the news about the testimony of Griswold and the others from the day before. This plan was no stroke of public relations genius on my part, just something I learned in my days as a wire-service reporter.

As it stood, Jack's statement was mostly an attack on the testimony of the other witnesses, and I couldn't be certain the media would find it especially newsworthy. But we were fresh out of major revelations about the case. The only way I could think of to give the statement news value was to denounce Kleindienst and declare him unfit to be Attorney General. In fact, I had done just that in the latest version of the statement. But during a break in the Wednesday hearing, something unusual had happened that made me wonder about this. Reporters and photographers were milling around the witness table, talking to each other and the witnesses. Kleindienst had gotten up and was standing near one side of the committee dais, talking to several reporters. Jack stood at the edge of the group listening. The next thing I knew the others had drifted away, and Jack and Kleindienst were left together. It was quite a sight. Both men were around the same age and height and both had developed paunches, although Jack's was far larger than Kleindienst's. There they stood, belly to belly, the two principal antagonists in the whole affair chatting amiably. Not a single photographer noticed it, though, and I wasn't going to rush around alerting them like a PR man. So I just walked over to join them. After a few seconds, Jack interrupted to introduce me.

"Oh, by the way," he said, "this is Brit Hume, my . . ."

"I guessed that," Kleindienst said, eying me coldly. "There's one thing I want you both to understand. If you ever have any information about Dick Kleindienst, I hope you'll get in touch with me before you use it."

I started to explain about the troubles we had been having with the Justice Department's public relations office, but he cut me off.

"I don't care about them," he said, looking first at me and then at Jack. "You call me directly. You won't have any trouble reaching me. That is, if I'm ever confirmed for this job."

"Oh, I'm sure you will be," Jack said reassuringly. "Heck, your nickname has always been 'clean dish.' My information is that there aren't more than ten or fifteen votes against you."

The conversation was making me uncomfortable, so I moved away. It was typical of Jack, though, that he felt no ill will toward Kleindienst. Jack simply didn't view issues on a personal level. He had been in too many fights in his twenty-five years in Washington for that, and, besides, he was too good-natured and easygoing. He liked people. He had a number of friends who never would have rated a favorable mention in the column had they held public office. So the fact that Kleindienst might have seemed too shady to be Attorney General mattered to Jack only for the purposes of the column. It was no reason not to be friends. It was the same quality in Jack that enabled him to offer words of comfort to the embattled Kleindienst in the midst of a scandal of Jack's own making that also enabled him to pursue remorselessly a damaging story about young Randy Agnew's private life. In public, Jack was the relentless muckraker bent on exposing wrongdoing whatever the human consequences. In private, he was a big softy whose wife once said she had seen him lose his temper only once in more than twenty years of marriage. In most people, there is at least some connection between their public posture and their private nature. But in Jack Anderson, there was virtually none.

In the taxi on the way back to the office, I asked Jack if he still wanted his statement to pronounce Kleindienst unfit.

"Well," he said, "maybe not. I don't know. What do you think?"

"After that conversation today with you predicting he'd be confirmed, I thought you might have changed your mind."

"Oh, that doesn't matter. I'm still willing to blast him, if you think I should. I'll leave it to your judgment."

The conversation shifted to the next morning's testimony. I was jumpy about it. As he had done before, Jack sought to reassure me.

"Look," he said, "you're gonna do fine. You're articulate and you're telling the truth. I'm not worried about you at all. Besides, I've contacted all the Democrats and they're not going to give you any trouble. They're on our side, except for Eastland, and I don't expect any trouble from him. We might get a hard time from some of the Republicans, but I'm not really afraid of any of those guys. I've talked to Hugh Scott and he's probably not going to be there, which is good news, because he's sharp and he could really be rough. I also talked to Mac Mathias and, although he has to be careful about it, I think he's on our side."

Charles McC. "Mac" Mathias was a liberal Republican senator from Maryland. He alone among the Republicans on the Judiciary Committee could be expected to be friendly to Jack Anderson. The ranking Republican was Nebraska's Roman Hruska, a devout conservative who was part of the Senate's cheering section for big business. Jack had embarrassed him in the column time and again. Once Les had gotten a transcript of a secret subcommittee meeting in which Hruska, Senator Hiram Fong, a fellow Republican member of the Judiciary Committee, and Senator Tom Dodd, the victim of Jack's greatest exposé, had been arguing vigorously for the suppression of a report exposing wrongdoing by an insurance company. Jack had a field day with it, labeling the trio "the three musketeers of the insurance industry" and recounting their dialogue with maximum colorful embellishment. That caused all three to rise as one on the Senate floor to attack the column. Jack's response was another column on the meeting which he called "Chapter Two of their exploits." In 1970, Les nearly cost Hruska re-election when he turned up the fact that, despite his denunciations of pornography, the senator was part owner of a chain of theaters that showed such films as *Wild and Willing—They Broke Every Speed Record in a Parked Car* and other sexploitation movies. None of us thought the column would be good for more than a few laughs at Hruska's expense, but the issue caught on in Nebraska, and, after being far ahead early in the race, the senator had to scramble to win in a squeaker. Of all the committee members, Hruska was the most certain to be gunning for Jack.

Fortunately, however, Hruska was perhaps the number-one bumbler in the Senate. At the height of the Senate debate over the confirmation of Judge G. Harrold Carswell, for example, Hruska said in a television interview that it didn't matter if Carswell was mediocre because "There are a lot of mediocre people in the country and they're entitled to some representation, too, aren't they? You can't have all Frankfurters and Cardozos and stuff like that there." This astonishing comment was later cited by opponents of Carswell as the turning point in the successful fight against his nomination.

The other Republicans on the committee were Fong, who had been present only briefly, Strom Thurmond of South Carolina, who had been there even less, Marlow Cook of Kentucky, and Edward Gurney of Florida. I didn't know what Gurney and Cook thought of Jack, but they had done much of the friendly questioning of Kleindienst and the other witnesses. And Cook was known to be a good friend of Kleindienst.

It was cold and windy the next morning as we rode in a taxi to Capitol Hill. The ITT story had brought a wave of publicity even greater than the India-Pakistan documents. Reporters from *Time* and *Newsweek* had been in the office working on major stories, and CBS had sent producer Phil Shefler and correspondent Morley Safer down from New York to gather material for a segment of the weekly "Sixty Minutes" program. Safer and Shefler were with us in the cab. I could tell that Jack was keyed up, but he talked cheerfully with them as he pored over the statement he would soon be reading to the committee. I was too tense to say much. I just sat and stared out the window, wishing the nervous twinge that kept recurring in the pit of my stomach would stop. As we were leaving the office, Les Whitten wished us well and said, a little enviously, "I sure wish I was going to be with you." I thought to myself, "I sure wish you were going instead of me."

Jack had cautioned me several times to be respectful and courteous to the senators. "If we get too smart with them," he said, "they might all turn on us." Jack didn't have to worry about me on that score. Whatever I might have thought of some—or even most—of the senators individually, I respected the Senate as an institution. Moreover, I would be testifying under oath, and I didn't take that lightly. I planned to choose every word carefully and to avoid injecting my own opinions unless pressed to do so. Ralph Nader had suggested in a phone conversation the night before that I parry every unfriendly thrust with a positive proposal for reform. That was all right for him, I thought, but not for me. Besides, Jack's statement contained enough remonstration for both of us. I intended it to be a blast of honest, unvarnished rhetoric that would clear the air of the elaborate circumlocution, euphemism, and dissembling that had characterized the hearings so far.

The senators had not come in when Jack and I took seats at the witness table. A gaggle of photographers and television cameramen gathered in front of us to get the only shots inside the hearing room the chairman would allow. Soon, the senators came in the rear door and Eastland pounded his gavel and Jack and I stood up and took the oath. I noticed that all the Democrats were present, except John McClellan, one of Jack's and Drew Pearson's greatest enemies, who had not attended any of the hearings. All the Republicans were present, except Strom Thurmond. Jack put on his reading glasses and started his statement. His deep, resonant voice made the hard-hitting passages sound far more blunt than they had while I was writing them.

"The public record on this episode is blotted with falsehood. The aura of scandal hangs over the whole matter . . . Mr. Kleindienst came here burdened by his previous emphatic statement that the ITT cases were 'handled and negotiated exclusively' by Mr. McLaren. Our report that he and Mr. Rohatyn had a series of private meetings on the case cast doubt, to put it mildly, on the truth of Mr. Kleindienst's statement. But instead of admitting manfully that his previous statement was misleading, Mr. Kleindienst sought to wiggle out from under his misrepresentation with a silly and artificial semantic distinction . . . He argued before this committee that he had done no negotiating. Perhaps more astonishing, Mr. Rohatyn and even Judge McLaren endorsed this transparent disclaimer. Webster defines "negotiate" as meaning 'to confer, to bargain, to discuss with a view to reaching agreement.' Can Mr. Kleindienst deny that he conferred with Mr. Rohatyn? Can he deny that they discussed the cases? Can he deny that the end result of their decisions was agreement? The answer to these questions is obvious. Yet these three grown men sat before this committee and insisted Mr. Kleindienst had not negotiated . . ."

The statement went on to attack the inconsistencies in the public comments made by ITT and John Mitchell and challenged the credibility of Ed Reinecke's about-face on his meeting with Mitchell. It noted pointedly that Dr. Liszka had failed to tell the committee, when asked, of what he had already said Mrs. Beard told him about her trip to New York. And it quoted press statements by Louie Nunn which conflicted with each other and with his testimony. The statement accused Nunn of having "perhaps the most erratic memory in the history of American politics," a memory which recalled vividly the Kentucky Derby party incident but thereafter again "turned to molasses." The statement ended with a final shot at Kleindienst.

"Mr. Kleindienst is a man who has trouble recognizing a crime when he sees one. Now, let us make no mistake about it. The contribution of $400,000 by a corporation to support a political convention is a crime. It directly and clearly violates the Corrupt Practices Act, which specifies it is 'unlawful for . . . any corporation . . . to make a contribution or expenditure in connection with any . . . political convention.' Yet when questioned about this, Mr. Kleindienst said he didn't have an opinion. He protested that it was 'customary' for political conventions to receive such donations. Do the American people want as their top policeman a man who thinks crimes are not crimes because they are customary?

"This is not all. When asked by Senator Tunney whether there might be a bribe in the ITT contribution, Mr. Kleindienst said his idea of a bribe was a situation in which someone walked into his office and offered a large political contribution in exchange for a favor. Yet this very scenario has already happened to Mr. Kleindienst. Robert Carson, a Senate staff member, walked into his office and offered a $100,000 political contribution in exchange for Kleindienst's going to bat for someone who had been indicted for stock fraud. We can all be grateful that Mr. Kleindienst didn't take the bribe. But he apparently didn't realize that it was a bribe. For not until a week later, when he learned the FBI was already investigating the offer, did he report it to the Attorney General."

As Jack read this last portion, I studied the face of Senator Fong for reaction. The reason was that Robert Carson had been Fong's aide. Because of the clubby custom of reciprocal courtesy among members of the Senate, no one on the committee had ever questioned Kleindienst about the incident, so as not to embarrass Fong. Remembering Jack's warning about turning the committee against us, I had deliberately left out Fong's name. He didn't react as Jack read the part about Carson, who ultimately was convicted of bribery.

"There can be no doubt," Jack went on, "that Mr. Kleindienst played a major role in the settlement of the ITT antitrust cases. He helped bring about a settlement experts have denounced as a sham. Having done this, he issued an utterly disingenuous statement about the matter indicating he had no role whatever. He then came before this committee and lacked the candor to admit his statement had been misleading . . . This country needs as its top law enforcement officer a man who understands the law and respects the truth. Richard Kleindienst is not such a man. He is unfit to be Attorney General."

The chairman posed no questions when Jack was finished and the floor went to Senator Ervin, who responded with one of his folksy tales.

"Well, Mr. Anderson," he said, "your analysis of various conversations convinces me that Lord Coke was right when he said that the scratch of a pen is worth the slippery memory of many witnesses.

"It calls to mind one of the first cases in which I participated in which my client was charged with murdering his wife by stabbing her in the neck. Four witnesses appeared at the trial and testified that they went to the jail together and that each one of them asked my client whether he had killed his wife. The first witness said my client did not say anything in reply to the question, but that he shook his head no. The second witness said that he answered the question with a simple yes and nothing else. The third witness said that he said yes, but that it was an accident. The fourth witness said that he answered yes, I took the knife and jabbed it in her throat.

"So I still have, as a result of your summation and analysis, a very profound conviction that Lord Coke was right that one scratch of a pen is worth the slippery memory of many witnesses. That is the only questions or observations I have at this time."

"Well, Senator," Jack said, not really knowing how to answer

Ervin's anecdote, "the Senator is known to have a strong sense of decency."

"Thank you," said Ervin.

"I might add," Jack said, "that I am concerned about the Senate's understanding of right and wrong. Sometimes I am concerned that there is not a clear appreciation for the difference between right and wrong, the difference between truth and falsehood."

Jack had been advising me to be respectful to the senators so they wouldn't turn against us. Yet he hadn't even been asked a question and he was already telling them, in effect, that they didn't know or care about the difference between right and wrong. Apparently, he meant his admonition against impertinence to apply only to me. The floor shifted to the Republicans, where the scowling Roman Hruska was waiting.

"Mr. Anderson," he began in his thundering tone, "on page 12 of your statement you make the flat and unqualified conclusion: 'The contribution of $400,000 by a corporation to support a political convention is a crime.' Are you a lawyer, Mr. Anderson?"

"No," said Jack, "but I understand the English language. And I will read some of the English language to you if you will allow it. Here is the Federal Corrupt Practices Act. It says: 'It is unlawful. . . .'"

Hruska interrupted to ask Jack to cite the section. Jack did, then proceeded to read it out loud to him. When he had finished, he said, "Now I don't think you need to be a lawyer to understand that, Senator."

"Well, that is your opinion," replied Hruska, "but, of course, you prefaced—"

"Well, what is your opinion?" interrupted Jack.

"You prefaced your statement most accurately that you are not a lawyer but that you can read the English language. That is not all that it does take," said Hruska.

Hruska produced a letter written by an official in the Justice

Department to a California law firm. The letter said the section of the Corrupt Practices Act cited by Jack did not apply to political conventions. As it turned out the law firm was Kalmbach, De-Marco, Knapp and Chillingworth of Los Angeles and Newport Beach, California, which was President Nixon's personal law firm and also the firm representing the Nixon Foundation. What's more, Herbert Kalmbach had quietly become one of the President's most effective fund raisers. This would later be brought out by Senator Kennedy, to the great embarrassment of the Republicans. For now, though, Jack would have to figure out a response of his own. I leaned over and whispered in his ear that Kleindienst hadn't cited the opinion when he testified. Jack nodded.

"Well," said Jack when Hruska had finished, "I heard Mr. Kleindienst respond to this question and he did not read any of these learned decisions that you cite."

"No, he did not," said Hruska, "and his testimony will speak for itself. Any lawyer questioned on as complicated matters as the many, many that he was interrogated upon, must be a little careful in what he says. Now you can have your opinions about it, but again I submit that the committee will probably have a pretty good idea of where the credibility lies with regard to whether the contribution by a corporation to support a political convention is a crime."

"Well, I am aware," Jack said sarcastically, "that the attitude toward political contributions on the part of the politicians has been somewhat fuzzy."

"It is not fuzzy at all," Hruska roared. "Conventions all over America are bought all the time by business communities, and everyone—"

Hruska never finished his sentence because the room exploded with laughter. Even the senators broke up. Jack shouted, "I subscribe to that." I tried not to show my amusement because Hruska was staring at Jack and me. When the room quieted down Hruska began again.

"Everyone in this room knows it," he stormed. "Every city in which any of the senators of this committee come from goes out and buys conventions, and how do they do it?"

The room erupted again, but Hruska went on with his description of what he considered legitimate fund-raising to attract political conventions. When he was finished, Jack spoke up.

"Well, I would just add this, Senator, and I say it with all the sincerity that I can bring to bear on this, I believe that our system of financing elections, our system of financing political campaigns is the most corrupt and the worst feature of our entire political process."

I didn't know what to make of all this. Jack had interrupted Hruska, shouted at him, lectured him. As their exchange went on, Hruska had become increasingly red-faced. His perpetual scowl was an expression of barely concealed rage. Like a snorting bull, he charged at Jack from another angle, demanding that he list the allegations against Kleindienst that Jack's statement had said the Attorney General designate had admitted.

"We said that he had told a lie," said Jack.

"Did he acknowledge that he told a lie?" snapped Hruska.

"Well," said Jack, "he came here and danced, as we said, around the mulberry bush on the word 'negotiate.' "

"That is not what I am talking about," fumed Hruska. "I am not talking about any dancing. We are talking about acknowledging. Did he acknowledge that he lied in terms of the charge that he made?"

Jack responded that Kleindienst had acknowledged having all the meetings with Rohatyn that we said he had. Hruska wanted to know what the other charges were. Jack offered to read our columns. Hruska said he wanted the charges. Jack began reading the column on Kleindienst out loud. Hruska interrupted and declared the answer unresponsive. Jack kept trying to read it and the senator kept cutting him off. Finally Eastland told Hruska to let Jack answer. But by now, Hruska's time had expired. The exchange accomplished nothing, except possibly to make Hruska look foolish. It had set the tone, though, for Jack's testimony. He had evidently planned all along to be just as contumacious as he thought necessary to keep the hostile Republicans at bay. His free swinging, of course, would not affect the credibility of our reporting because all questions of substance were referred to me, whom Jack had instructed to be precise and polite. It was an interesting strategy, I thought, but I wondered if it would work. My fear was that it would simply provoke the hostile Republicans even further and make things more difficult for us than Hruska had already shown they were going to be.

Soon, I was doing most of the talking. The Democrats tossed general questions about how I got the story, to which I gave long, detailed responses in a tone as dispassionate as I could make it. I referred often to the typed memorandum I had made after returning from Mrs. Beard's home. The Republicans soon seized on the memo in an effort to unnerve me. Senator Cook demanded it be made a part of the record. It had been typed in haste and it wasn't well organized and it contained some of Mrs. Beard's four-letter words. What's more, I was firmly of the conviction that newsmen should not be required to surrender their notes, tapes, film or the identities of their sources to any government body on demand. Reflexively, I refused. It was a decision I would come to regret later.

For the rest of the day, I filled in the record on my meetings with Dita Beard and the various other conversations I had had while digging up material for our columns on the ITT case. Intermittently, Jack fenced with the Republicans. Senator Gurney asked Jack to identify the source of the memo, but Jack refused beyond saying it wasn't Dita Beard. In the afternoon, Senator Cook led off by introducing into the record a batch of stories of Jack's that had been alleged to be inaccurate. Only one of them was, a totally untrue report that the chief of the anti-poverty agency had remodeled his office. Jack admitted the error openly and declared it "the most glaring" he had ever made. Cook said that it was an outright lie. Jack said it was an honest mistake. That exchange didn't get anywhere.

Late in the afternoon, under questioning from Senator Tunney, I reiterated something we had already reported in the column, but this time it had unexpected results. Dita Beard, I told Tunney, "said that the Attorney General told her during the discussion in the dinner party that the President had called him up and put pressure on him. She gave first the quote that the President said, 'Lay off ITT,' and that sounded so amazing to me that I pressed her. I said, 'He said, "Lay off ITT"?' And she said, 'No, I am sorry. It was more like "make a reasonable settlement." ' "

Eastland leaned forward and asked me to explain again. Then he asked: "Was that the President of the United States?"

In editing our first ITT column to make room in it for a last-minute statement from the company, the Washington *Post* had chosen to cut out this information. So while readers all over the nation had already seen it, it was news to the committee and to the press in the hearing room. I was surrounded by reporters during a recess and asked to repeat the story before the cameras and microphones outside. It made the network news that night and was a front-page story in the morning. In the words of the New York *Times*, "Brit Hume, a 28-year-old investigator for the syndicated columnist Jack Anderson, brought a stunned silence to the Senate Judiciary Committee chamber when he told about Mrs. Beard's alleged account of her conversation with Mr. Mitchell . . ."

Much had been made in news stories, before our testimony, of Jack's presence in the front row of the hearings—eager to testify, waiting, in the words of the Washington *Star's* Mary McGrory, to "finish Kleindienst off." But Jack and I had had no important new revelations to make and we feared our testimony would lack news value. Yet Jack's condemnation of Kleindienst had dominated the news early in the day, and my testimony, because of the earlier fluke in editing by the Washington *Post,* had hit the front pages by seeming to those present to implicate the President for the first time. I received a lot of favorable comment from other reporters about my performance, which they said compared well with that of earlier witnesses. It was nice to hear, but I sensed that if I had done well it was because I had a built-in advantage: I was telling the truth and it is easy to keep things straight when you are telling the truth.

The next morning, I met Jack at the office prior to going back to the Senate to continue testifying. It had been no fun the day before, but having gotten through it relatively unscathed, I felt more relaxed as we prepared to leave the office. But I realized that I had forgotten to bring the memo I had typed after returning from Dita Beard's home. I thought I would need it, but it was too late for my wife to bring it downtown to me in time for the hearing. Then I remembered that I had met with members of Senator Kennedy's staff at their request—and with Jack's specific approval—the night before the opening hearing. It seemed to me that I had shown them the memo and I wondered if I had let them copy it. I called the senator's office and left word that, if there were a copy, it should be left on the witness table for me so that I would have it when I arrived.

When we got there, there was no copy. The senators came in and the hearing was about to begin. Then a young man with long hair made his way through the crowd and quickly handed me a Xerox copy. I glanced around before opening it. Senator Cook had been watching me the entire time. I opened the document. It was the memo. Just then, Cook got up and walked over to Hruska, seated near the center of the dais. Glancing at me and smiling, he spoke a few words to him. Hruska, after looking at me, nodded. Now I was in a fine spot. Cook, the man whose request for the memo I had resisted the day before, was now obviously about to ask me questions which would reveal that I had earlier given it to Senator Kennedy's staff. Cook's request for the document had been withdrawn the day before, after I made it clear that I had no desire to withhold the information, only to avoid giving it up on demand. My intention had been to volunteer it for the record, but I had not gotten around to doing so, principally because I had only one copy and needed it for my own testimony.

I leaned over to Jack and explained the situation. "There's only one thing you can do," he said, "and that's tell them what happened."

Unfortunately, Cook did not get the floor immediately after the hearing began, so I had to wait through a series of other questions, knowing that I was in for some heavy weather when his turn came. Finally, the chairman called on him.

"Mr. Hume," he said, "just before these hearings started this morning—I presume you know what I'm going to ask you—a young man came into the room and was directed by one of the staff men from Senator Kennedy's office to deliver some papers to you, which you put in your briefcase. Is your organization supplying information to some members of this committee for the purpose of this hearing, and not supplying them to all members of this committee for the purpose of this hearing?"

I explained what had occurred, but Senator Cook was not satisfied. I knew he would not be.

"Therefore," he said when I was finished, "the notes which you did not want to give to the committee yesterday you had already given out anyway."

"Senator Cook," I responded, "I thought we had resolved that yesterday. As I tried to explain, my objections to giving the notes out was really more of a procedural thing and not a matter of substance. As I said, I had no objection to any member of this committee or its staff or any member of the public seeing these typed notes. It was just a question of the way it came about. Now, as I say, I have volunteered them to the committee; they'll be available to the committee and anyone on it; and I think that is as it should be."

Cook pressed on. "But at the time you refused yesterday, you knew that you had already given a copy of that memorandum to [Senator Kennedy's] staff," he said.

"Senator Cook, I'm sorry that's not so," I said.

"You had forgotten?" he asked incredulously.

I explained that I had forgotten and had only remembered that morning, which was true, but lame. I was trying to maintain a calm exterior, but I was squirming inside. Finally, Cook moved on to another subject, but he returned to this one when his next turn came. This time, Senator Gurney jumped in to say, incorrectly, that it was he who had made the request for the document and that he had never withdrawn it. So far, I had responded calmly and politely to all questions, but now I was beginning to get angry. The contretemps over my notes obviously had no relevance to the substance of my testimony and none to the issue before the committee. I turned to Jack, who was sitting to my right. He could see my mounting exasperation.

"There's nothing to do but take it," he said softly.

So I took it. I replied patiently and respectfully to every dig from Cook and Gurney, which took considerable restraint. Around the office, I spoke of public officials with far more scorn than anyone, especially Jack, who was generally tolerant of all but a few. Now, our attitudes were reversed. I was being reverent toward men for whom I had utter contempt and Jack was playing the blasphemer.

And he was even more aggressive about it the second day than he had been the first. At one point, he volunteered some decidedly unappreciated views, as far as the Republicans were concerned, about John Mitchell. "Now, those on the inside know as a matter of positive fact," Jack said, shaking his finger and speaking sternly, "that John Mitchell was serving as the President's campaign manager long before he stepped out as Attorney General; that he was making the decisions and performing the functions of the campaign manager, that he was calling the political shots from inside the Justice Department . . . We have the Lieutenant Governor of California, Ed Reinecke, calling upon John Mitchell, not as the Attorney General to discuss some legal matter, but as President Nixon's campaign manager, to discuss the convention. And for John Mitchell to come to this committee, as I presume he is going to do . . . and say under oath—if he does that—the same thing that he said in his unsworn public statement, that he has no knowledge of the Republican convention arrangements, that he had no knowledge of the ITT commitment, if he says that under oath, this is going to be one of the most arrogant examples of perjury this committee has ever had."

This, naturally, made Cook and Hruska indignant and they protested vigorously. It made me wince, because I thought it would only provoke the hostile Republicans. But it was consistent with the strategy of all of Jack's testimony, including his opening statement, which predicted further efforts to discredit Dita Beard. The idea was, that if we publicly predicted a tactic to be used by the other side, it would undermine its effectiveness in advance. Jack felt that Mitchell was going to lie about his involvement in the convention planning and sought to discredit his testimony in advance, or, perhaps to deter him from lying. There had been some thought at the beginning of our second day of testimony on Friday that Mitchell might be at the witness table before the end of the day. But Jack and I were kept the entire day. When it was finally over and we caught a cab back to the office, I experienced a feeling I haven't had since Friday afternoons in my school days. The worst was over, I thought, and now I could relax a little. Unhappily, though, the worst was yet to come.

NINE

Jack and I felt afterward that our testimony had been a success. It had dominated the news for two days. Jack's aggressiveness had put the Republicans on the defensive and his scathing opening statement had left the committee with a damning summary of the case, a sort of brief for the prosecution. Most reaction to my testimony seemed to be favorable. The mild-mannered, respectful approach, it seemed, had been effective. What's more, my triple-hearsay account of what Dita Beard said about what Mitchell said about what Nixon allegedly said had put the case a couple of notches higher on the Washington scandal scale. As the New York *Times* observed over the weekend after my testimony, "a controversy wins the brass ring when it implicates the President of the United States."

But there was one important drawback. Our testimony had left the committee with full knowledge of everything Jack and I knew about the case and how we knew it, except for the identity of our sources of information. Senator Gurney had questioned us both carefully on whether any of our information was tape-recorded and whether we had any other evidence dealing with the case. The answer, of course, was no. I had received about two dozen additional ITT documents from a source of my own which I had not had a chance to examine carefully. But a cursory look had shown me that they dealt with ITT's international operations, not with the antitrust action. In short, Jack and I were out of aces to play and this was now public knowledge.

There were signs, moreover, that the Administration and ITT were at last beginning to get their "ducks in a row." From Denver on Friday night, Dita Beard issued a statement denying that she had ever been told by Mitchell that he had gotten orders from the President to settle the ITT cases. The statement, which was read by her attorney, David Fleming of Van Nuys, California, also reiterated her earlier denials that there had been a deal to fix the antitrust cases in exchange for the $400,000 pledge. All this, of course, fit snugly with the statements issued earlier by John Mitchell also denying he or the President had any role in the ITT cases. David Fleming, we soon learned, was a Republican activist whose legal fees were being picked up by ITT.

Over the weekend, Senator Marlow Cook issued a statement charging that there was a "political conspiracy" between Jack, myself and Senator Kennedy. Cook made as much as he could in his statement of my having given my notes to Kennedy's staff before the hearings. This had been hashed over so thoroughly in the hearing that it didn't get much play in the press, but the statement was a sign some effort was under way to get Kleindienst and the Administration off the defensive. The statement came amid reports that the Administration viewed the attempt to destroy Dita Beard as a failure and were now considering trying to discredit Jack and myself.

I decided to stop regularly attending the hearings. Having lost a full week waiting to testify, Jack now had to turn to other matters and the ITT case once again fell into my hands. There was no way I could stay on top of it if I spent all day in the hearing room. I could keep track of the testimony through Reuben Robertson, who agreed to contact me at lunchtime and at the end of the day when anything important was said. This would leave me free to try to improve the depleted hand of cards that Jack and I were now playing. Being absent would also fit the posture of nonchalance I wanted to display toward other witnesses. I had testified truthfully, so there was theoretically no reason to be worried about what others might say, even if it contradicted my own testimony. If I were watching in the audience, it might seem that I was worried, which, in fact, I was. But I wanted to appear imperturbable.

John Mitchell was scheduled to follow Jack and myself to the witness stand on Tuesday, March 14. On Monday night, I flew to Texas to give a paid lecture in Texarkana the next afternoon. (The lecture was the first of many I would do over the next year, a result of the television publicity I had received from the ITT case.) The final edition of the Texarkana *Daily News* was on sale in a coin box when I walked into the airport to catch a flight back to Dallas after my lecture. The upper right quarter of the front page was devoted to an Associated Press account of Mitchell's opening statement before the Judiciary Committee. MITCHELL, said the headline, DENIES TIES TO ITT SETTLEMENT. At first glance, Mitchell's statement appeared to be a routine denial of impropriety. But deep in the story came the fact that in August 1970, Mitchell had met with Harold Geneen of ITT in the Attorney General's office. This was significant: Mitchell had supposedly disqualified himself from the ITT cases because of his law firm's former connections with the company. Now, however, the former Attorney General said he and Geneen had discussed the Administration's antitrust policy for about thirty-five minutes. But he insisted that they had not discussed the ITT cases. It was, instead, a general, philosophical discussion of over-all policy.

I guessed that must have caused some snickers in the hearing room. Harold Geneen was a busy, singleminded man whose every waking hour was devoted to the financial fortunes of the vast company he commanded. John Mitchell was also a busy man whose consuming interest was the political fortunes of the Nixon administration. It was a bit hard to envision the two of them sipping sherry in the Attorney General's office and debating the fine points of the Clayton Act.

Mitchell also acknowledged having had several meetings with Felix Rohatyn, but again, he said, these dealt with something else, not ITT. And he gave an account of the Kentucky Derby incident that squared perfectly with the one given the committee by Louie Nunn, which—despite several contradictory press statements beforehand—had squared perfectly with the position taken publicly earlier by Mitchell. As for his meetings with Reinecke, Mitchell had no recollection of ever discussing the convention plans with him—or with anyone else, for that matter, while still Attorney General.

"It is quite possible Lieutenant Governor Reinecke mentioned the convention in San Diego and Sheraton Hotel or something else," Mitchell said, "but it would have made no impression on me whatever, I not having that interest in it."

When I got home later that evening, I received a fuller account of Mitchell's testimony from Reuben. He told me Mitchell had also denied having any "re-election campaign responsibilities" before leaving the Justice Department to manage the President's campaign. This denial seemed especially brazen. Nearly everyone in politics, it seemed, had regarded Mitchell as the President's political signal caller long before he left the Justice Department. His office in the department had been considered a haven for frustrated Republican politicians who found they could not do business with the arrogant and politically insensitive men in the White House—mainly chief of staff H. R. Haldeman and domestic adviser John Ehrlichman—who guarded the entrance to the President's door.

Mitchell's testimony was not a surprise. It had been foreshadowed by his public statements and the testimony of other witnesses. But before he took the witness seat, I had not been able to completely dismiss the fact that he was the former Attorney General of the United States and that he would be under oath. I had grown up with the idea that when high government officials spoke under oath, they were bound to tell the truth because it was against the law to lie. It seemed clearer than ever now, though, that this idea was exactly backward. The highest officials of the government were *more likely* to lie under oath because they and their associates controlled the machinery by which such violations of the law are investigated and prosecuted. It was hardly likely that Mitchell's protégé, whose own fortunes depended so heavily on his testimony, would prosecute him for it. All this emphasized the disadvantage which Jack and I faced as the game got rougher: we had to play by the rules of law and the other side didn't.

Meanwhile, the White House's behind-the-scenes effort to counteract the scandal was intensifying. Senator Marlow Cook's "political conspiracy" charge against Jack and myself and Senator Kennedy had come after he was summoned to the White House on Saturday, March 11, for a meeting with some of the aides busy with the ITT problem, including lobbyist Wally Johnson and political troubleshooter Charles Colson. Cook was told that Dita Beard had been a longtime friend and drinking companion of Opal Ginn, Jack's secretary, that they met often at the Sheraton-Carlton Hotel bar for drinks and that Mrs. Beard had recently hosted a party at the hotel for a retiring bartender. Jack Anderson, Cook was informed, was the master of ceremonies at the party. Cook agreed to bring out this startling information and he was promised evidence, including a photograph of the party, to prove it. During an executive session of the committee just before Mitchell's testimony Tuesday, Cook raised the charges. "I bring this to the committee's attention in outrage," Cook said. "It illustrates that these men (Jack and I) have been less than candid with the committee, and in my mind it casts doubt on the veracity of Anderson's account of how he obtained the memorandum and perhaps on the origin and content of the memorandum itself." Cook distributed the statement he made in the executive session to newsmen and also gave out copies of a group photograph taken at the party to honor the retiring hotel employee. Dita Beard and Opal were both in the picture and so was Irving Davidson, Jack's hustling lobbyist friend from the floor below.

Cook's charges received little attention in the press because they were overshadowed by the news of Mitchell's testimony. I heard about them first on Wednesday morning. When I got downtown, I went into Opal's office.

"What about this stuff Cook is saying?" I asked. "It isn't true is it?"

"Hell, no," snapped Opal.

"Well, what's this all about?"

"I don't know. I haven't any idea where he got the information. I've only met Dita Beard once in my life and it was at that party. She didn't host it; nobody did. It was Dutch treat with a cash bar. Mark Kirkham, the resident manager of the hotel, suggested we do it for Bill—you must know Bill, he's been a waiter in the bar there for years. When I was introduced to Dita, she said, 'Your boss is a son of a bitch and I wouldn't touch him with a ten-foot pole.' "

"What about Jack?" I asked. "Was he at the party?"

"For about ten minutes. Bill's a great fan of the column and I asked Jack to come by and make a presentation to him. Olivia was waiting for him outside. He shook hands with Bill, gave him this picture which we all signed—it was a picture of the hotel the way it looked many years ago—and left. I don't think he even met Dita."

"What do you suppose Cook thinks he's doing?"

"I don't know, but it makes me damned mad. I don't want to get dragged into this f——ing scandal."

"Well, don't worry about that. If it's not true, it won't go anywhere."

I walked back to my desk in the kitchen. My first reaction was to forget about the incident. The press obviously wasn't paying much attention to it and a response might only give it more undeserved attention. But I hadn't forgotten my experience with Cook while I was in the witness chair. I was vulnerable then and he had taken advantage. Fair enough. Now, though, I thought he might be vulnerable. I telephoned Len Appel, one of the lawyers who represented Jack and the column, who had become a personal friend. Len had once been counsel for the House Judiciary Committee and I thought his advice might be especially valuable on this. Ordinarily, he said, it's better to let a charge that misses the mark be forgotten. But if it's demonstrably false, a counterattack might be worthwhile.

I went back into Opal's office and got a full description of the party, how it was organized and why Jack was present. Then I drafted two affidavits, one for Opal to sign, which included the salty quote about Jack from Dita, and one for Jack, recounting his side of it. Afterward, I drafted a strongly worded letter to Cook for Jack's signature. Cook had charged during our testimony that one of Jack's inaccurate columns was not an "honest mistake," as Jack had insisted, but a "bold-faced lie." So I included in the letter to him the following sentence: "Because I want to believe that you are a serious and sincere man, I shall assume that your statement was an honest mistake and not a bold-faced lie." Recalling his show of indignation of Senator Kennedy's staff having received my notes, I also wrote: "You have expressed great anguish about information pertaining to the current Judiciary hearings becoming available to some members but not to others. Therefore, I trust you will immediately read into the record of the hearings this letter and the two sworn affidavits which I enclose." The letter also contained a point-by-point refutation of his charges. "Your version is so wildly inaccurate that it is difficult to imagine how you got the facts so confused," it said.

I had Jack sign the letter and found a notary public in the building to witness the signing of the affidavits. They were dispatched by messenger to Cook that afternoon, but withheld from the press. My guess was that Cook would read the letter and the affidavits into the record the next day. He would know that if he didn't, Jack would then have grounds for blasting him either in a statement or in the column.

The next afternoon, Cook interrupted the hearing.

"Mr. Chairman," he said, "if I may just take a minute, I have a letter here I would like to read. I don't particularly look forward to reading it but I really ought to and ask that it be put into the record."

Cook then read the letter aloud, with evident discomfort. He did not read the affidavits, however.

187

"The affidavits merely affirm what is in the letter," he said. "I would say, Mr. Chairman, I, in all fairness, if I owe Mr. Anderson an apology, I certainly would extend it to him. But, I will submit affidavits during the course of the hearings . . ."

The White House, obviously, had given Cook information which no effort had been made to verify. His promise to produce affidavits in the future, or else apologize, was evidently the result of a promise from the White House that proof of the false charge would be forthcoming. By now, ITT had hired Intertel, a crack international detective agency, which had played a role in breaking the Clifford Irving–Howard Hughes autobiography hoax. We soon learned from Mark Kirkham, who had left the Carlton for a job in Florida, that he was contacted about the party by an Intertel investigator. He told us he corroborated Opal's version. And the waiter who had been honored at the party told the Washington *Post*'s Don Oberdorfer that he had been asked about the matter by a man from the internal security division of the Justice Department.

The ex-post-facto effort to buttress the charge came to little. Cook later told me he was given some material by the White House to back up his charge, but it was too weak to use. He never produced his promised affidavits. He never apologized either.

The day of Mitchell's testimony, Senator Thomas Eagleton, an exceptionally articulate and smooth young freshman Democrat from Missouri, rose on the Senate floor to attack Peter Flanigan. Calling Flanigan "the real missing witness," Eagleton said he was "a man who works in the shadows—but only at the highest levels, only with the fattest cats." The speech came after the liberal Democrats on the committee had begun suggesting that Flanigan's personal testimony was essential to the hearings, a suggestion that was not welcome at the White House. The word of Eagleton's planned speech reached the White House that morning. Flanigan telephoned Senator Norris Cotton, a senior Republican conservative from New Hampshire, and asked him to defend him against Eagleton. Cotton agreed. Two young Flanigan aides were then sent to the Capitol with a prepared text for Cotton to read. As he did so, they sat in the gallery and followed the speech with copies of their own. Newsmen watching in the press gallery spotted them. A White House lobbyist, Tom Korologos, saw what was happening and entered the gallery to tell the two young Flanigan aides to put their copies of the speech away. Later, Cotton was questioned about the origin of the speech. He acknowledged it had been sent from the White House for him to deliver. "Now don't you go saying I'm not competent to write my own speech," Cotton told the reporters.

A similar backfire occurred the same day when statements attacking Jack and myself and defending Kleindienst were issued on Capitol Hill in the names of Senators Paul Fannin and Barry Goldwater, both conservative Arizonans, like Kleindienst. Most press releases bear the name of a press representative of the person or organization issuing them. In Congress, they usually have the name and phone number of the member's press secretary. Both the Fannin and Goldwater statements carried the names of their press secretaries, but they were identified as employees of the Republican National Committee. This was noticed by the newsmen who received the releases, who quickly established that they had not been prepared in the two senators' offices, but by the Republican National Committee. The Republican counterattack was off to a bad start.

Harold Geneen followed Mitchell to the witness chair on Wednesday afternoon. He was a smooth and confident witness, according to the reports I received. He categorically denied that there was any connection between the convention pledge and the antitrust settlement. But he insisted that the convention pledge was only $200,000, thereby contradicting Dita Beard, Congressman Wilson, who had told me and others it was $400,000, and Leon Parma, chairman of a San Diego committee set up to raise funds for the convention. Further, he testified that the legal advice he had received was that ITT would probably win the antitrust cases in the Supreme Court. This, of course, was the exact opposite of what ITT's special counsel, Lawrence Walsh, had said in his letter to Kleindienst. And late in the day, Geneen ran into a line of questioning that was as embarrassing as it was inevitable.

"Are you aware," asked Senator Tunney, "of any public relations or executive people coming down and shredding documents?"

"I am aware of that, Senator," Geneen replied, thus confirming for the first time that the report of the shredding that Dita Beard had given me, and which we had published, was true.

"I know that some, or at least I am told that there were some kind of documents that were shredded . . . this was probably more a reaction to the feeling that our files were suddenly opened to the public or something, and certainly not any kind of an action to, you might say, prevent a review of our files by any legitimate agency, and I will get a report from our counsel of what actually happened, and I have no hesitation in turning it over to the committee."

The next day, ITT's lawyers made public a report on the shredding. A "substantial" number of memoranda had been destroyed, they said. "Many sacks of paper" were either shredded or thrown out, all on the day following my visit to ITT's office with the Beard memorandum. ITT's general counsel, Howard Aibel, explained what happened:

"At his regular weekly staff meeting on Thursday morning, February 24, Mr. Merriam discussed with the staff the fact that there was a possibility that documents were being turned over to Mr. Anderson. Mr. Merriam did not discuss the substance or subject matter of the Hume memorandum at the staff meeting. Mr. Merriam stated that because of the possibility that thefts had occurred, all members of the office staff should review their files to determine what, if any, documents were missing; at the same time they were told to remove any documents that were no longer needed for current operations *as well as documents which, if put into Mr. An-*

derson's *possession, could be misused and misconstrued by him so as to cause unwarranted embarrassment to the people mentioned therein.*" (Emphasis added.)

The admission of document-shredding was an unavoidable setback from which ITT would never recover. A group of panicky company officials dumping "many sacks" of the corporate files into a shredding machine less than twenty-four hours after a visit from a reporter carrying an embarrassing memo—that vision clashed with the protests of innocence by Geneen and his colleagues. And there was an element of comedy in it that gave it public appeal far greater than the tedious details of the antitrust settlement. The political cartoonists had a field day. Paul Conrad of the Los Angeles *Times* drew a document shredder with the rear half of a Republican elephant sticking out. The Washington *Post's* incomparable Herblock depicted a machine with a shredded Richard Nixon coming out the chute. A startled onlooker shouted the caption, "Quick, call Mrs. Beard's doctor." Corporate America had a new symbol, the document shredder.

All this could not have come at a more opportune time for us. Earlier in the week, I had asked Jeff Brindle, a student at Lehigh University who had been working for us as an unpaid intern, to go through the additional ITT documents I had received to see if there was a story in them. I hadn't had much hope the documents would be of help in the present controversy, even if they were newsworthy. The reason was that my quick examination of them had revealed that they had nothing to do with the antitrust case. I thought that if we began an exposé on an unrelated ITT matter, it would appear that we felt our original charges had fallen flat and that we were therefore trying to change the subject. The shredding, however, had made virtually any secret ITT documents newsworthy.

On Wednesday, Brindle came into my office to tell me what his study of the 25 or so memoranda, letters, and cables had disclosed. They dealt with the company's efforts to head off the election of

Salvador Allende, the Marxist, as President of Chile in 1970. The documents revealed a broad range of high-level contacts by ITT officials with powerful figures in the Nixon administration in an effort to enlist its support in the stop-Allende effort. The reason for ITT's concern was that it controlled several companies in Chile, including the telephone company, and ITT feared they would be seized by the government if Allende were allowed to take power. At the time the documents were written, Allende had finished first in the popular balloting and needed only the approval of the Chilean congress to become President.

"It looks like a pretty good story," Jeff said, "apparently they were dealing with the CIA."

"The CIA?" I exclaimed. "Let's see those documents."

We went through them together. They painted an extraordinary picture of a corporation utterly convinced of its right to interfere in the affairs of a foreign state in whatever fashion it chose in order to advance its own interests. The memos had a striking resemblance to the sort of documents that circulate at the highest levels of government; they bore various security labels—"Confidential," "System Confidential" and "Personal and Confidential." They indicated that ITT's representatives had no difficulty whatever in getting to see the top policy makers in Washington. (John Mitchell had even been approached on the subject during a wedding reception at the Korean embassy, according to one of the papers.) And, as Jeff had suggested, there were strong indications that ITT was dealing with the Central Intelligence Agency. This, above all, made the memos intriguing. There were several references to the "McLean Agency" (the CIA is located near McLean, Virginia, just outside Washington) and other references to a man named "Mr. Broe," who appeared from the context of the documents to be ITT's CIA contact. There were other references to a mysterious "visitor," who was apparently also "Mr. Broe."

The documents indicated that ITT and the CIA had plotted together to stop Allende by creating economic chaos in Chile, in hopes that this would trigger a military uprising that would avert Allende's election. They indicated that ITT had offered the U. S. Government as much as a million dollars to assist any move to prevent the Marxist from taking power. Read carefully, though, they revealed that ITT's overtures to Washington officials generally had been given a cool reception. Only at the CIA was there enthusiasm for taking extreme clandestine measures to stop Allende.

The key to the story was establishing that the company had actually been dealing with "The Agency," as the CIA is called in Washington. The references in the memos were too veiled to constitute proof. What was needed was certain knowledge of who the mysterious "Mr. Broe" was and what his occupation was. If he was a CIA man, we had it. If we couldn't show that, the value of the documents was greatly diminished.

My first phone call was to the person who had provided the material in the first place. He was glad to hear I was enthusiastic about them and assured me that they were real. "I'm absolutely 100 per cent sure of that," he told me. He said that he also had concluded that Broe was a CIA man, but couldn't prove it. So I would have to establish it on my own.

The Central Intelligence Agency is the most tight-lipped of all the executive departments. There are good reasons for this. Obviously, an organization engaged in gathering vital security information must protect its methods and sources of information from public view. But the secrecy had also been used to cover up the other side of the agency's operations—the so-called clandestine services, more popularly known as "dirty tricks." It is this section of the agency that was responsible for the abortive Bay of Pigs invasion and for the secret air war in Laos which the U.S. conducted for years. Few people outside the agency have known the extent of such activities, but they have been the subject of the most intense interest and speculation in Washington for years.

I checked with several friends familiar with Latin American affairs and with the CIA. They were able to identify some of the other persons in the memos whose names were unfamiliar to me, but no one could identify Broe. Finally, I called the public information office at the CIA itself to see if I couldn't wheedle the information out of an official spokesman. The man I talked to was named Angus Thurmer, and, as he was quick to tell me, he had been around a long time. He was willing to give me no co-operation whatever, even to the extent of telling me if the CIA had ever employed a man named "Mr. Broe." I pressured him, demanding to know, insisting we were going ahead with a story anyhow, so there was no use hiding the information. But it was no use. He hung up and I was stuck.

I began poring over the documents once more, searching for any clue that might enable me to establish Broe's identity. The texts of the papers revealed nothing new. But there were handwritten notations at the top and in the margins of some of the documents. On one of the papers, amid other scribblings, Broe's name turned up. Near it was a telephone number. I picked up the phone and dialed the number. A woman, presumably a secretary, answered.

"Is this Mr. Broe's office?" I asked.

"This is his former office," she said. "He has a new number now since he took his new job."

"Well, this was the office he had back in 1970, wasn't it?"

"Yes."

"What was his official title then?"

"Director of Clandestine Services for Latin America."

"I see. By the way, what is his full name?"

"It's William V. Broe."

I said thanks and hung up. Then I gave out a series of war whoops.

This was Thursday. Jack and I agreed that we should write at least one column on the Chile papers immediately. I went to work to produce two to be sent out the next day for publication the following Tuesday and Wednesday. The columns were easy to write. The shredding provided an obvious news angle and the documents themselves were most quotable.

"Secret documents which escaped shredding by International Telephone and Telegraph (ITT)," began the first one, "show that the company maneuvered at the highest levels to stop the 1970 election of leftist Chilean President Salvador Allende.

"The papers reveal that ITT dealt regularly with the Central Intelligence Agency (CIA) and, at one point, considered triggering a military coup to head off Allende's election.

"These documents portray ITT as a virtual corporate nation in itself with vast international holdings, access to Washington's highest officials, its own intelligence apparatus, and even its own classification system.

"They show that ITT officials were in close touch with William V. Broe, who was then director of the Latin American Division of the CIA's Clandestine Services. They were plotting together to create economic chaos in Chile, hoping this would cause the Chilean army to pull a coup that would block Allende from coming to power."

The column went on to quote from a hush-hush memorandum written by ITT's Washington vice president, William Merriam, to John McCone, a director of the company and a former head of the CIA.

" 'Today I had lunch with our contact at the McLean agency and I summarize for you the results of our conversation. He is still very, very pessimistic about defeating Allende when the congressional vote takes place on October 24.

" 'Approaches continue to be made to select members of the armed forces in an attempt to have them lead some sort of uprising—no success to date . . .

" 'Practically no progress has been made in trying to get American business to cooperate in some way so as to bring on economic chaos.' "

The column also quoted a confidential telex from ITT vice president Ned Gerrity to Geneen, following a visit from the CIA's Broe. It outlined a plan by which American businesses operating in Chile might create the conditions for an anti-Allende military putsch. The telex concluded as follows:

" 'I was told that of all the companies involved, ours alone had been responsive and understood the problem. The visitor [evidently Broe] added that money is not a problem. He indicated that certain steps were being taken but that he was looking for additional help aimed at inducing collapse.' "

Subsequent memos indicated that Geneen found this astonishing program "unworkable" but, as our second column revealed, ITT tried other ways to keep the Marxist from taking office, including its offer to Henry Kissinger to "assist financially in sums up to seven figures" in any anti-Allende effort led by the U. S. Government.

I didn't finish the two columns until late that evening. I had agreed earlier to appear on the inaugural broadcast of a new TV talk show in Boston, which was to be taped the next day, Friday. So I left the two draft columns with Jack with a request that he phone ITT for whatever comment the company might want to make. I doubted ITT would say anything to us at this stage, but I wanted to make sure the company couldn't later claim it wasn't given the chance. I phoned Jack from Boston before the taping of the show. He said he had called Bernie Goodrich at ITT for comment. "I told him that if they had shredded all their copies of these documents, we'd be glad to let them look at ours," Jack said, chuckling. Goodrich, however, had not called back with a response, so the columns had been sent.

The talk show went smoothly and I was in good spirits when I boarded the plane for my return to Washington. ITT and the White House had tried to mount a counterattack but, so far, it was going nowhere. And now we had some more ammunition in the form of the Chile columns, which had turned out to be nearly as sensational in their way as the original stories on the antitrust case. They seemed certain to add impetus to the scandal and to keep ITT on the defensive. The committee had still to hear from Dita Beard, but it had voted to postpone its trip to Denver for another week. There was no telling what she might say, but the statement made through her lawyers gave no indication that she would contradict me. For the first time in weeks, I felt relaxed. I drank two vodka martinis on the flight and was feeling most agreeable when the plane arrived in Washington. I was running late, so I stopped at a coin telephone in the airport to call Clare.

"Hi," I said cheerfully when she answered.

"Oh, hi," she said. "Everyone's been trying to get you. I guess you heard what happened."

"No," I said. "What?"

"Dita Beard has issued a sworn statement that says the memo is a hoax and a forgery. It's all rather mysterious. Senator Scott read it to reporters from the back porch of his house here. No one seems to know how he got it."

The twinge in the pit of my stomach was back again. I phoned the office. Opal answered.

"Will you kindly get your ass in here and start taking some of these calls? It's after six and I've got a date and the phone's been ringing off the hook. Jack's here, but everyone wants to talk to you too. There goes the phone again. Bye."

I caught a cab. It had been three weeks and a day since I first confronted Dita Beard with her memo. Two weeks of hearings had been held and neither she nor anyone else had suggested the memo was not genuine. Indeed, my possession of the memo had touched off an orgy of document destruction in the Washington office, which ITT had admitted was intended to keep other embarrassing memoranda out of our hands. At this point, Dita's disclaimer seemed like a desperate gamble. Although I didn't know her well, I suspected she had been reluctant to take it. The writing of the memo was no crime, but the denial under oath of doing so was perjury. What's more, she had struck me as a forthright person, capable perhaps of some shady political dealing, but not of criminal lying. My guess was that she had been pressured into it by the White House and ITT, possibly with the connivance of her lawyers. The thought made me angry.

If I had known the truth, I would have been even angrier. Several days earlier, Dita Beard was visited in her hospital room by a man named E. Howard Hunt. He was a former CIA agent, an ultraconservative and one of the leaders of the abortive Bay of Pigs invasion. He had been a member of the Nixon White House's Special Investigations Unit which had been established to find and plug the sources of news leaks of supposedly vital national security information. One of his confederates with the special unit was George Gordon Liddy, the man who hustled Dita Beard out of Washington following our first column on the antitrust case. Liddy had left the White House to become an official of the Committee to Re-Elect the President, but Hunt remained on the President's payroll as a consultant, with an office in the old Executive Office Building.

Hunt's trip to Denver was made on orders of special presidential counsel Charles Colson, one of the White House aides most preoccupied with the ITT case. Hunt arrived bearing forged identification papers, furnished him by the CIA, which gave his name as "Edward Warren." He was wearing an ill-fitting wig, which Mrs. Beard's son Bull later told newsmen "looked like he had put it on in a dark car." Colson would later insist that he only wanted Hunt to encourage Mrs. Beard to tell the truth. But the fact is that she did the opposite after his visit. Both Hunt and his cohort Liddy would later become famous, or infamous, when another of their covert operations was discovered, triggering the biggest scandal in American political history. But for now, their activities would remain secret.

There was a copy of Dita's affidavit at the office when I arrived. I had nursed the faint hope as I rode in from the airport that perhaps it was a more equivocal statement than Clare had made it sound. No such luck. "I did prepare a memo at about the time indicated, at the request of Bill Merriam, to him, concerning plans for the Republican convention in San Diego," the affidavit said. "However, it was not the memo Jack Anderson has put in evidence before the Senate. Mr. Anderson's memo is a forgery, and not mine. I did not prepare it and could not have since to my knowledge the assertions in it regarding the anti-trust cases and former Attorney General Mitchell are untrue. I do not know who did prepare it, who forged my initial to it, how it got to Jack Anderson's hands or why. But I repeat, I do know it is not my memo and is a hoax.

"I want the opportunity to tell the Senate Judiciary Committee the true facts about this false and fallacious document. I am ready to testify from my bedside at any time. I have done nothing to be ashamed of, and my family and I—and in a greater sense the whole American government—are the victims of a cruel fraud. I only wish I could make this statement firmer and stronger and still get it printed in the public press."

While I knew nothing of the clandestine events that had preceded the affidavit, I knew the moment I read it that I was in for some heavy weather. For no matter how preposterous her three-week-late disavowal might seem, the press would have to treat it in a straight-faced manner. Thus Dita Beard's memo would henceforth be Dita Beard's "alleged" memo. And my testimony, which had gone unchallenged except for Senator Cook's bungled attempts, would from now on be a principal point of contention in the case. I was on the spot.

I found Jack issuing heated statements in response to the affidavit. He told the New York *Times* man who called from Denver, for example, that it was "about the most bizarre and blatant and incredible lie in a whole litany of lies." Privately, though, he took the whole thing with a cheerful smile and a shake of his head. "This is the stupidest thing they could have done," he said. "They'll never get away with this."

So once again, Jack was inwardly calm and outwardly indignant. And again, I was inwardly troubled, but needed more than ever to be outwardly calm. Jack sensed my apprehension. "Hey, look," he said in his most reassuring tones, "I've been through these fights before and I can tell you there's no way they're going to turn the tables on us now. We're just too far ahead. Besides, the press is on our side. The press was never on Drew's side. He was always stirring up something like this. I guess I was about your age when I got caught up on one of these things for the first time. And I felt just the way you do. And I had more reason to worry than you do, because Drew could be terribly careless and sometimes we'd be in the middle of one of these flaps and he wouldn't have his facts straight. But somehow, he always survived them and got stronger as time went on. He just bulled his way through."

I didn't question the truth of what Jack said. But there was another side to the lessons of his experience. Pearson's bitter struggle against Senator Joseph McCarthy, for example, showed that politicians threatened with destruction will fight like cornered rats to save themselves. McCarthy succeeded in intimidating the company that had sponsored Pearson on ABC radio for years into withdrawing its support. Pearson was back on the air in syndication a week later, but somehow his radio show started downhill after that and never again regained its enormous popularity and impact. And Jack's struggle against Senator Thomas Dodd proved that the government's investigative resources are frequently used more diligently against the whistle-blowers than the culprits. Those who had helped Jack uncover the evidence of Dodd's profound corruption were the objects of intensive FBI investigations while Dodd's felonious conduct, reported in great detail by Drew and Jack, went unpunished. Finally the Senate itself investigated, but only when asked to do so by Dodd himself. Even then, the inquiry focused on the most peripheral of the charges against him. One member of the committee acknowledged publicly that the panel steered clear of any misconduct that "impinged" on existing law. So when

Dodd's behavior was so outrageous as to be illegal, the Senate looked elsewhere.

Richard Kleindienst was perhaps not in the same league with Joe McCarthy and Tom Dodd, but there were important parallels. If Kleindienst's nomination were defeated, he would be ruined and so would others, like McLaren, who had cast their lot with him. It was an election year and the political stakes were high. The arena was a congressional committee, whose majority was hostile to Jack and myself. Indeed, this was not even an investigation. Not a single subpoena had been issued, except for Dita Beard's testimony, and not a single investigator had been put on the trail of the leads Jack and I had furnished. Instead, the witness list had been packed with pro-Administration witnesses and the schedule had been conveniently juggled by the chairman to lend their testimony maximum impact. Jack's words of encouragement were some comfort, but not much.

I got my first sample of the impact of Dita's affidavit that night. Carolyn Lewis, congressional correspondent for WTOP-TV, a large Washington station owned by the *Post*, asked me to appear on the 11 P.M. news for a live interview. Lewis had covered the ITT case from the beginning and, like most of the press, had been friendly to Jack and myself. I found her as pleasant as ever when I arrived at the studio for the show. But when the interview began, she was all business, firing one tough question after another. Why should people believe me? Did Dita Beard ever really confirm writing the memo? Hadn't I gotten a lot of personal publicity out of the whole affair? Wouldn't publicity be a motive for a hoax? These, of course, were all fair questions and no professional reporter would have failed to ask them in the aftermath of Dita's affidavit. That didn't make them any more fun to answer, though.

Fortunately, this was not my first broadcast interview. I had done a number already on the ITT case and many others before that in connection with my book on the United Mine Workers and with other stories I had reported for the column. My two days at the witness table had given me some extra seasoning. And what was more, ITT had supplied me with an obvious answer to questions about the authenticity of the document by shredding the files. So I countered with that, knowing it was still fresh in the public's mind. And I said I was willing to testify again under oath. I was careful not to criticize Mrs. Beard; indeed, I expressed sympathy for her plight. I suggested she and I should testify side by side.

I was particularly eager to do well in the interview, because I knew many of those who counted in Washington would be watching or would quickly hear about it. If I became flustered or reacted with an outburst of any kind, the impression would be unavoidable that I was rattled. That would only make me a more tempting target. I left the studio that night feeling that I had held up well enough.

But these were only the first of many skeptical questions I would be asked in the weeks ahead. The next day, for example, CBS asked me to visit its Washington bureau for an interview with reporter Bernie Shaw to be used on the Saturday evening network news. This time, the questions were even rougher. Among them: "Are you lying?" and "If you were lying, would you admit it now?" I responded much as I had the night before, striving to sound confident, not defensive, reasonable but not indignant. It wasn't easy. I had reported the ITT story carefully. I had told the truth under oath and had done so without resort to such lawyerly hedges as "to the best of my recollection" and "as nearly as I can recall." My testimony was voluntarily given and I had weathered two days of sometimes harsh cross-examination. Now Dita Beard, from behind the walls of a distant hospital to which she had fled and where she was guarded by a platoon of doctors and lawyers, was answering with perjurious statements issued through spokesmen for the Republican party. I was vexed and frustrated, but I dared not show it. Angry young men may win the applause at campus rallies, but, if Marshall McLuhan can be believed, they come over badly on television.

Carolyn Lewis' question about publicity being the possible motivation for a hoax had surprised me, although she was not the first person to comment on the notoriety I was getting. I was hearing by now from many friends I had not spoken to in some time and they all seemed to have the same reaction: I was getting "marvelous exposure." It was true, I supposed, but somehow I didn't see anything very marvelous about this controversy at this point. For me, one of the joys of journalism had been that I could have an influence on events without having my own personal fortunes tied to their outcome. This was one of the differences between being a newspaperman and being a politician. Politicians could wield more power, but to acquire it, they had to play a game that was too savage and compromising for me. Yet now I was caught up in a political controversy whose outcome would affect my reputation forever.

Dita Beard said in her sworn statement that her initial had been "forged" on the memorandum I had shown her. As I thought about this over the weekend, it made me curious. She was going to have to explain this statement when the senators visited her in a week. She had not seen the memo, as far as I knew, since I showed it to her in her office. The penciled "D" Xeroxed badly, so it would be difficult for her to claim she reached any conclusions from studying a copy. I wondered if the original had not been sent to Denver for her perusal. If it had, this would raise questions of possible tampering, particularly since the initial was penciled and could be easily and indistinguishably erased. On Monday, I called John Holloman, chief counsel for the Judiciary Committee. He was a likable Mississippian who had no evident sympathy for what I was doing, but was, like many in Washington, perfectly willing to be friends offstage.

"John," I asked, "is the Beard memorandum still in Washington?"

"Yes," he said, "it's still in Washington and has never left Washington."

The answer made me even more curious. "Well, is it still up there with the committee?"

He paused. "I thought you wanted to know if it was still in Washington," he said.

"I did. But now I want to know if you've still got it up there."

There was a longer pause. "That document is in the hands of the Federal Bureau of Investigation."

"How long have they had it?"

"Since Friday."

"What are they doing with it? How did they get it?"

"I don't have any comment."

I was on to something and I didn't want to let go. I tried to bluff him with a question indicating I knew that the Justice Department had sent someone up to get it. I asked if this weren't true. He knew I was bluffing, but he told me the truth.

"I hand-delivered it to an official of the Justice Department."

"Who?"

"John Duffner. He asked for it. I hand-delivered it to Duffner."

Holloman refused to discuss the matter further, referring me to Eastland, who was in Mississippi. I tried to reach him but failed. Nevertheless, I had little difficulty in establishing that John Duffner was an assistant to Kleindienst. I also quickly learned that the document had been given to him without the knowledge of the rest of the committee.

So the principal piece of evidence in the case, submitted formally by Jack and myself, had, in effect, been slipped secretly to the defendant. Ostensibly, this was done to allow FBI's laboratories to test the document. This was hardly reassuring. The method by which the bureau got it left open the possibility it could be tampered with along the way. Besides, the FBI, for all its autonomy, was still part of the Justice Department. And J. Edgar Hoover detested Jack Anderson.

We later learned that the Beard memorandum had been handled in an even more irregular manner than I had discovered. Not only had it been given to a Kleindienst aide, but it was subsequently passed to the White House, where presidential counsel John Dean promptly handed it off to ITT, which wanted to have it tested by some "experts" of its own.

I didn't think I could get the press much interested in Eastland's under-the-table play with the Beard memo, but I wanted to do something to chasten him—and perhaps J. Edgar Hoover as well. I drafted a letter of protest for Jack's signature, which I had delivered to Eastland and distributed to the press. "I should not need to point out to you, Mr. Chairman," it said, "the extreme impropriety of allowing a party in interest in a congressional investigation to take possession of a vital piece of evidence." My hope was that the letter would discourage any funny business with the lab report on the document. It would also prepare the way for Jack to denounce a dishonest report, if one were made. I had never been a great fan of J. Edgar Hoover, but before this controversy I would have strongly doubted any suggestion the FBI might produce a phony laboratory report. Now, though, I was not willing to bank on the integrity of anyone connected with the Department of Justice.

That afternoon, ITT summoned newsmen to its Washington office to receive what it called "new and important evidence" of its innocence. It consisted mainly of an affidavit from a young woman named Susan Lichtman, who had been a temporary secretary to Dita Beard at the time of her disputed memo. Mrs. Lichtman had been visited in Toronto, where she now lived, by Russell Tagliareni, one of the ITT security men who had been in on the shredding. Tagliareni had gotten an affidavit from her which said that she remembered typing the first portions of the memo, but not later, more incriminating parts. (Tagliareni, it later developed, had also been told by Dita Beard that she wrote the memo, but he wasn't saying anything about that, naturally.) In addition, ITT announced it had found another memo addressed to William Merriam from Dita Beard, written on the same date, in which she said the Republican convention in San Diego would result in "unbuyable publicity" for Sheraton Hotels but said nothing of any deal involving the antitrust cases. This, the company said triumphantly, was the "genuine" memo.

At first, it looked as if ITT had really come up with something, and some news agencies rushed out stories to that effect. But a closer look revealed that something funny was going on. Susan Lichtman, interviewed by several reporters by long distance, said she was "puzzled" by the so-called "genuine" memo. She hadn't been shown it by Tagliareni, she said, and her affidavit had nothing to do with it. At first, ITT balked at releasing the newly discovered memo. When it finally did, the document turned out to be a job description which the company required employees to submit each year for its files. The reference to the San Diego convention was part of Mrs. Beard's effort to list her activities and their significance to ITT. So the memo Susan Lichtman remembered typing and the "genuine" memo just discovered by the company were not the same. ITT's Bernie Goodrich admitted that the memo Mrs. Lichtman recalled was still "missing."

The Lichtman affidavit turned out to help us more than it did ITT. For now there was additional corroboration of part of the memo in question. Although Lichtman couldn't recall some of the more incriminating parts, she did remember the early paragraphs in which a host of Republican big shots, including John Mitchell, were said to be in on the convention pledge. Mitchell, of course, had testified to the contrary under oath. I told reporters who asked me that if Jack and I had had Susan Lichtman's affidavit, we would have released it ourselves.

The day after the Lichtman affidavit was released, the first of the columns on the Chile documents was published. It created an immediate sensation, and, within days, representatives of virtually every major news organization in town had come to the office to obtain a set of the papers. The result was a spate of follow-up stories that helped stir a remarkably quick official reaction. The Washington *Post*, for instance, published a blistering editorial, while its veteran reporter Stanley Karnow prepared a lengthy story on the papers for Monday's editions. Tad Szulc, the well-known diplomatic correspondent of the New York *Times*, wrote news accounts on each of our columns and also did subsequent stories based on the documents and his own reporting. Before the week was out, a subcommittee on Latin America of the Senate Foreign Relations Committee voted to hold extensive hearings later into the role of all multinational corporations in foreign policy. ITT, of course, protested its innocence, but it challenged neither the authenticity nor the specific revelations of the documents. They were a direct hit.

Almost simultaneously, *Life* magazine dropped a bombshell on the Justice Department. "The Nixon Administration," the magazine reported, "has seriously tampered with justice in the city of San Diego. In an effort to protect certain of its most important friends there from prosecution, the Administration has in several instances taken steps to neutralize and frustrate its own law enforcement officials." The article was based on a lengthy investigation by Denny Walsh, a Pulitzer Prize-winning reporter who belonged to the magazine's special investigative unit. It charged that Harry Steward, the U. S. Attorney for San Diego, had interfered in federal investigations of possible tax cheating and illegal political contributions by individuals and companies associated with a man named C. Arnholt Smith. Smith, one of President Nixon's most ardent supporters, was a multimillionaire businessman who was easily the most powerful figure in San Diego. Indeed, Harry Steward had gotten his job on the recommendation of Smith, who was so close to the President that he was invited to watch the 1968 election returns with Nixon and his family.

The *Life* article reported in exhaustive detail how Steward and others had acted to block the investigations of Smith's associates and his companies. But the most explosive revelation was this: when the FBI reported Steward's actions to his superiors as a possible case of obstruction of justice, a serious federal crime, Richard Kleindienst excused him and allowed him to stay on the job.

The *Life* story came at a crucial time. The hearings had been suspended, pending the visit of a seven-member subcommittee of the Judiciary Committee to Denver to take bedside testimony from Dita Beard. Now that Mrs. Beard had disavowed the memo, the Republicans were eager to hear from her. They made no secret that once she had been heard, they would press for an immediate end to the hearings, contending that the key evidence against Kleindienst had been discredited. Of course, the memo was not the key evidence against Kleindienst. He wasn't even mentioned in it. The case against him rested upon the fact that he had interfered in the antitrust case and then lied about it, and that the whole settlement had been brought about in a highly irregular way, whether a $400,000 promise from ITT to the GOP was the reason or not. There was also Kleindienst's questionable behavior in the Robert Carson affair, where he had failed to report a bribery attempt until a week after it occurred and the FBI was already on the trail. In addition, there was the selective and self-serving recollection which Kleindienst had displayed in his testimony before the committee—a recollection that required repeated "refreshing" to save him from what would have looked very much like perjury. And now there was the *Life* story. It didn't have anything to do with the ITT affair, but it had a lot to do with Richard Kleindienst and it would give the liberal Democrats on the committee far greater leverage in their efforts to prolong the hearings. Senator Tunney announced promptly he would ask the committee to broaden the inquiry to include the *Life* charges. Not surprisingly, old Jim Eastland was opposed. "I don't see where they involve Kleindienst," he said. It would come to a vote after the Denver trip.

On Friday, March 24, the FBI released the findings of its tests of the Beard memo. The bureau said the memo appeared to have been typed on Mrs. Beard's typewriter and, while it couldn't state positively that it was done on the date specified on the memo, "nothing was found . . . to suggest preparation at a time other than around June 25, 1971." The FBI tests, thus, tended to corroborate the authenticity of the memo. Asked to comment by the Washington *Post*, Mrs. Beard's lawyer, David Fleming, said from Denver that the FBI report was "exactly as we suspected." Fleming didn't say how it squared with his client's condemnation of the document as a hoax, but he asserted mysteriously that the memo had been prepared by "one or more persons" besides Mrs. Beard in the ITT offices. So Dita's lawyer, at least, was apparently ready to concede that the document was written in her office. When that was put together with Susan Lichtman's sworn recollection of typing part of it and the FBI's conclusion that Mrs. Beard's typewriter was used to prepare it, the evidence began to seem overwhelming, at least to me, that the memo was genuine.

But Fleming insisted that he would call a news conference in Denver shortly after the Senate subcommittee arrived to offer "proof" that Mrs. Beard was telling the truth. I had no idea what his "proof" was, but I had suspected he might have something up his sleeve for the press when the big day of Dita's testimony arrived. So I had quietly acted to give myself another card to play when the time came.

I don't remember who thought of it first, but Jack and Reuben both suggested it independently in the days after Mrs. Beard issued her "hoax" affidavit. At first, the idea was that I should offer to take a lie-detector test and challenge Mrs. Beard to do the same. Then Reuben suggested I take one privately as a "dry run." Jack returned from a speechmaking trip to say that the lie-detector idea had even been advanced by members of the audience who accosted him after his lecture. At first, I balked. I didn't trust the polygraph. The theory of it is that it is more stressful to lie than tell the truth. The polygraph measures pulse rate, blood pressure, and, in some cases, perspiration, as the subject answers a variety of questions ranging from insignificant queries about age and address to the central matters at issue. The machine gauges the subject's reactions to the varying stimuli. The examiner makes a subjective judgment after studying the results of whether the subject is telling the truth or lying and about what. I had always thought that a highly nervous person telling the truth might flunk such a test, while a brazen liar could pass. So I was reluctant.

But the idea had undeniable appeal. If I were to take the test (and pass), we could release the results, then challenge Mrs. Beard to take one. If she didn't, we would be one up. If she did, and flunked, the contest would be over. If she did and also passed, there would be no damage, except to the reputation of the polygraph as a gauge of veracity.

Dita Beard had had weeks to plan her testimony and she had the added advantage of knowing in advance my side of the story. Whatever she said, her testimony was certain to create a sensation. She was the long-awaited missing witness and she would be heard under the most extraordinary circumstances. If she made a frontal assault on my testimony, it would be up to me to refute it. Of course, she had some severe credibility problems. But that didn't change the fact that I didn't have anything new to say, while everything she was saying would be new—indeed, the falser it was, the newer it would be. So, on the theory that you can't beat something with nothing, I agreed to take a polygraph.

The next question was who would give the test. At first, we considered using a big-name polygraph institute in Chicago. But time was of the essence, since we wanted to have the results by the end of the week. So we decided to have it done locally. Les suggested a man named Lloyd Furr whom he had once used when he was trying to determine the credibility of a source. Furr, it happened, was the same man who had caught Jack and an investigator from the House of Representatives electronically eavesdropping from the room next door on the hotel suite of the New England industrialist Bernard Goldfine. This occurred during the famous scandal, broken by Jack, involving Goldfine's gifts to President Eisenhower's chief of staff, Sherman Adams. At that time Furr, who was a private eye in addition to being a registered polygraph examiner, was working for Goldfine's lawyer. Jack's red-handed apprehension was a celebrated incident, which Senator Gurney had brought up during our testimony in an effort to embarrass Jack. The idea of using Furr appealed to Jack, because, he reasoned, he would then be able to say he hired an old adversary to assure that the polygraph was done impartially.

It was about 9:15 on the morning of Thursday, March 23, when I pulled into the driveway beside Lloyd Furr's home on a quiet, secluded street in McLean, Virginia. Les Whitten had arranged the appointment a couple of days earlier, which had given me plenty of time to work up a good case of nerves. At the door, Furr held back his barking dog, greeted me in a friendly way, and showed me to his office, a small wood-paneled room in his basement. Furr looked remarkably like William Conrad—the actor who plays Cannon, the private eye in the CBS television series—except that Furr had a full head of white hair and a white mustache. He was a striking figure. He seated me in a chair next to his desk while he busied himself setting up his polygraph, which was stored in a portable case; Furr did a lot of lie-detector work for department stores trying to curb stealing by their employees, a task that required him to give the tests on location. I gave him a typed list of twenty quesions on the central issues in the dispute over the Beard memo. As Les had recommended, I had written them so that they could be answered yes or no. Furr read them over, made a few penciled changes, then remarked:

"These look like they were written by a polygraph examiner."

"Well," I said, "Les told me to do them that way."

There was a period of silence. I was so nervous I felt I should say something about it. I was afraid my nerves might make me so jumpy I could flunk the test.

"I don't know why I feel so tense," I said. "I guess if you're telling the truth, there's nothing to be nervous about. But I can't help it."

"I can tell you one thing," he said with a short laugh, "if you're not telling the truth, you've got no business being here."

Furr strapped a flexible rubber cable across my chest. This was apparently designed to measure my heartbeat electronically. Then he wrapped a blood-pressure bag around my left arm, which was resting on his desk. He warned me that the bag would be inflated longer than I was accustomed to and that it would become uncomfortable. When it did, he told me to say so, and he would let the air out and give me a rest.

"All right," he finally said, "I'm ready to start."

He began by asking me questions about my name, occupation, and age. He was standing behind his desk, watching the needle on the polygraph make its scribbles on the narrow strip of graph paper that rolled across the machine. I could hear the scratch of the needle against the paper. He spoke to me in a measured, soft voice that took on a mysterious quality, since I couldn't see exactly where he was standing. Occasionally, he would intersperse the irrelevant questions with one from the list I had given him, or with a series from the list. Soon my arm began to feel weak from the pressure and the blood vessels on the back of my hand were bulging. It hurt. I told him and he stopped and let the air out of the bag. This process was repeated several times. Soon he had gone over all the relevant questions a number of times, repeating some of them more often than others. One question he repeated frequently dealt with my first meeting with Dita Beard. It was: "Did you invite her comment on the memo?" The reason, he explained later, was that the graph showed my having a strong reaction to the question. As it turned out, this was fortunate. For there was no dispute over whether I had asked Dita Beard to comment on her memo; it was the whole purpose of our meeting. So when I reacted far more noticeably to this question than to other, more crucial ones, Furr concluded that I was telling the truth. Among the questions to which he found I had little reaction were: "Did Mrs. Beard identify the penciled initial on the memo as "my own little 'D'?" (Yes.) "Did Mrs. Beard explicitly confirm during this second meeting that she had written the memo?" (Yes.) "Did Mrs. Beard ever at any time tell you the memo was a forgery?" (No.).

When it was done, Furr had taken me through five separate polygrams and found my answers to be consistently truthful. I felt a wave of relief as I drove back to town afterward. Furr had promised his report by the next day. It would be a detailed analysis of the results of the polygraph, signed by him and notarized. A nice, official document to buttress my position. Of course, there would be questions. Hadn't the questions been prepared by us? Wasn't the examiner paid by Jack Anderson? The answer, of course, was yes in both cases. But I thought I saw a way to insure that the polygraph was not questioned too aggressively.

I prepared a letter for Jack to send Eastland along with a copy of Furr's report, requesting that the report be made part of the record. It contained a list of Furr's credentials, which included polygraph work for the U. S. District Court in Washington, the Justice Department, and the old Senate Crime Committee under Senator Matthew Neely. It also contained this sentence. "If any questions should arise about this examination and Mr. Furr's conclusions, he is an experienced witness who would be well able to explain the intricacies of his examination to the committee." The last thing Eastland or the Republicans would want was a competent witness before the committee telling the world how he had expertly concluded that I was telling the truth. Our suggesting it made it even more certain it would never happen.

The next question was how to release the story. It would be Friday when we got the report. One possibility would be to hold it until Mrs. Beard testified, which was expected to be on Sunday. Releasing it Sunday in Denver might seem an effective way to counter direct contradictions of my testimony. But there was the danger it would be buried under the avalanche of news about Mrs. Beard and her dramatic sickbed testimony. So I ruled out Sunday. I also ruled out waiting longer, because that might seem a little too calculating.

Putting out the report on Friday would mean it would land in the news that night and in Saturday's papers. But the trouble with Saturday was that in a running controversy of this kind, news has almost no half-life. A day is like eternity. My lie-detector test would be old hat by the time Dita said her lines, and I would be empty-handed again. So releasing Lloyd Furr's report and Jack's letter to Eastland on Saturday became the only choice. That way, it would make the late Saturday news and the Sunday papers, but would still be fresh enough to merit a mention in stories about what Dita said. And I could still talk about it without sounding as though I was harping on an old theme. What's more, Dita and her lawyers wouldn't find out about it until the last minute and it might make it more difficult for them to cook up a reply. Perhaps it would even throw a scare into her and have a chilling effect on any really extravagant lying.

Dita Beard's affidavit seemed to put her on a collision course with me, but I still had hope it wouldn't turn out that way. It occurred to me that if her lawyers were trying to keep her out of trouble, they would advise her to avoid direct clashes with my testimony wherever possible. She could do this and still contend that the memo was not real. She could testify, for instance, that during her meetings with me, she had believed the memo to be genuine because she remembered parts of it and the initial appeared to be hers. Only later, after careful reflection, had it dawned on her that the document must be a phony. This, of course, would not be terribly plausible. But I thought it would be a lot more believable than trying to pretend she thought it was a fake from the start, but kept silent about it for three weeks.

I had originally planned not to go to Denver, in keeping with my unworried posture. But several reporters told me they thought it would be helpful if I were there, so they could get immediate responses from me on major points of dispute. When I thought about it, I realized that it would be wise to make the trip, not so much for the convenience of the press as for "getting my licks in," as Jack called it. If Dita Beard contradicted me seriously and I were on the scene, the TV networks—with their scrupulous attention to fairness and balance—could hardly fail to put me on camera to give my side of it. So while Dita might dominate the day as far as the senators and most of the press were concerned, I could make up some of the ground by getting equal time on national television.

Nevertheless, I didn't relish going out there. I thought the whole idea of her bedside testimony was an outrageous setup, designed to enable Dita Beard to utter her lies under the most pitiful circumstances and to escape any heavy cross-examination because of her health. Before and after her appearance, her lawyers would no doubt be scurrying around making statements, issuing challenges, and defending her version of events in overblown lawyers' rhetoric. It was going to be Dita's show, staged by her handlers in her territory, and I was going to be the lone, unwelcome voice of opposition.

I caught a mid-afternoon flight on TWA to Denver, together with a handful of other reporters with whom I had become particularly friendly. Given the situation, I especially welcomed their company. At the outset of the affair, all the press corps had treated me as one of them. Later, though, I had clearly become a principal in the case, and since the moment my testimony had been challenged, I had noticed a marked change in the way a number of reporters acted toward me. There was a glimmer of skepticism in their eyes and a trace of coolness in their greeting. I told myself over and over that this was only natural, even proper. But still it made me feel empty and alone. It reminded me further how much my own reputation was tied to the outcome of the case.

Inside Story

I wondered on the flight to Denver how I should react if Mrs. Beard sharply challenged me. Perhaps now was the time for some righteous indignation. After all, I was being called a liar. My sworn testimony was being disputed by a witness who had fled and kept silent for three weeks. Wouldn't people expect me to be angry? Maybe, I thought. But it was too risky. It might sound shrill. It was better, I decided, to maintain a calm posture and avoid blasting Mrs. Beard. The TV cameras would not be allowed to film her testimony, but they would probably be allowed to take some silent film of her as she lay in bed before the hearing. I didn't want to be a nasty young man saying bad things about a sick old lady.

But what to say? I sat, gazing out the airplane window for a long time, trying to formulate some answer that would be firm, yet reasonable. The best I could do went this way: "I hesitate to criticize Mrs. Beard because she's under a lot of pressure, but she's simply not telling the truth." Then I could go on to cite the most significant falsehoods and mention that I had taken a lie-detector test. Someone might ask if I were accusing Mrs. Beard of perjury, which I would be, of course. But that was a word I wanted to avoid, because no matter how I said it, it would still look harsh in print. So I decided I would duck the question by saying that perjury was a legal issue I wasn't competent to judge.

The press, the members of the committee, and the committee staff were all quartered at the Denver Hilton, a large modern building that stands in the shadow of the Colorado State Capitol at the edge of downtown. Dita's lawyer, David Fleming, and his partner, Harold "Hack" White, were also staying there. But Fleming had announced no press conference to produce the proof he had been promising. A few reporters had called or visited his room, but no one had been able to get in touch with him. And as the press corps gradually converged on the hotel, no one outside the small group I had arrived with seemed to be in any hurry to track Fleming down. Later, though, as we were eating dinner in the taproom, Tom Gallagher, one of Senator Tunney's aides, came in and said he had just seen Fleming and White leave the hotel. My friend Bob Walters of the Washington *Star* and I got up and went after them. We spotted them outside the hotel, then followed them a couple of blocks to the Brown Palace Hotel, an old Denver landmark. I stopped Fleming and White in the lobby, where they were buying cigarettes, and introduced myself. Fleming appeared to be in his late thirties. He had a boyish, slightly bulbous face and close-cropped dark hair and wore slightly modish, but not flashy, clothes. White, who wore a bow tie, was older, ruddy, and graying. I told Fleming that I and some other reporters had some questions to ask him. He said he hadn't had dinner and started to leave. I persisted, speaking softly but staring at him coldly. White broke in, announcing self-importantly that he was "co-counsel" and that he thought whatever we wanted could wait. They went into the grill just off the lobby and took a table. Walters took a seat at the bar and I walked back to the Hilton to round up some other reporters.

By the time I and the others got back to the Brown Palace, Fleming and White were in the middle of dinner. The reporters congregated around the bar, waiting and drinking. Bob Shogan of *Newsweek* took me aside and told me gently he thought it would be a good idea for me to stay in the background during any questioning of the two lawyers. He said he had heard some of the other reporters wondering aloud if they were being rounded up to quiz Fleming and White or to watch a confrontation between those two and me.

Shogan was right, I realized, and I immediately felt embarrassed. I was so caught up in this affair that its every intricacy seemed of utmost importance. I found great significance in the fact that these two men were being paid by ITT and yet were supposed to be representing one of its employees. And I was suspicious of their Republican connections. The whole situation in Denver seemed to me to cry out for aggressive and skeptical questioning to tear down the carefully arranged setting in which Dita Beard was about to testify. But the rest of the press didn't share my sense of urgency, and that was understandable. I had my reputation on the line. They merely had a job to do, namely to cover Dita's testimony. Except for a handful of them, the reporters undoubtedly regarded Saturday night as an opportunity to relax after a long trip and have a few drinks. But here I was, dashing around, exhorting them about how to do their job.

Finally, some of the newsmen drifted over to Fleming and White's table. Soon, all of them were grouped around. I remained at the bar. As the brief session began to break up, though, I gave in to temptation and walked over. Fleming was talking in impassioned tones about his client.

"She wants vindication," he said, "and she's going to get it." He went on to tell how sick she was, how worried he was about whether she could get through the next day's ordeal. I leaned over and put my palms on his table and looked at him.

"If you're so worried about her health," I asked, "then why are you allowing this to go forward?"

"Because," he said, "I'm between a rock and a hard place. I don't know whether it would be worse for her to testify now or to have to wait any longer to be heard."

He was giving me an icy stare as he spoke and I gazed back at him as sternly as I could. Nothing more was said. The reporters began to leave and head back to the Hilton. I went with them. Later, as I lay in bed, I thought how ridiculous the whole scene had been, especially the last part. Fleming and I had been glowering at each other like a couple of prize fighters at a weigh-in. I went to sleep with the conviction that I had begun my performance in Denver—by making a thumping ass of myself.

TEN

The Rocky Mountain Osteopathic Hospital turned out to be a squat, red-brick building located in the midst of Denver, and surrounded by one of the largest complexes of modern medical facilities I had ever seen.

A pressroom had been set up in a vacant apartment on the ground floor of a building across the street from the hospital. Only one reporter was to be allowed in the room while Mrs. Beard testified. The rest would have to wait until the lunch break, when a tape recording of the testimony would be played in the pressroom. The same procedure was to be repeated at the end of the day. Dan Thomasson of the Scripps-Howard Washington bureau had been elected as the so-called "pool" reporter to witness the testimony. He would give a briefing after each session. It was a cumbersome arrangement, but it didn't matter as much as it ordinarily might have, since this was Sunday and no one except the wire services had to meet early deadlines.

The pressroom was filled with metal folding chairs which surrounded a table on which microphones had been placed. Their wires led to the rear of the room where a battery of TV cameras was set up. Reporters milled about in the room and on the patio outside its glass doors. I saw many familiar faces from the hearings in Washington and a number of new faces, whom I took to be members of the Denver press.

The hearing was scheduled to begin at nine-thirty and, just beforehand, a member of the Senate staff walked in with a stack of copies of Mrs. Beard's prepared statement, which Fleming was going to read into the record as the hearing opened. Newsmen swarmed about the table, reaching for copies. I had been in suspense for days, wondering what Mrs. Beard would say, but the copies were gone before I got one. Someone—I don't remember who—loaned me one and I sat down in an empty row, my heart pounding, and began reading.

The statement began with a denial that there had been any attempt on her part to "run away, hide, escape or make myself unavailable to this committee." Then came a solemn statement of how "sacred" she considered the oath she had taken to be. "What I am about to say is the truth, the whole truth and nothing but the truth.

"I did not write, compose or dictate the entirety of the memorandum which Mr. Hume presented to me in the Washington office of ITT last month. I do recall similar language in the first part of that memorandum which I wrote at sometime in late June or early July of 1971, at the request of Mr. Merriam . . ."

There followed a summary of my first meeting with her which, except for a few details, was accurate. So far, so good—particularly since she had admitted writing part of the memo.

"The following day," the statement went on, "Mr. Hume called and requested another meeting with me. I was extremely distraught. I felt certain that someone was deliberately putting me in a position to be used as a vehicle to embarrass the administration, embarrass my company, and to destroy me. Mr. Gerrity called me and I reported to him that Mr. Hume wanted to talk to me again. I asked Mr. Gerrity that I not be required to talk to Mr. Hume until we got to the bottom of this. He insisted I meet with Hume and tried to assure me that I could somehow explain it. I told him, 'I couldn't.' He told me, 'You've got to.'

"Hume called my house early in the evening of February 24, 1972, and said he was coming over, and arrived a few minutes later. In the meantime, I called my doctor and asked him to come by. I was highly distressed. I have had a heart condition for some years, and I was, frankly, afraid of what a prolonged encounter would do. I had taken a Valium tablet, which is a barbiturate. My doctor had prescribed them.

"I could picture the total ruination of myself, my family, our financial security, together with incredible detriment to my company and to a man I revere and respect, my company's president, Mr. Harold Geneen. I was in a state of total despair. I know all too well the viciousness of certain reporters in Washington and the fact that they care nothing of damaging human beings, but only of getting a 'story.' I began to drink. By the time Mr. Hume arrived, I had a feeling of utter desperation."

In fact, Mrs. Beard had returned my call that day and made an emotional appeal to Les Whitten, which Joe Spear overheard, to find me so that she could "tell the truth." And when I reached her that evening, she was eager to talk to me. My coming that night was a suggestion she readily accepted. Still, these distortions didn't bother me. She was telling a sob story and I wasn't going to quibble over small points. But when I read the next paragraphs, I realized this would be no ordinary sob story, embellished here and there for effect.

"Walter Benning was in town. He works for ITT in Fort Wayne, Ind., and we have known each other for some years. He, along with my secretary, Beverly Sincavage, were with me at the house throughout the time Hume was there. My youngest son was present in the kitchen from time to time and Dr. Liszka arrived later on in the evening.

"Mr. Benning and Beverly heard my conversation with Mr. Hume."

The implications of that sentence—set apart as a paragraph by itself—were immediately obvious to me, although not to the others in the room. Dita was claiming she had witnesses to back up her version. And both were her friends and fellow ITT employees. I felt the color drain out of my face as I read the next passages.

"I recall Hume saying that there was someone trying to set me up. I kept saying I didn't know what it was all about. I asked

Mr. Hume where he got the memo and he said, 'Who did you give it to?' I told him again and again the memo wasn't mine.

"I said, 'Who in their right mind would write something like this? This isn't mine.'

"He said over and over again, 'I don't care what you say—I'm going to prove a connection between San Diego and the settlement, I'm going to use you to prove it. . . .' For 2 hours, despite the fact that I again and again asked to be left alone, he continued to grill me . . ."

Dita Beard was no longer just twisting the truth. She was making up lies from scratch. She had never denied writing the memo. Indeed, she explicitly confirmed writing it. I had never said anything even remotely resembling the threat she described. In fact, it had been part of my strategy to deliberately avoid committing myself about what Jack and I intended to do with it. She had never begged me to leave her alone. She had seemed reluctant to let me go and hugged me at the door.

I looked around the room. It was quiet except for the sound of pages being turned as the reporters read the statement. To no one in particular, I said, "Let me know when you're finished and I'll tell you where the perjury is." There were some chuckles, but I immediately wished I hadn't said it. I had promised myself to avoid the word "perjury." Although my composure was deserting me, I didn't want to show it. I read on.

"On Monday, February 28, I was instructed by Mr. Gerrity to come to New York. I spent part of Tuesday and Wednesday, February 29 and March 1 in New York. I told Mr. Gerrity and others that I could not explain the Anderson memorandum, in spite of Mr. Gerrity's assertions that I had written it.

"It was my impression that they did not believe me. I knew it was not my memo but I had no way to prove it without assistance which had to come from ITT and which was not tendered at that time.

"I asked time and time again to talk to Mr. Geneen, but was

prevented from doing so. On Wednesday afternoon, March 1, I announced to Mr. Gerrity and Mr. Jack Hanway, Mr. Geneen's assistant, that I was going away for a rest to West Yellowstone. I had not had a vacation in many years. I was told to keep Bill Merriam informed as to where I would be. I could not reach Mr. Merriam that night, but I had told Mr. Gerrity I could be reached through my daughter. I returned to Washington that night and on Thursday, March 2, I left by plane with the intent of changing planes in Denver to fly to Bozeman, Mont., and taking ground transportation to West Yellowstone. I suffered another attack on the plane. I was attended by a stewardess. This is the reason for my presence in Denver."

This was followed by an account of the Kentucky Derby party which squared perfectly with that of John Mitchell, whose version had been backed up by Louie Nunn. But Mrs. Beard did not deny telling me she had made a deal with Mitchell at the party. Instead, she said she didn't remember what she told me.

Obviously, Dita's story was full of holes, even without its direct contradictions of me. The idea that ITT was told by Mrs. Beard that she didn't write the memo and the company wouldn't believe her was utterly fantastic. When the memo surfaced, the company had shredded sacks of documents and put out a false statement that only lawyers had been authorized to conduct the antitrust negotiations. Would the company have failed to rush out a sworn statement from Dita that the memo was phony if she were willing to give one, even if they thought she was lying? And what about her claim that she had told Gerrity where she was going and left word that she could be reached through her daughter? ITT had claimed that she had disobeyed orders by skipping town and that the company didn't know where she was or how to reach her. And the defiant pose she struck toward the company looked like an effort to overcome skepticism caused by the fact that both she and her lawyers were on ITT's payroll.

But the inconsistencies were not of much comfort to me as I

sat waiting for the other reporters to finish reading the statement. Dita had chosen to attack my testimony directly, which I had hoped would not happen but had prepared for. What I was not ready for was her assertion that there were other witnesses to our conversation. Walter Benning and Beverely Sincavage had remained in the living room, which was on the other side of the dining room from the kitchen of Mrs. Beard's modest house. I had not been able to overhear what they were saying, even during pauses in my conversation with Mrs. Beard. It was impossible that they could have heard our conversation clearly. And even if they had, they would have to lie to back her up. The trouble was that they were her friends and co-workers. She would not have mentioned it, I felt sure, if she and her lawyers had not arranged for them to testify in her favor. Until this moment, the fact that I was telling the truth had, by itself, been a great tonic for my morale. It gave me a sense of righteousness. Also, I reasoned, the truth is easier to remember, to keep straight under cross-examination. Lies, of course, are complicated because one usually requires another to support it and the second requires others until there is the proverbial web of falsehoods that must be made to stick together. But Dita Beard had narrowed the area of her lies about me to things that had happened in her home, things for which my version had no support besides my memory and my typed notes. Against this, she now posed her own testimony and that of two others—three if her son were to be counted. It isn't much comfort to know you're telling the truth if you're outnumbered three or four to one.

Throughout this affair, Jack and I had enjoyed a considerable measure of good luck. ITT and the Justice Department, together with the strategists in the White House, had made blunder after blunder in their efforts to cover up the scandal. The trouble was that we never could be sure that, at some point, one of their stratagems might not work. Not only would it end the scandal, but it might leave Jack and myself badly hurt. Since it was I who had done all the work, since the facts in dispute were my facts, I was the one with the most to lose. My spirits plunged and, for the first time, I felt a touch of panic.

Bob Clark, the congressional correspondent for ABC News, called to me from across the room. "Brit, why don't you take a seat up here and we'll get your comments on this now?"

I sat down behind the table with the mikes arranged in front of me. Some radio station reporters came up to turn on their portable tape recorders, which were sitting on the table. The klieg lights went on. I adjusted myself to suit the cameramen. I heard their machines rolling. Someone asked a question about Dita's statement.

"Well, I hesitate to criticize her," I said, glad that I had rehearsed these lines on the plane a day earlier, "because she's in the toughest spot of anyone in this controversy. But she's simply not telling the truth."

There were more questions. I went over the areas of disagreement, speaking as confidently as I could, explaining that she had never denied writing her memo but had explicitly confirmed it, relating for the first time how, when I called her the day after the meeting, she had not denied making a deal with Mitchell at the Kentucky Derby, as her statement claimed, but had told me, "Why don't you tell them [the Justice Department] that old Dita's told you the truth so they won't lie to protect me?" No, I said, the others in the house had not overheard our conversation because they were a couple of rooms away. Besides, I said, there was nothing new about their being there; I had mentioned it in my own testimony.

The reporters seemed satisfied. A number of them went downstairs where another room had been outfitted with tables and telephones. The wire-service reporters and network newsmen filed stories. I wandered around, striking up conversations here and there. For me, Dita's prepared statement contained the most ominous and important testimony yet heard. I was eager to find out how the others reacted to it. I wanted to hear them say they thought it was shot through with holes and an insult to the public's intelligence. But no one was saying much of anything about it. The reports I heard the broadcast newsmen dictating over the telephone were brief, straightforward accounts, for use on hourly network news reports.

It seemed like hours before Dan Thomasson came in to say that the morning session was over and to brief his colleagues on what had happened. Dita Beard, he said, was in a large room, propped up in a hospital bed, flanked left and right by doctors and lawyers. Oxygen tanks were beside the bed and plastic tubes led from the tanks to Mrs. Beard's nostrils. The senators faced her at an L-shaped table, with Senator Philip Hart, the subcommittee chairman, in the center. Thomasson said Mrs. Beard seemed to get stronger as the morning session went on. There was laughter when he recounted some of her responses, especially one to a question from Senator Kennedy. The senator had asked about the last sentence of the first paragraph of Mrs. Beard's memo. It said, "John Mitchell has certainly kept it on the higher level only, we should be able to do the same."

"Well," Mrs. Beard had said, "the whole first paragraph is not mine. The last sentence, I don't know where in the world that mother came from."

Throughout most of the afternoon, the reporters listened and took notes as Mrs. Beard's morning testimony was replayed on a tape recorder. There was one possibly significant new revelation when Mrs. Beard was explaining how she came to write the memo in the first place.

"I remember that Mr. Merriam asked me one day—that he had gotten a call from somebody at the White House, wanting to know —on this commitment, underwriting commitment, which is all in the world it was, there in San Diego, and I never did know the exact amount because I didn't stay that long, had suddenly jumped—'Is this $600,000 going to Nixon's campaign?'"

The original figure discussed had been $400,000. That was the figure in the memo and Bob Wilson, who had been present at the meeting where Geneen had agreed to it, had confirmed it. A check for $100,000 had been sent as a down payment. Geneen had subsequently insisted that no more than $200,000 had ever been promised. Now Dita had upped the ante to $600,000 and raised the possibility that it had been planned as a straight campaign contribution for Nixon at some point.

The hearings remained in recess until 3 P.M. when another hour and a half of testimony was to be taken. On this abbreviated schedule, the subcommittee expected to finish by Thursday. Shortly after 4 P.M., though, a breathless Dan Thomasson burst into the pressroom. "Where are the wire services?" he said. "Find the wire services!"

After a long series of searching questions from Senator Kennedy, Mrs. Beard had been addressed by Senator Gurney. He had barely begun when she slumped back against the bed, moaning in pain. She was having another attack of chest pains and the hearing was over.

A short time later, Senator Hart and the co-chairman, Senator Cook, arrived. Hart looked stricken. His face was ashen and damp with perspiration. This was characteristic of Hart. He was one of the most intelligent and gentlemanly men in Washington. But that was the trouble. He had no taste for the brutal nature of this case. Where his colleagues, Kennedy, Tunney and sometimes Ervin and Bayh had bored in with tough questions, Hart tended to back off and make philosophical statements, lamenting the loss of faith such affairs caused the American system. Furthermore, he had had a warm relationship with Richard McLaren. Hart was the Antitrust and Monopoly Subcommittee chairman and McLaren had tried to be a vigorous enforcer of the antitrust laws. They were both decent, honorable men, cut from similar molds. Hart had not enjoyed watching his dignified friend roast in the heat of scandal. In short, Phil Hart had turned out to be a weak sister in a tough fight and I had long since lost patience with him. He was in a position to do our cause considerable good because he was widely respected among his colleagues. For example, it seemed that Marlow Cook almost couldn't bear to get into a disagreement with him. Cook was a brawler, an unrefined courthouse politician. But he became lamblike in the presence of Hart. At one point earlier in the hearings, a dispute with Hart had ended with Cook's making some mush-mouthed comment about how anything Hart did was "just great" with him. The effect of Hart on Cook was like that of an exorcist. But because Hart went soft, his influence ended up helping Kleindienst and hurting our cause.

The two senators said the hearing had been adjourned pending a further report later in the evening from Mrs. Beard's doctors. From the looks of Hart and the circumstances, I doubted any more would be heard from Dita Beard. Senator Cook turned aside a question about whether Dita's contradiction of me meant that one of us has committed perjury. After the senators left, Mrs. Beard's two doctors took the stand. They were quite a pair. One of them, Dave T. Garland, was a tall, light-haired man with popped eyes that seemed to roll back into his head on occasion. I thought he was spooky. The other, a cardiologist named Louis Radetsky, was an inarticulate, dark, little man, also balding, who answered most of the reporters' questions in a way that had them all looking at each other and shaking their heads. Five minutes before the attack, he said, the cardiac equipment monitoring Mrs. Beard's condition indicated she was having contractions in "the right ventricle of her heart." But he decided not to call off the questioning unless she showed contractions in the left ventricle, "which could have been a signal to stop." The left ventricle contractions came when the attack occurred, he said. I didn't say so, but my reaction to all of this was that I wouldn't let either of them cut my toenails. They were followed to the table by David Fleming and "Hack" White. Fleming got the reporters scribbling when he told how he had visited his client shortly after the seizure and she had grasped his hand and whispered, "Don't let them go," meaning the senators. Fleming didn't want anyone to think old Dita had hoked up this heart seizure to get out of further cross-examination.

I had strongly suspected all along that Mrs. Beard's condition was much exaggerated, if not invented. Although they didn't say it in so many words until later, the heart doctors who had examined Mrs. Beard for the committee had found no objective evidence of heart disease. I had been told that this was the essence of their findings by one of Senator Kennedy's staff members who had had a doctor friend translate the medical jargon in the cardiologist's report.

A group of reporters asked me for my reaction to Dita's collapse. I was tempted to say I thought the whole thing was a fraud, but I decided not to. "I leave it to you to say whether there is any justice in this," I said. "I had to undergo rigorous cross-examination before the Judiciary Committee in Washington. Now, with Mrs. Beard having made her accusations against me without cross-examination, it appears the committee is going to leave it at that." I brought up the fact that during my own testimony I had urged that the committee wait until Mrs. Beard had had ample opportunity to recover before testifying because I feared just such a thing might happen.

When the tape of the afternoon session was played, it seemed clear to me that Mrs. Beard's seizure had occurred just after her story had begun to come apart under Senator Kennedy's questioning. He took her through the portions of the memorandum which she admitted recognizing as familiar. Then he compared her answers with the contents of the second June 25, 1971 memo, the one containing her job description, which ITT had released to the press. There was the following sequence:

SENATOR KENNEDY: Could you tell us whom you talked to in the Republican National Committee about these arrangements? Did you talk to anyone?

MRS. BEARD: No one of any great importance, not Bob Dole or Lyn Nogziger or anybody.

SENATOR KENNEDY: Could you just tell us, though, whom you did talk to?

MRS. BEARD: Well, members of the finance committee.

SENATOR KENNEDY: Who were they?

MRS. BEARD: Trying to remember whether it was Bobbie O'Dell or whether it was Jerry Milbank himself. I think everyone was trying to get clear in his mind, is this going into the national committee or whose pocket it was going to wind up in. . . .

SENATOR KENNEDY: All right, could I get back to the first paragraph, Mrs. Beard, the mention in the third line there. "Other than permitting John Mitchell, Ed Reinecke, Bob Haldeman and Nixon (besides Wilson, of course) no one has known from whom that $400,000 commitment had come."

MRS. BEARD: Now, that is a misleading sentence, which I shouldn't have written the way it is, because I did not know from the first time I talked to Ed Reinecke—I did not know to whom he had spoken, when how or if. He had simply told me that these are the people, the only people who would be aware of our attempt to take the thing to San Diego after the site selection committee met in Denver.

SENATOR KENNEDY: When did he tell you that?

MRS. BEARD: On the first meeting.

SENATOR KENNEDY: When was that?

MRS. BEARD: January or February, I don't remember. He came in to Washington and said, "I need your help on something of the utmost confidence."

SENATOR KENNEDY: Did he say he was going to or that they had talked, that they were aware of these negotiations which you were involved in?

MRS. BEARD: He told me only, "This is very confidential. Nobody is discussing it. We know we can have faith in you. Do not talk to anybody about it. At some point eventually those will be the people who will be involved with it." But he did not say clearly or distinctly that he had spoken to any one of these people. In fact, I rather imagine he had not, but when he tells me it is in complete confidence, I don't ask questions I don't need to know answers to. . . .

SENATOR KENNEDY: Well, you assumed when you wrote it that those gentlemen did know about it?

MRS. BEARD: Somebody would have to be in the know then, because I already asked ITT what they planned to do, but—

SENATOR KENNEDY: But you assumed—

MRS. BEARD: He never told me "I went to see Mr. Mitchell. I spoke to Mr. Haldeman." He never said anything like that at all.

SENATOR KENNEDY: But when he spoke to you in January, he indicated those would be the people he would talk to?

MRS. BEARD: That would know about it if there was to be any possibility or feasibility.

SENATOR KENNEDY: Now, going back to after May 10th, after the luau or the meeting when you indicated to the ITT group there the possibility of the Republican convention going to San Diego, am I correct in understanding your testimony that was the end as far as your participation?

MRS. BEARD: This is what I thought would be the end as far as my participation. Yes, I had found—

SENATOR KENNEDY: Did you ever have any conversations after that May date with ITT officials or with Mr. Reinecke or—

MRS. BEARD: As I said, Ed Reinecke came to Washington a couple of times, but we never discussed any details. I think I know what you are trying to get at, but—

SENATOR KENNEDY: Well the point I was trying to get at was in the job description memorandum on the bottom it says, "The negotiations for the 1972 convention being held on ITT properties in San Diego have been wholly my responsibility," and that was admittedly the June 25th date which you agreed to?

MRS. BEARD: Yes.

SENATOR KENNEDY: And if, after May 10th, you didn't have anything further to do with it, then I would wonder why you would—

MRS. BEARD: Well, now, this was relating to getting the hotel built. This wasn't relating to any financing.

SENATOR KENNEDY: That isn't really what it says, Mrs. Beard. It says, "The negotiations for the 1972 convention being held on ITT properties in San Diego have been wholly my responsibility."

Inside Story

A few questions after this exchange, Senator Kennedy yielded to Senator Gurney and Mrs. Beard collapsed.

Mrs. Beard had admitted writing part of the memo. She had said the contribution at one point had been conceived as $600,-ooo, which would go into the President's campaign coffers. She had done poorly under cross-examination. And she had been unable to finish testifying. The day had thus contained plenty of developments to keep the scandal brewing. But I had trouble thinking about anything besides the fact that Mrs. Beard had claimed there were friendly witnesses who overheard her conversation with me at her home. Later that evening, the subcommittee announced that, after conferring with Mrs. Beard's doctors, it had been decided to postpone further testimony from her indefinitely.

The next morning, as I prepared to leave, I learned that David Fleming had scheduled a press conference for late in the morning. I toyed with the idea of staying to attend it but decided against it. I ran into Fleming and White on the elevator. I smiled and said good morning, trying to sound cheerful and confident. They murmured greetings and looked at me coldly. I asked how Mrs. Beard was feeling. One of them said she was better. I said I was glad to hear that.

I caught a ride to the airport with Al Hunt, a reporter for the *Wall Street Journal*. He had been talking to Fleming the night before and had a good idea what would be said at the press conference.

"They're going to claim these other witnesses will support Dita and demand that they be called," he said.

"Yeah," I protested, "but they were out of earshot. They couldn't have heard."

"I believe you," he said. "I'm only telling you what they told me. They're going to claim that you can't support your testimony and that you were just out for a story and didn't mind going after a sick old lady."

"But that's preposterous," I broke in. "Why the hell didn't she say something about it at the time . . ."

"Hey," said Hunt, laughing. "Take it easy. I'm just telling you what they told me."

I subsided for a moment. But I was too rattled to keep quiet. "Well, what else did they say? What did they say about the lie-detector test?"

"Somebody asked Fleming that, whether Dita would take a lie-detector test since you did. He didn't really answer. He said they had not seen your test but they were in the process of getting it."

On the plane, Hunt and I sat together in the forward part of the coach cabin. I noticed as we got on that several of the senators, including Tunney, Kennedy, and Cook were aboard, traveling first class of course. There were a number of other newsmen on the plane also and some members of the Senate staff.

After we took off, I continued to pump Hunt about his conversation with Fleming the night before. I suppose the questions got pretty repetitious, but he answered them patiently, sympathetic, apparently, to my anxiety. The essence of what he told me was that Fleming planned to take the offensive, demanding that the others in the house the night of my meeting with Mrs. Beard be called to testify. The center of his strategy was to challenge my credibility and to appeal for public sympathy for Mrs. Beard. "They're going to paint you as the heavy in this, there's no question about that," Hunt said.

After a while, Hunt got up to sit for a while in the rear of the cabin where smoking was permitted. I looked around and found a copy of the new *Time* magazine. Jack Anderson stared sternly from its cover. Inside was a five-page spread, critical in parts but favorable in tone. "Now the most celebrated practitioner of the muckraking tradition," the article said, "Anderson has conquered the shadow of his late employer and friend, Drew Pearson." My version of how I went about verifying Dita Beard's memo was recounted as fact and described as a "memorable" job. My spirits lifted slightly.

To my surprise, Dave Huber, the young aide to Senator Cook who handled his Judiciary Committee duties, came over and sat down with me. He made a show of friendliness, telling me how impressed he had been with my testimony. I sensed he was trying to find out how I had been affected by Dita's testimony. I said I had been disappointed she had committed perjury. He asked if the differences in our testimony could be resolved. I said they couldn't and added, sounding as nonchalant as I could, that it was obvious they were going to make me a target.

"Well," he said smugly, "when you get into something like this, you have to be prepared to take the heat."

That irked me, but I suppressed the urge to reply with an insult. "After three years of working for Jack," I said, "I am used to taking heat."

After Huber went away, Senator Kennedy left his seat next to Tunney's and ambled back into the coach section. He stopped at my seat and stood over me in the aisle talking for a few minutes. He seemed to want to continue the conversation, so I moved over to the window seat and he sat down next to me, by the aisle.

"I think it turned out very well," he said, "I think we should try to pursue the $600,000 question with other witnesses. I think that will help to keep things going, don't you?"

"I guess the Republicans will try to cut the hearings off," I said.

"They will, but I think we can keep them going," he replied.

At this stage, I would have been just as happy to see the hearings end, before Mrs. Beard's witnesses could make things worse for me. I mentioned my concern to Kennedy, but he didn't seem too worried about it.

A short time later, Senator Cook came back into the coach section and stopped to talk.

"Senator," I said, "I just spent about forty minutes with your staff man, so I think I've earned my time with Senator Kennedy."

Cook laughed good-naturedly. He cocked his head to the side to look at the cover of *Time,* which was on the seat between me and Kennedy. I couldn't resist the opportunity. I picked up the magazine and handed it to him.

"You see that," I said, "that's Senator Marlow Cook on the cover."

Kennedy laughed, but Cook acted as if he hadn't heard. When he looked up, he said, in his most earnest tones:

"You know, that's nice. That's really nice. This country really needs someone like Jack Anderson around. He does a lot to keep people honest. I really mean that."

I felt embarrassed. Kennedy is ruddy, but I thought I even detected a flush of embarrassment in his face. The next thing I knew Cook had spotted a baby traveling with the couple in the row in front of us. He stopped oozing and began gushing. It was quite a sight, this raunchy, burly politician grinning and winking and saying cootchy-coo to a strange baby that wasn't even from his home state.

Marlow Cook had given me ample reason to dislike him, and I did. But there was one thing about him that I liked. He was given to flashes of blunt candor that were refreshing. When he stopped flirting with the baby, the conversation between Kennedy and myself had turned to Mrs. Beard's health.

"I think Dita Beard could probably have testified again today," Cook said. "I don't think she's so sick. But I wasn't going to be the one who insisted we stay. If something happened to her, I don't want to be known for the rest of my life as 'Killer Cook.'"

My car was parked at Dulles Airport, where we landed, and I gave Bob Shogan of *Newsweek* and Ron Ostrow of the Los Angeles *Times* a ride home. During the last hour of the flight, I had been considering asking for a chance to testify again before the Judiciary Committee to respond to specific points in Mrs. Beard's testimony. I mentioned the idea to Shogan and Ostrow, who both advised strongly against it. They argued that it was poor strategy to try to contest every point. I was better off letting my testimony stand. I decided they were right.

I went home that afternoon planning to sleep away the rest of the day. But I was awakened by Clare, who told me CBS News was calling. I knew before I picked up the receiver what the call was about—Fleming's press conference had followed the scenario outlined by Al Hunt. CBS wanted to know if Sincavage and Benning could have overheard my conversation with Mrs. Beard. I said I doubted it and added, "If these witnesses were available and had something to say, why didn't they come forward weeks ago?" On the CBS evening news that night, Walter Cronkite reported Fleming's demand, then quoted me in response.

If the press had at first failed to catch the significance of Dita Beard's claim about the two witnesses, it was certainly catching on now. The next morning's Washington *Post* carried a front-page story on the press conference. In addition to his demand for the testimony, Fleming had choice words for Jack and Senator Kennedy, whom he accused of a "complete ruthless and obsessive disregard of anything save the attainment of their own objectives, whatever they might be." He added, "That a sick and distraught woman, responsible for the upbringing of five children, has been driven to the point that she would risk her very life to insure that the truth be made public is a sad and disgusting commentary on the almost untrammeled power of Jack Anderson and his pathetic, mud-raking investigator Brit Hume."

A group of friends of mine later held a luncheon and gave me a plaque. Most of them were reporters who had covered the United Mine Workers while I was writing my book on the union. The press and the union's critics had been attacked in the organization's newspaper as part of a "motley Washington cabal parading under liberal banners" which was seeking to destroy the union. The framed cardboard plaque read: "The National Press Building Chapter of the Motley Washington Cabal is pleased to present its coveted Pathetic Mudraker of the Year Award to Brit Hume for an outstanding demonstration of 'complete ruthless and obsessive disregard for anything.'" Printed below was an enlargement of the section of the Washington *Post* story containing the lawyer's remarks about me and Jack. At the bottom, in small print, it said, "Destroy this, huh?"

The next word Dita Beard's doctors gave on her condition was that she could not testify again for at least six months. But by the next weekend, she turned up on CBS's "Sixty Minutes," being interviewed by Mike Wallace. The interview took place not in her hospital room but in a nearby apartment, to which Mrs. Beard went wearing street clothes. When she got there, though, she put on her hospital gown for the interview. Asked about Dr. Liszka's testimony that she had told him she wrote the memo, she responded, "Did Victor say that? Poor Victor. He has to translate from English into Hungarian and back into English again and it never works." Her doctors said afterward that the interview was "unauthorized."

Meanwhile the Judiciary Committee held another day of hearings so that the questioning of Harold Geneen, which had been interrupted for the Beard trip, could be continued. He was asked about the call from the White House relating to whether the ITT contribution would be a $600,000 gift to Nixon's campaign. "I don't know anything about the damn call," he said. "And I know of no commitment that would fit this description. I don't think it makes sense . . . It's not logical . . . It's ridiculous."

Geneen was accompanied by the company's general counsel, Howard Aibel, who was questioned about Mrs. Beard's assertion that company officials appeared to be "delighted" to think she wrote the memo and refused to accept her denials. Aibel said he had checked on this and found "no overt basis for her belief."

The same week, ITT released reports from independent document experts which the company claimed supported the contention that the Beard memo was fraudulent. But one of the expert's reports concluded that the memo was typed in ITT's offices on

Mrs. Beard's typewriter, although it claimed that the typing could have been done as late as January 1972. At first, the company refused to release the so-called experts' reports. When they finally did release them, most of the press decided, as the Washington *Star*'s Bob Walters put it, that "neither report offered any substantial documentation" in support of its findings. Senator Eastland announced he was accepting the FBI's conclusions. Another ITT maneuver had failed.

After the Geneen testimony, there were no further hearings scheduled pending a vote on whether to continue them at all. During the lull, I worked on some other stories and worried privately about the prospect of Dita's two friends being called to testify.

I didn't find out about it until much later, but this period was one of even greater worry inside the White House. The Securities and Exchange Commission had begun an investigation into charges that ITT officials, acting on inside information, had traded the company's stock during the period surrounding the merger with the Hartford Fire Insurance Co. The practice, known as "insider" trading, is illegal in cases where the officials have information not available to other investors. Conviction can bring a fine and a jail term. The SEC had subpoenaed documents from ITT and had obtained a number related to the company's lobbying on the three antitrust cases. No one on the Judiciary Committee knew what documents the SEC had. But Reuben Robertson had been promoting the idea that the committee should obtain the agency's ITT file to see if it contained anything of relevance to the Kleindienst case. The fact that there was discussion of obtaining the SEC documents quickly got back to the White House. It caused great apprehension among several senior officials: Fred Fielding, assistant to White House Counsel John Dean, and presidential advisers John Ehrlichman and Charles Colson. The three, with the co-operation of ITT, had investigated to find out what other administration or ITT documents might be in existence which could add fuel to the scandal. They had concluded that the SEC documents could be highly damaging, as would several others.

What's more, as was revealed much later, bickering had broken out between Kleindienst and his friends, mainly John Mitchell and Robert Mardian, and members of the White House staff, chiefly Colson, and lobbyists Clark MacGregor and Wally Johnson, over how the embattled nomination should be managed with the Senate. Kleindienst & Co. were eager to press for an up or down vote in the full Senate by June 1, then about two months off. Colson, aware of the possibility of further disclosures, wanted to remain flexible, even to the point of considering withdrawing the nomination to avoid more embarrassment. On March 30, Colson dictated to his secretary a confidential memorandum for the President's chief of staff, Bob Haldeman.

> Setting June 1 as our deadline, [he argued,] merely puts the hard decision off to a time when it will be considerably more volatile politically than it is today. Kleindienst's withdrawal will then be an admission of defeat but it will come two months closer to the election . . .
>
> The most serious risk for us is being ignored . . . there is the possibility of serious additional exposure by the continuation of this controversy. Kleindienst is not the target; the President is . . . but the battle over Kleindienst elevates the visibility of the ITT matter and, indeed, guarantees that the case will stay alive . . .
>
> Neither Kleindienst, Mitchell nor Mardian know of the potential dangers. I have deliberately not told Kleindienst or Mitchell since both may be recalled as witnesses and Mardian does not understand the problem. Only Fred Fielding [assistant to John Dean], myself and Ehrlichman have fully examined all the documents and/or information that could yet come out. A summary of some of these is attached:
>
> 1. Certain ITT files which were not shredded have been turned over to the SEC; there was talk yesterday in the Committee of subpoenaing these from ITT. These files would un-

dermine Griswold's testimony that he made the decision not to take the appeal [of the Grinnell case] to the Supreme Court. Correspondence to [Treasury Secretary] Connally and [Commerce Secretary] Peterson credits the delay in Justice's filing of the appeal to the Supreme Court of the Grinnell case to direct intervention by Peterson and Connally. A memo sent to the Vice President, addressed "Dear Ted" from Ned Gerrity tends to contradict John Mitchell's testimony because it outlines Mitchell's agreement to talk to McLaren following Mitchell's meeting with Geneen in August, 1970.

It would carry some weight in that the memo was written contemporaneously with the meeting. Both Mitchell and Geneen have testified they discussed policy only, not this case, and that Mitchell talked to no one else. The memo further states that Ehrlichman assured Geneen that the President had 'instructed' the Justice Department with respect to the bigness policy. (It is, of course, appropriate for the President to instruct the Justice Department on policy, but in the context of these hearings, that revelation would lay this case on the President's doorstep). There is another internal Ryan to Merriam memo, which is not in the hands of the SEC; it follows the 1970 Agnew meeting and suggests that Kleindienst is the key man to pressure McLaren, implying that the Vice President would implement this action. We believe that all copies of this have been destroyed.

2. There is a [Herb] Klein to Haldeman memo dated June 30, 1971 which of course precedes the date of the ITT settlement, setting forth the $400,000 arrangement with ITT. Copies were addressed to [Jeb] Magruder, Mitchell and Timmons. This memo put the AG [Attorney General] on constructive notice at least of the ITT commitment at that time and before the settlement, facts which he has denied under oath. We don't know whether we have recovered all the copies. If known, this would be considerably more damaging than the Reinecke statement. Magruder believes it is possible the AG transmitted his copy to Magruder. Magruder doesn't have the copy he received; he only has a Xerox of the copy. In short, despite a search, this memo could be lying around anywhere at 1701 [Pennsylvania Avenue, address of the Committee to Re-elect the President].

3. The Justice Department has thus far resisted a request

for their files . . . One is a memo of April, 1969 from Kleindienst and McLaren to Ehrlichman responding to an Ehrlichman request with respect to the rationale for bringing the case
against ITT in the first place. There is a subsequent April,
1970 memo . . . to McLaren stating that Ehrlichman had discussed his meeting with Geneen with the AG, and suggesting
to McLaren that Mitchell could give McLaren "more specified guidance." There is another memo of September, 1970
from Ehrlichman to the AG referring to an "understanding"
with Geneen and complaining of McLaren's actions. There
is a May 5, 1971 memo from Ehrlichman to the AG alluding
to discussions between the President and the AG as to the
"agreed upon ends" of the ITT case and asking the AG
whether Ehrlichman should work directly with McLaren or
through Mitchell. There is also a memo to the President in
the same time period. We know we have control of all the
copies of this, but we don't have control of the original
Ehrlichman memo to the AG. This memo would once again
contradict Mitchell's testimony and more importantly, directly
involve the President. We believe we have absolute security on
this file within Justice, provided no copies were made within
Justice and provided there are no leaks. We have no idea of
the distribution that took place within Justice.

No single document could have been more revealing than Colson's memo to Haldeman. The entire history of the ITT settlement
and the extensive effort to cover up the scandal it caused were outlined in the starkest terms. John Ehrlichman, with the apparent
knowledge of the President, had pressured McLaren both directly
and through John Mitchell to accommodate ITT. Mitchell, who
had officially disqualified himself from the case, not only discussed
it with Ehrlichman but with the President and Harold Geneen.
Under oath, Mitchell had denied it all and so had Geneen. Mitchell had also denied having any knowledge of the ITT convention
money until after the settlement of the case. Yet a memo explaining the deal had been sent to him before the settlement. Then
there were the ITT documents crediting two members of the
President's Cabinet for successful intervention to delay the filing
of the Grinnell appeal to the Supreme Court—a delay that the

esteemed Solicitor General Erwin Griswold had said was his doing.

So what had begun as a case of corporate influence at high levels had now become, in addition, a possible case of perjury by the former Attorney General and the president of ITT. And the documents further suggested that both McLaren and Griswold may have lied in their testimony. As a result, senior presidential assistants were diligently trying to round up and cover up the remaining evidence.

Unfortunately, neither the remaining evidence nor even the fact of its existence were known to me as I sweated out the interval before the resumption of the hearings. On Wednesday, April 5, I flew out to Bloomington, Illinois, to speak at Illinois State University in the neighboring town of Normal. Traveling the lecture circuit was a new experience for me, and I was flattered by the attention from students and the local media. It would have been more fun, though, if I hadn't been preoccupied by the nagging worry about the outcome of the ITT affair. It was late when I got to my motel room after speaking, but I put through a call to Clare, as was my custom every night when I was away. I was not prepared for the news she had.

"Bob Walters has been trying to get you," she said. "Apparently there's a story out about some tape-recorded interview with Congressman Wilson where he talks about the memo and says Dita told him it was real."

"Did Bob say he had the story, or what?"

"No, he said tomorrow's Baltimore *Sun* has it, but it's on the wire. I didn't catch all the details. He called from the office and he said he'd be there a while. Why don't you call him?"

"Okay, I'll call him right now."

"And call me back."

"Okay."

Bob Walters' extension in the Washington *Star*'s newsroom rang only once before he picked up the phone with a curt "Hello."

"Bob," I said. "It's Brit."

"Hume!" he said, laughing. "You're vindicated."

"Clare told me. What's this all about?"

"Well, Walter Gordon went out to San Diego, apparently just to snoop around. While he was out there he found out that a reporter named Cox who's with the San Diego *Union* had done a tape-recorded interview with Wilson just after the memo came out. Wilson had talked to Dita and he said the memo is real. Apparently, the San Diego *Union* wouldn't let this guy use the interview. But Gordon heard the tape and the story's on page one of the *Sun*. The AP picked it up."

Walter Gordon was the Justice Department and Supreme Court reporter for the Baltimore *Sun*. When I first met him, I had thought he was a pest, because every time I saw him, he came up and asked about a dozen questions. Later, though, I began to read some of his stories. He did as good a job as anyone in covering the hearings. His analysis of testimony was lucid and complete. He never failed to point out inconsistencies and he somehow kept straight all the different versions. I had come to respect him as one of the two or three best reporters covering the case. Now he had come up with a scoop that made me want to send him some roses.

The Wilson interview, given to Robert Cox of the San Diego *Union* on March 3, could hardly have been more helpful to me. First of all, there was no question that Dita and Bob Wilson were good friends. Thus there was no reason to think that she would lie to him about the authenticity of the memo. What's more, Wilson was an ideal person from whom to have additional confirmation that Dita had admitted writing the memo. He was the chairman of the Republican Congressional Campaign Committee and a personal friend of Harold Geneen. And there was no way he could disavow his own tape-recorded words.

The key quotes from the interview with Cox, which covered other subjects besides ITT, were as follows:

> WILSON: That thing's blown up way out of proportion to its importance, but I'll admit that that note from Dita is the thing that stirs people up, and it should. But you have to

know her to—you haven't seen a copy of it?—well, she just went rambling on and—she's a very unusual person and she's got a lot of animosities within—it's sort of a—it's an inter-political fight.

Cox: In the company?

Wilson: Yeah, inter-company fight. . . .

Cox: Where is she? How come she's so hard to find?

Wilson: I don't have any idea where she is . . . She called me Wednesday evening [March 1] in my office and said that she'd been up to New York and that they were putting her on a leave of absence and that she was going to get out of town. At that time, there was no mention of subpoenaing her . . . And I said, "Where are you going?" and she said, "I have no idea, but where I'm going, they won't be able to find me and I won't be able to talk to them," or something like that . . . She's a real, real top woman lobbyist, you know and she cusses like a man, but a very effective person. . . . There's no question that she was mouse-trapped by, in my book anyway, by Gerrity and Merriam, who works for Gerrity. . . . I just know as sure as can be that Gerrity released that—that Merriam who's scared to death of Gerrity and scared of everybody—when he got that memo that Dita tells me she typed up at Merriam's request and she said, "Why do you want to put it in writing?" And he said, "I don't understand the ramifications." In the memo she was talking about—Merriam had come to me and said . . . "It's going to be in services, not cash." And I had complained to Dita. I said, "My God, what's he trying to do, screw up the deal?" And so she said she went to him and complained. And he said, "Put it in writing for me so I'll understand it." She said, "Well, I'm telling you," and he said, "No, write it down." He said, you know, "Just an inter-office memo." So she hand carried it, she said, to Merriam. And at the end it says, "Please tear this up, huh?" So there it is. Jack Anderson had the original. Not just a copy, but the original memo.

Cox: It had to come from Merriam.

Wilson: It had to come from Merriam.

The congressman went on to say that Merriam had told him he received the memo but had given it back to Dita. Now, of course, Merriam was saying that he never received it.

The San Diego *Union,* one of a group of papers run by the ultra-conservative James Copley, was the alma mater of President Nixon's communications director, Herb Klein. It was dismaying, if not surprising, that the paper would have sat on information bearing on a major issue before a Senate committee. But at this point, I was too happy that the information had surfaced to worry about the ethics of the San Diego *Union.* I felt a sense of relief as great as any I have ever experienced. Now no matter what Dita's friends might say, no one would doubt that Dita had told me—as she had her friend Bob Wilson—that she wrote the memo. And no matter what the outcome of the hearings, I would survive them with my credibility intact.

The next morning was crisp, clear and cold. I was driven to the Champaign, Illinois, airport about sixty miles away, to catch a non-stop flight to Washington. The Baltimore *Sun's* revelation of the Wilson tape was on every newscast I heard along the way. I couldn't keep from smiling.

The next day, the Judiciary Committee agreed to hold nine more days of hearings on the Kleindienst nomination and to take up, at least to some extent, the charges raised in the *Life* magazine article on San Diego.

The first witness was Bob Wilson, who wriggled and balked under questioning, but found himself unable to shake free of his own tape-recorded words, which by now were in transcript form and were part of the hearing record. In addition, he insisted that the ITT commitment to the Republican convention had indeed been $400,000 as Dita's memo had indicated and as Wilson had earlier told me. This, of course, contradicted Geneen's testimony that his company never expected to put up more than $200,000.

The next witness was Bill Merriam, and his performance will never be forgotten by any who saw it. It was late in the game now and the issues were clearly framed. Merriam had had an opportunity to study the record and to prepare his testimony with the assistance of the squad of lawyers which hovered about all the ITT witnesses. By now, though, the committee had invited presidential assistant Peter Flanigan to testify. The White House had indicated the invitation would be declined on the grounds of "executive privilege," the doctrine which holds that the President's advisers must be immune from being summoned before congressional committees because such appearances would undermine their confidential relationship with the President. Sam Ervin didn't think much of the doctrine of executive privilege and he was spoiling for a fight over it. So his interest in the ITT case had grown much sharper. He had some things to ask Merriam.

"Who issued the order to the Washington office of ITT," Ervin inquired innocently, his face twitching, eyes ablink, "for the Washington office to destroy any records which might be embarrassing to the company or to any individuals connected with the company?"

"I did, sir," said Merriam.

"Is that a policy of the ITT?" asked Ervin.

"It is when you have a memo like this one we are talking about that has escaped your files and been distributed to the press."

"Well," reasoned the senator, "you could not destroy that memo because you did not have it."

"No," said Merriam. There was a pause. Then he blurted, "That is right, but there might have been a lot of others in there like that."

The room erupted in laughter. But Ervin, his face now redder than usual, pressed on, obviously irritated.

"Now," said Ervin, "you stated that after you had gone to see Congressman Wilson, Mrs. Beard called on you for information about what transpired between you and Congressman Wilson?"

"No, sir," said Merriam, "I do not believe I said that."

"Who did you say you fudged on, what did you say you fudged about, did not make a complete report?"

"I said I fudged on whether or not I had seen the memo that we are talking about."

"You mean you fudged on Congressman Wilson?"

"Yes."

"Well, now, Mr. Merriam, if you had no recollection of having seen the memorandum, you could have been sure of having no recollection of having seen the memorandum, could you not?"

"Yes, you are right, I could have."

"Yes. I just wonder why you did not tell him that."

"Well, I know him so well I did not know whether he would have bought that recollection."

"Well," said Ervin, a little exasperated, "do you fudge on people you know well or strangers?"

"Well, that is a bad word, 'fudge,' I meant by that simply that I did not know for sure when I told him whether I had seen the memorandum or not. So I hedged is a better word than fudged."

"Well," said Ervin, "you concealed the truth."

"What, sir?"

"You concealed the truth."

"No, I did not, honestly, I did not."

"When you hedge, do you not conceal the truth when you hedge on a statement?"

"Well, you slip a little bit—well, I cannot describe it."

"In other words, you tell part of the truth, but leave most of it out, is that what you mean by hedging?"

"Well, there is an unfortunate word, both of them, and I would like to correct it. You are putting me in a box now."

William Merriam, soon thereafter, was reassigned to ITT's office in Rome.

Other witnesses in the final days of the hearings included Ed Reinecke and his aide, Edgar Gillenwaters. They gave the committee an elaborate explanation of why they both at first confirmed, then denied, having informed John Mitchell of the ITT convention pledge before the settlement of the antitrust cases. Their story was received with skepticism, and in some instances, outright disbelief. Senator Birch Bayh, irritated at Gillenwaters' flippant responses to his questions, finally blew his top.

". . . somebody is not telling the truth, or somebody is making a misstatement," Bayh said, staring at Gillenwaters, "and I have to say here just as one senator, and I do not make this statement lightly, just listening to this conversation over the last couple of hours that your credibility has gone from 100 to damn near zero."

While Bayh spoke, Gillenwaters was smirking. After beginning another question, Bayh interrupted himself.

"You may smile, sir," he said, reddening, "but if my impression is correct of what you have said both to the press and here under oath, you have committed perjury. I am only one member of the Senate, but that is my gut reaction to what you say."

Gillenwaters was not cowed. "Senator," he said, "if I smiled I am sorry. But if our credibility has gone to zero in your eyes then it must have shot up considerably elsewhere."

That reply, for sheer impudence, matched anything the committee had heard since Jack's exchanges with Roman Hruska, and the room filled with laughter. There was laughter at another point, as Senator Kennedy questioned Reinecke on what prompted him to change his story and to issue a statement contradicting his earlier assertion that he and Gillenwaters had discussed the ITT convention cash promise with John Mitchell in Washington in May. Reinecke said he changed his story after his office received a phone call, but he didn't volunteer any information on where the call came from.

"There was a call that came in," he said, "that asked that we check our records."

"Who did that call come from?" asked Kennedy.

"I have no idea," said Reinecke.

"Who was it to?"

"I was not in the office, so I presume it was addressed to me."

"Well, then, how do you know about it?"

"Well, because my secretary told me about it."

"What did she tell you?"

"She told me that somebody called and said that the testimony

248

of Attorney General indicated that I did not see him in May and I should check my records."

"And she just said someone from the Justice Department?"

"I am sorry," said Reinecke. "It is true. I do not know."

"What about it, Mr. Gillenwaters?" asked Kennedy.

"Excuse me," interjected Reinecke, "I am not sure she said the Justice Department. We got a call. I do not know; it could have been someone in Sacramento. It could have been anyone."

"I am sorry," said Kennedy. "What did your secretary tell you: 'We got a call and someone said we ought to check our records'?"

"I am sure," responded Reinecke, "she said, 'I will deliver the message.'"

This exchange continued for a while, with both Reinecke and Gillenwaters professing ignorance of the origins of the phone call. Finally, Kennedy asked: "You mean your secretary is not in the habit of checking who is calling?"

"Senator," responded Gillenwaters, ever the wise guy, "we do not have a staff the size of the Senate staff."

The response drew a laugh. Kennedy's next question got a bigger laugh.

"How big a staff do you need to get a secretary to ask who is calling?"

The senators also heard from Henry Petersen, head of the Criminal Division of the Justice Department, and Harry Steward, the United States Attorney for San Diego. Petersen acknowledged that Steward's handling of the case referred to in the *Life* magazine article was grossly improper, but defended his and Richard Kleindienst's decision not to dismiss Steward. Firing him, said Petersen, would have undermined public confidence in the department at the time of another important court case Steward was trying. The IRS and Justice Department investigators who had been the key sources for the *Life* article were not allowed to testify. Denny Walsh, the investigative reporter who dug up the facts, would certainly have been heard if Time, Inc. had been willing to request it. But the company let the opportunity pass. Harry Steward gave a terrible account of himself with halting testimony in crude English, which included a denunciation of the "scurlious" *Life* article. He said he had not acted improperly, but if he had it all to do over again, he would handle it differently.

By now, though, it didn't matter what these witnesses said as long as they didn't admit to anything utterly reprehensible. The hearing record was replete with the most direct contradictions and admissions of the most obvious irregularities and indiscretions. The Administration and ITT had failed to prove their innocence, but they had succeeded in so muddling the issues that no clear picture of guilt was visible. Kleindienst said at the time he asked for the hearings that he wanted to remove the cloud from above his head. The cloud was still there, darker and heavier than ever. But the United States Senate does not require presidential appointees to cabinet posts, even to the most senior law-enforcement jobs, to be free from clouds; they need only be free from hurricanes. So, despite his evasions, his repeated need to have his recollection "refreshed," despite all the loose ends that the committee had never even tried to resolve, it appeared the Kleindienst nomination had been saved. But even at this late stage, the Administration nearly threw it away. The committee wanted to hear from Peter Flanigan, and the President and his counsel John Dean said that would violate "executive privilege." So Sam Ervin said he would oppose the nomination unless Flanigan testified. Ervin, being a Southerner with great seniority and impeccable credentials in the clubby old guard that dominates the Senate, was quickly joined by Robert Byrd, the majority whip and a committee member, and Russell Long, the chairman of the Finance Committee. For several days, it appeared the White House was going to let the nomination go down the drain to keep Flanigan from testifying. Finally, though, a compromise was worked out. Flanigan would testify along limited lines and the committee would agree to release the hostage nomination for a vote by the full Senate.

Flanigan appeared, said absolutely nothing the committee did not already know, and refused, citing the agreement under which he appeared, to answer other pertinent questions. Sam Ervin, having already claimed victory, said nothing. The hearings were over.

There was one final incident that grew out of this protracted affair that seems worth mentioning as an example of the kind of intrigue that occurs in Washington. One of the last witnesses was Jack Gleason, the former White House aide and Republican fund raiser who had become a public relations adviser to ITT and other clients. I had spoken to Gleason early in my investigation of the case and he had leveled with me far more than I had expected. It was evident to me that he was in no way culpable in this case and I kept in touch with him throughout the ensuing weeks.

When the hour of his testimony approached, he and his partner in the consulting firm, Robert Conkling, were apprehensive that some of the Democratic senators might try to delve into embarrassing information concerning Gleason's earlier fund-raising activities. They were eager to avoid this. Not long before Gleason was to appear, Conkling spotted one of the Democratic Committee members' cars parked outside Conkling's house in Georgetown. An attractive divorcee with whom the senator—Gleason has refused to tell me which senator—was rumored to be having an affair lived next door. Seeing an opportunity, Conkling pulled his own car up in front of his house, double-parked next to the senator's car and opened his hood. After a while, the senator came outside. Conkling, a boyish chap, apologized profusely for his car's having broken down. Then he pretended sudden recognition of the senator and made a gee-whiz show of awe and rushed into his house to get his Brownie camera. While inside, he telephoned friends in the area and told them to drive by and take note of who was outside with him. The flashbulb in his camera didn't work, but several of his friends did pass by and spot the senator, giving Conkling the witnesses he thought he might need. Finally, after delaying the impatient senator awhile, he got his car running and moved out of the way. Senator X drove off into the night. Gleason told me he planned, if the circumstances indicated he would be in for heavy questioning, to have his partner seated next to him at the witness table. He said he thought it would have a chilling effect. No doubt it would have, but by the time Gleason appeared, time was running out on the ITT affair and it didn't appear he would be given a hard time. He wasn't.

The Kleindienst nomination reached the Senate floor on June 8, and by then there was no suspense over what would happen. A month beforehand, Senator Philip Hart had announced that he would vote for Kleindienst despite the fact that, as one of Hart's aides put it, Kleindienst had used bad judgment in the ITT matter. Hart's position, of course, was support for his friend Richard McLaren whose own behavior would have been impliedly censured if the ITT affair resulted in Kleindienst's rejection. Republicans on the committee were thereafter able to refer doubting colleagues to Phil Hart for an endorsement of Kleindienst. The nomination passed 64 to 17.

The ITT affair was the best thing that ever happened to my career. I was virtually unknown before it began, despite several years with Jack and the publication of my book. Now I was well known throughout the news business and even known to some outside it. Magazines were interested in my free-lance work and my agent reported expressions of interest from book editors. My lecture agent was booking more dates than I could keep and still fulfill my duties with the column. I had to ask him to limit the engagements. Kleindienst might have survived the ITT affair in one piece, but I had come through it much better. I had no reason to complain from a personal standpoint.

But still there was something discouraging in those final weeks about watching the system grind inexorably toward the vindication of the guilty. The Senate Committee had not seriously investigated the charges against Kleindienst; it had merely provided a forum at his request where some witnesses could be questioned. The liberal Democrats had made a good try, but without subpoenas of additional records—such as those unshredded by ITT or on file at the Justice Department and the SEC—the full truth about the case could not be ascertained. Many witnesses had lied, but there seemed to be no hope they would ever be brought to justice for it. Other witnesses had never been called and some, like Peter Flanigan, had refused to answer pertinent questions. As a sort of parting shot, Senator Tunney got the Judiciary Committee to refer the hearing record to the Justice Department for a perjury investigation. Everyone snickered at the idea that anything would come of that.

As the election approached, the efforts to keep the lid on the case continued. William Casey, chairman of the Securities and Exchange Commission, found himself confronted with an effort by the House Commerce Committee to obtain the SEC's ITT files. Instead of making it available, Casey had the material—all thirty-four cartons of it, including the documents revealing the high-level ITT contacts on the antitrust case—sent to the Justice Department. The Department promptly turned the material over to White House counsel John Dean.

After the election, though, unexpected things began happening. The Washington *Post's* dogged pursuit of the facts behind the June 17 break-in and burglary of the Democratic National Committee by agents of the President's re-election committee finally paid off. A special Senate committee formed to investigate the incident began pressing for testimony from White House aides. A federal grand jury held an investigation in which presidential aides were likely to be indicted for conspiracy to cover up the truth about the break-in. Damaging details of the cover-up spilled out during Senate hearings into the nomination of acting FBI director L. Patrick Gray to be permanent FBI director. President Nixon bowed to the pressure and admitted there had been serious misconduct by members of his staff. Richard Kleindienst resigned and Elliot Richardson was named to replace him. As a condition of his confirmation, the Senate insisted upon the appointment of a special prosecutor, independent of the Nixon administration, to handle the Watergate affair. Archibald Cox, a Harvard law professor and former Solicitor General, was named special prosecutor and promised full autonomy. And, in addition, Richardson gave him responsibility for the ITT perjury investigation.

Cox named a special division of his investigative task force to deal exclusively with ITT. The ITT cover-up began to unravel. A memo to ITT officials from Russell Tagliareni, the company's security officer who obtained the Susan Lichtman affidavit, was obtained. In it, Tagliareni told his superiors that Dita Beard had told him her memo was authentic. Ed Reinecke told the San Diego *Union* that he had discussed the ITT convention promise with John Mitchell in May of 1971, thereby recanting his own flat testimony to the contrary and contradicting Mitchell. Reinecke, in effect, admitted he had committed perjury. The Cox investigators obtained all the SEC documents, which by now were public record and pressed the White House for its files on the case. The Senate Watergate Committee turned up the explosive Colson to Haldeman memo outlining all the other known documentary evidence in the case.

Among those who came forward to co-operate with the investigation was Richard Kleindienst, apparently in the hope of avoiding indictment for his false statements about White House interference in the Grinnell appeal. In a statement issued October 31, 1973, he acknowledged receiving the calls from Ehrlichman and Nixon. The intervention was also confirmed by the White House, which claimed the President acted for "policy reasons." This was a curious statement, in view of the fact that the ITT cases had been in the courts for some time and were known everywhere to be a centerpiece of the Administration's anti-trust policy.

The Cox task force, which later became the Leon Jaworski task force, appeared to be in a position to obtain a series of indictments for perjury, conspiracy and obstruction of justice.

ELEVEN

One line in the *Time* cover story on Jack meant more to us than all the rest. "The column," it said, "now has a far better reputation for accuracy than it did in Pearson's time." This, of course, was the sort of judgment we had all been striving for. And there was no doubt that, in the aftermath of India-Pakistan and ITT, it was shared by others besides *Time*. The disdain and occasional suppression we had received from the Washington *Post* vanished. Now the *Post* watched the column closely, followed up its more important revelations, and praised Jack editorially. The public, it said, was "indebted" to Jack for his India-Pakistan reporting. The *Post* said Jack was "indefatigable" and possessed "phenomenal investigative resources." When Jack reported that U.S. ambassador to France Arthur Watson had gotten drunk aboard a flight back from Paris and made crude passes at stewardesses, the *Post* promoted the column in a box on the front page. That had never happened before.

The same week *Time* published its cover story on Jack, *Newsweek* also carried a piece of similar length on the column, which emphasized its newly won credibility. *Life* magazine, in its death throes, ran a favorable feature on the flock of young student interns who competed for places on Jack's staff. The New York *Times Magazine* assigned Susan Sheehan, a *New Yorker* writer and specialist in profiles, to write a definitive piece on Jack.

And there were more major stories in the column. The Arthur Watson affair created a remarkable stir, far greater than any generated by earlier columns on the private conduct of public figures. Watson denied he was drunk, but the State Department, in effect, confirmed that the story was true. Jack got ahold of the diplomatic portions of the Pentagon Papers, which Daniel Ellsberg had never made available, and published excerpts in the column. Once again, reporters lined up to get their own copies. The result was a spate of additional stories on the documents, crediting Jack with making them available.

Joe Spear developed a source who had access to the dossiers maintained by the FBI on private citizens and, over a period of weeks, obtained, copied, and returned a large number of them. For years, of course, it had been generally assumed in Washington that the FBI had kept files on prominent persons. But the bureau had consistently denied it. The documents Joe obtained, however, proved that the FBI had been keeping tabs on the private affairs and/or political activities of people ranging from Ralph Abernathy to Tony Randall. There were FBI files on James Baldwin, the famed black writer, Coretta Scott King, widow of Martin Luther King, and even the singer Eartha Kitt. Joe also learned that the Secret Service was keeping an eye—and a dossier—on Groucho Marx, which led to some wisecracks in the office about the government's paranoia about Marxism of any kind. The documents Joe obtained showed the bureau was keenly interested in the sex lives of some of those it kept files on. One dossier, whose subject we never identified, began with the assertion that this person, an actor, had never been the subject of an FBI investigation. But it went on to quote "reliable sources" to the effect that the person was a homosexual. There was no criminal record, only a list of reports of homosexuality. The person was not and has never been a government official. The stories on the FBI papers were picked up by a number of other news organizations, though they didn't create the same sensation as India-Pakistan and ITT. Joe and Jack ended up testifying before a House committee on the subject. Then L. Patrick Gray, newly appointed as acting FBI director, announced that there were no such thing as "secret files." But many of the papers Joe had obtained were marked "secret" and "no foreign dissemination." So Jack promptly wrote a column offering to give Gray the numbers of some of the files so that he could look them up for himself.

The height of this harvest of praise and scoops came when Jack was awarded the 1972 Pulitzer Prize in national reporting for the India-Pakistan revelations. The trustees of Columbia University refused to concur in the awards to Jack and to the New York *Times* for the Pentagon Papers, but they did not set them aside. The controversy only added publicity to the award, and Jack liked that just fine.

Jack Anderson was now the hottest attraction on the lecture circuit and his fee had more than doubled from the $1,000 plus expenses he had been getting. What's more, the Mutual Network took over the little-heard syndicated radio show he and Les had been doing once a week and converted it into a daily broadcast. Jack's five-times-a-week television commentaries for Metromedia and several other stations continued, but with new hope they would become more widely broadcast. He signed a contract with Random House for $100,000 for a book on his major stories of recent months.

Without counting his occasional article for *Parade* magazine and his book, Jack now had to produce at least eighteen fresh news items a week to feed the furnace that his various enterprises had now become. There were seven columns a week, many of them containing more than one story, five television commentaries, and a daily radio show with several stories. Jack's emergence as a major national figure, instead of easing the burdens on him and the staff, increased them markedly. This was all the more so since all of us, taking advantage of our increased opportunities, were now busy much of the time with outside endeavors, including lecturing, books, and magazine writing.

Jack's successes did not tempt him to rest on his laurels. He seemed determined to live up to his new billing as the nation's foremost investigative reporter. He insisted upon attending both political conventions and taking part of the staff with him. I have always thought political conventions are a dreadful bore and I was thrilled to be the one left behind. Although there was no way to keep the column current on the fast-breaking events at the conventions, Jack came back from both satisfied that he had stayed ahead of most of the press on his radio show and in the nightly television commentaries he did for a Miami station with which he had an old and friendly relationship.

For my part, the temptation to rest on the year's achievements was great. Clare and I went to Bermuda for a week in May, just at the close of the ITT affair and we spent a week with the children at the Delaware shore in June. As the summer wore on, we went to the shore on weekends whenever we could, a couple of times staying in Jack's newly purchased $110,000 house in Rehoboth Beach. I wrote a long piece for *Harper's* on the ITT case, a book review, which involved considerable reporting, for the Washington *Post*, and an article on the same book for (*MORE*), the journalism review. The lecture dates continued into June and kept my pockets fuller than they had been. I began to wonder, during those weekends at the shore, whether it wouldn't be possible for me to make it on my own.

On Tuesday, July 25, Senator Thomas Eagleton of Missouri, the man selected by Senator George McGovern as his running mate on the Democratic presidential ticket, held a news conference in a resort lodge in the Black Hills of South Dakota where McGovern had been resting before the campaign. Two reporters for the Knight Newspapers, Robert Boyd and Clark Hoyt, had established that Eagleton had three times been hospitalized for mental disorders in the past. With the Knight papers poised to break the story, Eagleton and McGovern decided to make a public confession immediately. Eagleton's statement to a roomful of stunned reporters contained assurances that he was fully recovered, that his problem had been "nervous exhaustion" and that he had learned to "pace" himself so that he would not have the problem again. Nevertheless, he acknowledged that he had undergone electric-shock treatment on two of the occasions when he had been hospitalized. There could be no doubt that it was a devastating development for the Democratic ticket. Eagleton was an attractive and articulate man, considered a remarkably talented politician by his colleagues. But would the public place a man with a history of mental illness a heartbeat from the presidency? Most people doubted it. The headlines the next morning were very large.

I stopped in Jack's office the next day before going to my own. He had just done his morning radio show and was going through some papers at his desk.

"It seems to me," I said, "that this Eagleton press conference left some questions unanswered."

"Oh?" said Jack.

"Well, in a separate interview with the Knight papers, he said something about still taking some 'little blue pills.' I wonder if they are barbiturates and, if so, what kind. That raises questions about when they were prescribed and if they were prescribed by a psychiatrist. And that makes me wonder if he isn't still seeing a psychiatrist. You can't tell how the press will react. They may decide to drop the subject. They might press it all the harder. But if they drop it, there might be an additional story there."

"Well," said Jack, "I think you're right. Why don't you go after it."

I called Eagleton's office to reach his press secretary, not knowing where the senator and his traveling staff were. I was told he could be reached at the Century Plaza Hotel in Los Angeles. I called the hotel and left a message with a message operator for the press secretary. As it turned out, I never heard from him.

About three o'clock that afternoon, Jack crossed the hall into my office. "I just talked to True Davis," he said. "I don't know why I didn't think of it before. He says Eagleton was arrested eleven times for drunk driving in Missouri."

"Has he got proof?" I asked.

"No, but he's seen photostats of the citations," Jack said.

"Has he still got them?"

"No. But he says if you reach the man who was the prosecutor in the county just north of Jefferson City in 1968, he will know all about it."

"God, it's a hell of a story," I said. "Eagleton has denied over and over that he's ever had a drink problem."

"True has never misled me before," Jack said. "I've got to go out and I'm going straight home later, so why don't you try to reach this prosecutor and call me at home tonight about it. I'm afraid this won't keep for the column, but we might be able to use something on radio."

True Davis was a somber figure, old-fashioned and formal, who had been ambassador to Switzerland and Undersecretary of the Treasury during the Johnson administration. He and Jack had become friends during Davis' years in Washington. In 1968, Davis ran in the Democratic primary for the Senate from his home state of Missouri, where he had accumulated a large fortune in business before deciding to go into government. Davis finished third in the primary behind Thomas Eagleton and the incumbent senator, Edward Long. Now he was the president of the National Bank of Washington, which was owned by the United Mine Workers. The corruption in that union, of course, was the subject of my first book, *Death and the Mines.* Jack had assured me of Davis' personal probity and said he thought his present job was just something to keep him in Washington while he awaited another opportunity for a political post. I had only met Davis once, during lunch with Jack in the Montpelier Room, a swanky French restaurant in the Madison Hotel in downtown Washington. Jack wanted to get some confidential information from Davis for a story we were working on. According to plan, I sought to soften Davis up with polite but skeptical questions about his role with the union and the bank. Jack then intervened with praise for Davis' integrity and remarks about what old and close friends they were. Then came his pitch for the information. The next day, Davis came through. His information turned out to be absolutely accurate and it made an excellent story. Since then I had never seen Davis, except in the society pages of the newspapers. A widower, he entertained lavishly and often at his huge home in Washington's embassy district. Davis struck me as such a colorless, solemn figure that it seemed strange that he would emerge as a leading light of society.

I began making calls to try to find out the name of the prosecutor of whom Davis had spoken. There turned out to be two counties side by side just north of Jefferson City, which doubled the number of calls I had to make. Everyone I spoke to seemed to remember one case, in 1962, when Eagleton had been arrested for speeding in a radar zone and paid a fine. Gene Hamilton, the present prosecutor in Calloway County, told me that other reporters had asked about the drunk-driving reports. He said he had never heard of any such thing. So eager was Hamilton to convince me that the 1962 case was actually speeding, and not a reduced charge stemming from a drunk-driving arrest, that he dug out the ticket itself from the county records and read the details to me over the phone. Eagleton had been driving 85 in a 65-mile-per-hour zone, had been pulled over at 8:45 P.M. March 11, 1962, on State Highway 40, a two-lane road, near the town of Fulton. Soon after I finished talking to Hamilton, a newsman with a Washington television station called to ask me if we had heard the drunk-driving rumors. I said I had. He told me that all he and other reporters digging into Eagleton's past had found was a 1962 speeding arrest. I told him that was all I had found. More calls turned up no information on drunk driving. After two hours, though, I still had not reached all the present and former prosecutors in the two counties in question. But this story just didn't feel like one that was likely to pan out.

Late in the afternoon, Mike Kiernan came into my office. Mike was a young reporter who had originally been recruited by Jack to do research for a college of ecology Jack was supporting. When the enterprise failed, Mike joined the staff. He was welcome. Bright, energetic, and resourceful, he took over a variety of tasks, including preparing TV and radio scripts and did them well and reliably. Mike had a mordant sense of humor and I enjoyed his company.

"I'm looking for something on Eagleton for radio tomorrow," he said. "Can you help?"

I told him what I knew. He seemed glad to get what little I had.

"That will be fine," he said. "I want to be able to write an item that will have Jack sitting here in Washington giving the inside dope on what all these other reporters out in Missouri are trying to get. The story will be that reporters are swarming all over Missouri checking out these rumors of drunk driving, but all they have found is this speeding arrest. That doesn't make a bad little item."

I kept trying after Mike left but still hadn't reached all the possible officials by the time I left to go home for dinner. I still hadn't turned up a thing to support the drunk-driving story. After dinner, I got on the phone again but made little progress. I finally called Jack and asked him to get back to Davis for more details. He agreed to, but at first was unable to reach him. When he called back later, he seemed to have less than he had before.

"True can't remember exactly how many photostats he received," Jack said, "but he had a stack of them and the figure eleven sticks in his mind. He said it could possibly have been as few as six. A couple of them were definitely drunk driving. They were given to him by a state trooper. The reason he didn't give me the state trooper's name is that he didn't know him. True never showed the photostats to any member of his staff. He agonized over what to do with them, whether to use them in the campaign or not and finally decided to tear them up. He isn't sure which county is the one, but he said there is a prominent

Democrat who owns the largest funeral home in Fulton who would probably know something about this."

I told Jack I still had not reached all the prosecutors who might be the one Davis was talking about. But so far, I said, I had turned up nothing to substantiate the drunk-driving report. Jack sounded as if he was unsure I was giving it my best. (He has since told me he was a little irritated by what seemed to him a half-hearted effort.) But I was doing the best I could. For example, I tried to reach one ex-prosecutor through his home telephone listing. His daughter, who sounded like a young teen-ager, told me, though, that he no longer lived there. I pressed her, and reluctantly she told me he now lived with another woman in St. Louis. Even more reluctantly, she gave me the woman's name. But I couldn't find such a person listed with information in St. Louis, so I called the young girl back to find out where her mother, who was not home, might be reached. She gave me the name of a local night club, "Mr. B's." I called there, hoping the mother would know how to reach her husband—or ex-husband, I couldn't be sure. The man who answered said over the noise and laughter that he had no way of paging anyone, but if I could tell him what the woman looked like, he would try to find her. I called the daughter again. She told me her mother was wearing black slacks, white sandals, a white and black long-sleeved cotton blouse. She had jet black hair with gray streaks. She was in her mid-thirties. I called the night club again. The man looked, then returned to the phone to tell me she had just left. I would have to wait until morning, when I could reach the man himself at his office in St. Louis.

I wasn't ready to give up on this story, but I wasn't optimistic about it. From those I had spoken to, I had gotten virtually unanimous recollection of the one speeding charge and unanimous ignorance of any drunk-driving charges, although several people said there had been persistent rumors that Eagleton had a drink problem. At the time of the supposed arrests, Eagleton was attorney general, then lieutenant governor, of the state. It wasn't hard to believe that he could have been stopped for offenses which were promptly and thoroughly covered up because of his office. But plausibility and provability are not the same. Jack, though, had a different feeling about the story.

"I'm inclined to go ahead with something about this on radio," he said. "When a guy like True Davis says he saw those photostats, there's obviously something to it. Someone's going to get this story, so I'm inclined to move ahead with something so we don't lose it."

I didn't disagree. True Davis had been a reliable source and Jack told me he gave this information most reluctantly. Although he had been a political opponent of Eagleton's, he was now supporting him and Davis' son was working for Eagleton. True Davis was certainly not one of my heroes, but he seemed too much the solid citizen to fabricate a story of this kind and feed to a reporter whose friendship he clearly valued. Carefully hedged, Davis' information could be a legitimate story.

When I got to the office the next morning, Jack and Les had not returned from taping the radio show at the Mutual Studios farther downtown. Shortly after I sat down at my desk, one of Mutual's correspondents called me.

"Listen," he said, "I just heard Jack's report that he has located the photostats on Eagleton's drunk-driving arrests. Some of my sources in the Senate have told me the same thing. I'm sure it's true, and I think it's great that Jack's got the documents. Is he going to make them public?"

"Well," I said. "I don't think he's actually located them. He's learned about them from a pretty good source."

Moments later, an NBC radio reporter called. It seemed the word was out all over town that Jack had the goods on Eagleton's drunk-driving record. I put the NBC man off with a promise his call would be returned by Jack. Just after I got off the phone, I heard Jack and Les come in the front door of the office. I walked out to the reception room. The morning's radio scripts were lying on the desk. The Eagleton item was on the top of the stack. It began as Mike Kiernan had indicated it would, telling how reporters were "streaming into Missouri" to check out "rumors" of Eagleton's being nabbed for drunk driving. Mike had gone on to say that the reporters had found nothing but one speeding violation. But Jack had drawn a line through that with a black felt-tipped pen. I suppressed a gasp when I saw what he had written in its place. The Mutual man had not been paraphrasing when he told me Jack had said he had "located" the photostats. That is exactly what Jack had just recorded for broadcast on the largest radio network in the nation.

"Hey," I said, "you can't say you've 'located' the photostats, can you?"

"I don't know," Jack said. "Les and I were just talking about that."

"I don't think that's the word you want. Don't you want to say you've 'traced' them or 'traced their existence'?"

"Traced!" said Les. "That's the word we want."

"You're right," Jack said. "I'll go and phone in a correction." The correction Jack phoned to Mutual might have been enough to soften the impact of the story if he had made it before the taping. But Mutual had been calling all over town to say that Jack Anderson, their new star attraction, had the documents on Eagleton's drinking. The press was beginning to descend on the office as it had done in the ITT and India-Pakistan cases. It was the lead item on the hourly network radio news broadcasts. The fact that Jack was now saying that he had "traced" the documents instead of "located" them was not enough to quell the interest, even though Jack's correction made it clear that he had not seen the photostats himself. The correction attributed the story to a "former high official from Missouri whose reliability is beyond question."

What's more, Jack seemed to have no doubt that the story would be vindicated, even if he had exaggerated it originally. He was not the least reluctant to be interviewed by television or the newspapers. He gave each interviewer the most ringing assurances of the reliability of his source.

Eagleton, who was by now in Honolulu, quickly called a news conference to denounce the story as a "damnable lie." Les seemed surprised when he heard that. Later in the afternoon, Jack stepped across the hall to get a glass of water, between interviews.

"Are you worried about this?" I asked.

"No problem," he said, smiling. "Look, True Davis is a reliable guy. If he says he saw the photostats, then they existed. In a situation like this, the truth has a way of coming out. So I'm not worried about it. Besides, this shows we're willing to go after liberal Democrats."

In Missouri, though, the drunk-driving report was getting no substantiation. E. I. Hockaday, the State Police Superintendent, said the files of his department revealed no drunk-driving arrests of Thomas Eagleton. I finally got through to all the other people I had planned to call and some others as well. They all had heard of the speeding charge, even state troopers who worked in other parts of the state. But no one knew anything about drunk driving. As before several people said there had been rumors that Eagleton had a drinking problem. But the rumors had never been confirmed.

One of the last interviews Jack held that day was with Channel 5, the local Metromedia station where he taped his television commentaries. Asked if he should have waited until he had the proof in his hands before going ahead with the story, Jack conceded that he probably should have. It was the first sign that he was becoming a bit uncertain about the story.

Both Jack and Les, however, were elated about one development. The New York *Times* had asked to interview Jack's source, with the promise that the name would not be revealed. Jack felt that Davis would inspire confidence and the result would be a story tending to support him. He talked Davis into it. The interview was to be held the next morning.

I got into the office later than usual that Friday morning, be-cause I had to attend a court hearing in which a close friend was involved. From the courthouse, though, I phoned Jack at the office. The New York *Times* interview with Davis, he said, had gone badly. Although Davis repeated everything he had told Jack, he acknowledged under questioning that he had not authenticated the traffic citations himself and, what's more, the state trooper who had handed them to him at a political rally was not in uni-form and he could not prove that he really was a trooper. Jack thought the *Times* reporters had been antagonistic toward him. He did not expect the *Times* story to be favorable.

"They were asking things like, 'Do you think this kind of re-porting is worthy of a Pulitzer Prize winner?' " he told me ruefully.

"I've been thinking about it," I said, trying to be as tactful as possible. "And it occurred to me that the best thing to do might be to apologize to Eagleton. That way, you'd be out of this thing clean."

"Maybe so," Jack said. "We can talk about it when you come in."

When I got to the office, I sat down at my typewriter and drafted a statement. It took the tack that the report was based upon limited evidence and was intended for only limited use. But instead, it had created a sensation and done an injustice to Eagle-ton. It ended in an apology.

I personally felt that an outright apology as succinct and com-plete as possible would have been preferable, but I doubted I could sell it to Jack. He believed the citations had existed and that Eagleton was lying. I thought he might be willing to go along with an apology that fell short of being an assertion that the story was absolutely false. And I felt that the impact of it would be the same, anyway. Jack Anderson would have apologized. Eagleton would say he was vindicated. End of incident. If the story later turned out to be true, Jack might appear foolish, but not irre-sponsible.

It was about noon by now, and the first edition of the Washington *Star* was on the streets. On the front page was a story by Bob Walters under the headline "Anderson Backs Off." It quoted his remarks on the interview on Channel 5 the night before, which the rest of the press had missed. The office was immediately besieged with calls from newsmen wanting to know if Jack really was backing off.

Jack read the statement I drafted, then turned to his typewriter and began to fashion his own. About thirty minutes later, it was done. It ran about a page and a half, double-spaced. I thought it was too long, too full of explanations and defenses. But it ended with an apology to Senator Eagleton for not waiting until the story was fully verified before using it. I thought it was probably enough to extricate Jack from this worsening jam. I sensed that he was in for some severe criticism for this story. An apology, no matter how hedged with explanation and defense, would take the sting out of any outraged comment. Jack would stay ahead of the reaction, apologizing before he was forced to.

Jack called the staff into the office and read the statement. Opal was strongly in favor of the apology.

"I just don't want you to act like Drew used to," she said. "He refused to ever apologize, even if he was wrong."

Joe and I agreed. But Les, who wasn't aware that I had tried hard and without success to confirm the story, thought it was likely to pan out at any time. He thought Jack ought to ride out the storm.

"Why do you have to make any statement at all," he said. "Why don't you act like the Russians did when Napoleon was advancing. Just sit tight and let them wear themselves out."

"That option is foreclosed," I said. "The *Star*'s out with a story saying Jack's backing off. The entire press corps has been on the phone wanting to know if it's true. Jack has to give an answer."

A heated argument ensued. It was typical of the office. A roiling squabble over substance, with no hard feelings. Jack listened to everyone, but I could tell he was finding Les persuasive. The reason was not that Les was giving the best argument, but because Les was saying what Jack, at this point, wanted to hear. Jack didn't want to back off when he thought the story might be vindicated at any moment. After an extraordinary streak of major stories, Jack didn't want the humiliation of announcing he had blundered when events might still bail him out.

Les argued that Jack had done something any reporter might have done—gone out fast with a story to stay ahead of the competition. The press, he said, would understand that.

I argued that that was the worst possible justification, but to no avail. Jack had made up his mind. The statement would be rewritten and the apology would go.

One of the reasons I was so eager for Jack to back down was that I suspected the rest of the press, which had also been hearing reports of drunk driving by Eagleton, was beginning to doubt that those reports were true. For example, I had received a call from Paul Duke of NBC News, who had become a friend during the ITT case. He was appalled that Jack had gone with the Eagleton story without the documents in hand.

"What the hell is going on?" he asked. "In the ITT case, you had the memo. But he hasn't even seen these documents."

The Washington *Post* that morning reported that one day before Jack went on the air with his report, it had gotten a strikingly similar tip. "The Washington *Post*," the story said, "received a report from a former Missouri official that a highway patrolman approached him at a 1968 political rally with a sheaf of traffic citations allegedly issued to Eagleton. Repeated checks with authorities in Missouri did not substantiate the report."

Jack's statement began just as Les had urged: "For competitive reasons, we went out fast yesterday with a story that Senator Tom Eagleton has been cited for drunken and reckless driving. The story was based on the recollections of a competent source, who personally saw photostats of the traffic citations. We also discussed the story with other responsible sources who had been told of Eagleton's traffic violations."

The statement went on to explain how newsmen are accustomed to relying on confidential sources. As an example, he said, "The Washington *Post* quoted an unidentified former Missouri official as saying, 'that a highway patrolman approached him at a 1968 political rally with a sheaf of traffic citations allegedly issued to Eagleton.' " That, of course, was a quote from the *Post* story mentioned earlier, which had gone on to say that no substantiation had been found for the report. It was not a good example for Jack to cite.

The statement said, in closing, "In retrospect, I believe I broadcast the story prematurely and should have waited until I could authenticate the traffic citations personally. Nevertheless, I have faith in my sources and stand by the story. If this faith should ever turn out to be unwarranted, I will issue a full retraction and apology."

I thought the statement was not likely to get Jack off the hook, but I hoped that it would. Everyone in the office continued to follow leads in an effort to find the elusive proof that Eagleton had been caught driving drunk. But at the end of the day, no proof had been uncovered.

Meanwhile, Eagleton was counterattacking hard against Jack. In the ironic way things often work in politics, Jack's story was helping Eagleton, not hurting him. Eagleton's acknowledgment that he had undergone shock treatments put him on the defensive and raised the question of whether, in originally concealing the fact, he had placed ambition ahead of judgment and thereby gravely wronged McGovern and damaged the party's chances of winning the election. But as long as no proof of drunk driving was forthcoming, Eagleton appeared to have been wronged by Jack. He now had an issue to get himself off the defensive. "I'm not going to let a lie drive me off the ticket," he told cheering crowds upon his return from Hawaii.

I was still asleep when the phone rang at eight-thirty the next morning. It was Opal.

"You might as well get up, it's worse than ever," she said. "You should see the Washington *Post*. I thought everything was fine when I read the *Post*'s story on Eagleton. Then I turned to the editorial page. And now Jack's agreed to go on 'Face the Nation' with Eagleton tomorrow."

"Let me look at the *Post* and I'll call you back," I said.

It could hardly have been worse. A large portion of the editorial page was taken up with a piece by Maxine Cheshire, the *Post*'s redoubtable society columnist, whose reputation for accuracy was roughly equal to Drew Pearson's. The article was headed: "Anderson on Eagleton: A Charge That Didn't Stand Up." It began as follows:

"Columnist Jack Anderson does not reveal his sources and I don't reveal mine. So we will probably neither of us ever know for sure whether we both received from the same individual, almost simultaneously this week, the same piece of gossip about alleged drunken driving incidents involving Sen. Thomas Eagleton. This city being the giant rumor mill that it is, it is entirely possible that our sources were not the same.

"What is clear, however, is that the information we both received was remarkably similar, down to quite specific details. What also is clear is that it did not stand up under the sort of examination that any responsible news reporter would be obliged to give it before making it public.

"The Anderson charges, in short, are a classic example of precisely the sort of reporting practices that have brought the news business under increasing attack."

Cheshire went on to set forth in considerable detail her own efforts to check out the drunk-driving report, which undoubtedly had come from True Davis—someone she would know well from covering the city social scene. Her chronicle was almost an exact copy of the steps I had taken in trying to verify Davis' information.

She had spoken to virtually the same officials and the same state troopers. And she had achieved the same results—nothing. At the end of the piece, she wrote:

"Meanwhile, Anderson yesterday was still holding press conferences and issuing statements and making headlines, defending himself and the 'veracity' of his source on the one hand, and conceding on the other hand that he 'probably should have withheld' the original report until he had checked it out . . . By way of added justification for what he had done, he said the Washington Post, in a dispatch in last Friday's editions, had quoted an unidentified former Missouri official as saying that a highway patrolman had approached him at a 1968 political rally with a sheaf of traffic citations allegedly issued to Senator Eagleton. Anderson apparently did not think it necessary to add that the Post went on to say, in the same dispatch, that 'repeated checks with authorities in Missouri did not substantiate the report.' "

Whew. And Cheshire's piece was accompanied by an equally scathing editorial. "Mr. Anderson," it said, "aired the story without supporting evidence, managed to do an incredible disservice to Senator Eagleton, and now seems to be backing off with a series of lame excuses. Metaphorically speaking, it is Mr. Anderson, not Senator Eagleton who should be charged with reckless driving at this point."

The New York *Times* story, carried on page one, was as unfavorable as Jack had feared. It emphasized that Jack's source had never verified the authenticity of the citations. And the *Times*, too, ran a sharply critical editorial.

I called Opal back to commiserate. She was worried about Jack's going on "Face the Nation" the next day with Eagleton. He had told her that morning that he planned to really "go after" Eagleton. The assumption was that they would both be guests. She thought the panel of reporters would chop Jack to pieces. I agreed. But it occurred to me that Jack might yet redeem himself with an apology to Eagleton on the show. It would be dramatic, occurring live on national television and it would make Eagleton and the panel seem churlish if they were rough on Jack afterward.

The worst thing about this episode now, it seemed to me, was that the longer it continued without some acknowledgment of major error on Jack's part, the more it would look as if he didn't know when a story was proved and when it wasn't. Far from being America's number one investigative reporter, Jack would appear a dimwit with no conscience and no recognition of the distinction between a soft fact and a hard one.

After I hung up with Opal, I talked about it with Clare. She thought Jack's behavior had been outrageous and saw nothing but disaster coming from the incident. She agreed with me that he should use the "Face the Nation" as an opportunity for a dramatic apology and not a chance to clobber Eagleton again. She encouraged me to go out to Jack's house and to urge him to take just that course. I left right away.

Jack was finishing breakfast in the kitchen when I arrived. In the years I had known him, I had never seen him as tense. He was wearing the seedy, threadbare bathrobe he often wore around the house and which was a symbol to us in the office of his easygoing, unpretentious ways. But there was nothing relaxed about him that Saturday morning. He looked drawn and the muscles in the back of his jaw were working visibly as he sat listening to my entreaties, his mouth a tight line. His hands shook, not much, but noticeably.

I have always been loud and opinionated. One of the elder statesmen of the Hartford *Times* once told me when I worked there that I would fare much better in life if I could learn to keep my voice down. I have never tried. Nor have I ever seriously tried to curb what many people, Clare included, have said was my least appealing habit—profanity. Jack Anderson, the gentle and non-swearing Mormon, had always tolerated my obstreperous ways, even seemed amused by them. But I could see he was having a hard time taking my pitch for going on the air with an apology.

He had heard a lot of noisy advice from me in the past days and it hadn't been what he wanted to hear. He was close to losing patience and it was hard to blame him. Then I managed to make things worse by seeming incredulous when he told me he had all along possessed evidence besides the say-so of True Davis that the Eagleton story was true. Two state troopers, one retired, the other still on the force, had told him confidentially that Eagleton had gotten the tickets, that the arresting officers had kept their own copies and the others had been quietly disposed of.

"You mean," I said, "that you had this before you broadcast the story?"

"Of course!" he snapped.

There was a period of silence. Jack looked at the newspaper and I just sat there. I didn't know what to say. I had worked on this story with him. I could recall no case where he hadn't filled me in completely on a story we were doing together. What's more, I couldn't think of any thing in his public statements that indicated the existence of any source besides True Davis. Yet Jack was indignant that I had questioned him about it. The worst thing was that I wasn't sure I believed him. My impulse was to cross-examine him, but I knew that would never do. The important thing was to try to persuade him to use the Sunday television appearance to get out of this jam.

I went into the den and called Opal. I told her about Jack's mood and said I was afraid he might go on the air and blast Eagleton.

"Suppose I threaten to quit if he doesn't apologize," I suggested.

"No, that wouldn't work. It would just make him mad."

"Well, look," I said, "why don't you come over here?"

She agreed to come. I then called Joe Spear and Les and urged them to come over so the whole staff could discuss the matter.

Soon, they began arriving. Opal came with George Clifford, a veteran Washington newspaperman who had helped Jack with books and was a close friend. Then Joe and Les arrived. Jack was visibly touched at seeing his staff rally around at a time of crisis. We all sat in his living room.

"First let me say," he began, "how much I appreciate your coming. It means a lot."

Even now, I couldn't resist being loud and opinionated and I jumped in with my argument for an apology, dramatic and gracious, at the beginning of the show. Opal, as I knew she would, agreed. George Clifford thought it might be a good idea to duck the appearance, but Jack was unwilling. He interrupted to explain all the reasons he was reluctant to back away from the story completely.

Everyone else was as ignorant as I had been about Jack's conversations with the two state troopers. He had also spoken to ex-Senator Edward Long, who said he remembered someone in his campaign staff being given some photostats, but the senator couldn't remember which staff member and had never seen the photostats, according to Jack.

"I'm being criticized for only talking to one source," Jack said. "But that isn't all I did. I've talked to these other sources. They won't let me use their names, but their stories all add up to the same thing. If we can't quote competent sources, we'll go out of business. The other papers are doing it, but we're the only ones who are catching hell for it. The story we had was technically true."

"No, it wasn't, Jack," I said. "You said you'd located the documents when you hadn't located them."

"I was out with a correction of that within ten minutes," he said.

"I know, but the correction didn't do the job," I said. "On the news that night, everyone was saying simply that you had reported that Eagleton had been arrested for drunk driving."

"I can't be responsible for that," Jack said. "If they don't report what we say accurately, it's not my fault."

And so it went, for the better part of an hour. I kept raising my voice and George kept asking me not to shout. Everyone, Jack included, seemed to agree that an apology was in order. But beyond that, there were differences.

Les was eager for Jack to outline all the steps Jack said he had taken to check the story. I argued that this was all "mumbo-jumbo" that added up to a chronicle of how we had failed to get a story. The public wouldn't be interested in such details, I said. But Les, himself the most careful reporter of us all, didn't agree. There was no way for me to signal to him my doubts about Jack's version of what had happened. Jack said he thought it was still worth trying to confirm the story. George agreed to go to Missouri to see what he could come up with.

The meeting broke up with Jack again expressing his gratitude to everyone for coming. But there was no certainty of what he would do.

Later that afternoon, True Davis did something very peculiar. He went to the CBS studios in downtown Washington and made a public statement that he was Jack's source. Davis said he had "very reluctantly come to the conclusion" that he was the source. He said that he had "discussed some of the things that went on in politics" with Jack back during the 1968 campaign and, at that time, had shown Jack the photostats of the drunk-driving citations "without realizing it might be made public without verification."

Jack also went to the studio and confirmed that Davis was the source. He said also that he apologized to Eagleton and "to the American people" for making the story public without further checking.

Davis, of course, was lying. How could he "reluctantly come to the conclusion" that Jack was now using some four-year-old information when he had discussed it with Jack two days earlier and been interviewed about the matter by the New York *Times* only the day before. What's more, he was now saying that Jack had seen the photostats in 1968, though Jack professed to have no such recollection. Of course Jack, having sworn by Davis' veracity, was in no shape to start calling him a liar. He had to go along.

The "Face the Nation" appearance now took on ever greater importance since Davis had emerged as the source and claimed that Jack was using information imparted four years earlier. The show was to be broadcast at noon but was taped ninety minutes earlier. Shortly after eleven, Opal called.

"Jack apologized to Eagleton," she said. "And he accepted it graciously and praised Jack for his 'moral character.' "

"That's great," I said. "But how do you know?"

"I just heard a slice of it on the CBS radio news at eleven," she said. "It sounded great."

When Clare and I tuned in at noon, we were expecting to watch some very favorable developments. And the show began much as the radio report had indicated. Jack asked Eagleton some other questions, then began the following exchange:

"This is the first time I've had a chance to face you," he said, "and I do owe you an apology. I've always told my reporters, Senator, that a fact doesn't become a fact for our column until we can prove it. Now I violated my own rule, and I want you and the nation to know that I violated it."

Jack went on with some explanatory remarks about how he had gotten the story, but he concluded by saying, "I went ahead with a story that I should not have gone ahead with, and that was unfair to you, and you have my apology."

"Well," responded Eagleton, "let me say, Mr. Anderson, that the true test of moral character is, I guess, to admit when one makes a mistake . . . it takes quite a man to go on nationwide television to say he made a mistake and I commend you for your courage."

Clare and I were shaking our heads in relief and elation. It could not have gone better. A humble apology and a gracious acceptance.

But the next thing we knew, the subject had been raised again and Jack was talking.

"I wish I could retract completely the story and say there's nothing to it. I can't—I cannot in good conscience do that."

I had repeatedly urged Jack to say nothing about retraction, just to apologize and let that speak for itself. But he had raised it and he was giving Eagleton a lengthy explanation of why he couldn't "retract the story completely."

"I cannot do that yet," he said. "My conscience won't allow me to . . ."

Eagleton, incredulous, began to question Jack about why he could not retract and Jack responded with reasons why he still thought there were unanswered questions raised by information he had obtained from sources.

". . . they have given me specific incidents which I would like to go over with you. In addition, the St. Louis *Post-Dispatch* has quoted a former Missouri official as saying that he personally stopped you three times—"

"Nothing to do with drunken driving," Eagleton protested. "That was never mentioned."

"Well," said Jack, "I would like to exhaust these. I really would prefer to retract everything right here, but I cannot retract a story that still hasn't been pursued to a final end . . ."

I was stunned. Clare and I looked at each other in horror. Jack had seemed to be out of trouble but now he had gone so far to make clear that his apology wasn't a retraction that it sounded as if he had retracted the apology.

The phone rang. It was Jack. "What did you think?" he said.

"Well, it was fine," I stammered. "But I wish you hadn't brought the whole thing up all over again."

"Believe me," he said, "I was tempted not to. That would have been the easiest thing to do. But I think I did the right thing."

There was no use arguing. "Well, I hope so," I said.

What I hoped, of course, was that the apology part of the show would overshadow all the other discussion. And the next morning's papers seemed to indicate that it might. Jack and Eagleton were shown together in the studio after the show in a front-page picture in the Washington *Post*. The *Post*'s story mentioned the retraction disagreement, but placed more emphasis on the apology.

Still, though, a number of other newsmen told me they thought Jack had acted terribly on the show. I had to agree. Invoking conscience as justification for clinging to this discredited story was outrageous.

The next morning, the Washington *Post* criticized Jack as he had never been criticized before. In an editorial entitled "Jack Anderson's 'Apology,'" the *Post* said that Jack had revealed "some very peculiar and unsatisfactory notions concerning journalistic responsibility—and some absolutely bizarre notions concerning 'conscience.'" The editorial went on, "Having first invoked competitive pressures as an excuse for his behavior—which was no excuse at all—Mr. Anderson proceeded . . . to offer the Senator an apology. Or something." It went on to explain how Jack had apologized and Eagleton had accepted and even praised Jack. "Whereat—or shortly after—Mr. Anderson announced, positively stricken with more-in-sorrowism, that he only wished he could 'retract the story completely.' . . . The point, to the extent that one was discernible, seemed to be that Mr. Anderson's conscience would not permit him to retract the story (for which he had already apologized) because it might still prove true.

"The logic in all this really devours itself," the editorial continued. "What exactly was Mr. Anderson refusing to retract if not the allegations which, by his own account, it had been irresponsible to broadcast? We do not know how Jack Anderson's reporters—the staff upon which he claims to have imposed such strict journalistic standards—are meant to receive this latest bit of delphic instruction from the master. But for our part, we believe Senator Eagleton was right on the money when he objected to the distinction and observed that it hardly seemed equitable to him.

Sunday's exchange on the television program did nothing to alter our opinion that the Anderson performance has been a reckless and wholly regrettable excursion into the worst kind of 'journalism.'"

I found Jack at his desk when I came into the office. I have never seen him looking so depressed. He looked up at me.

"Well," he said softly, "your advice was right all along and I wish I had taken it. I want you to know that I appreciate your giving it."

There wasn't anything to say, so I left the room.

The mail that poured into the office in the days after the Eagleton broadcast was overwhelmingly angry. There was too much to count it all, but someone did take one day's worth and tally it. There were sixty-seven letters denouncing Jack, five praising him or telling him he was on the right track.

The reaction among Jack's colleagues that I spoke to was also overwhelmingly negative. Mary McGrory, the columnist for the Washington *Star*, told me she couldn't believe it was Jack she was seeing on "Face the Nation."

"I've always loved Jack," she said. "He was always so down to earth, so unassuming—a man who remembered where he came from. Suddenly here he is apologizing 'to the American people.' The word for it is 'hubris.'"

That morning, Jack went up to Senator Eagleton's office to play out the last inevitable scene in this dreary drama. Jack raised the questions he had mentioned on "Face the Nation" and Eagleton gave his answers—all of them denials, of course. Outside Eagleton's office, Jack walked up to a battery of microphones and television cameras to announce that he was giving a "full retraction" of his story. The next morning, he went on the "Today" show and repeated the retraction in a thirty-minute, mea-culpa interview with Frank McGee.

I admired Jack for taking his medicine publicly. But I felt, as Mary McGrory had, that I hadn't been dealing with the same man I had known the past several years. There was something about his compulsion to come up with something on the Eagleton story, about his stubbornness in backing away, and his insensitivity to his own standards that was unfamiliar and unexpected. It seemed that Jack had had an upside-down reaction to his own success. Instead of feeling more secure, he felt more compelled. And once he had slipped, it was more difficult than ever to accept the humiliation of admitting the error.

Certainly, I thought Jack had behaved disgracefully in the Eagleton affair. But in the end, he had faced the facts and taken his lumps—publicly. And Eagleton, whatever he said, did not lose his place on the Democratic ticket because of Jack's unsubstantiated charge. He lost it because of his own misjudgment of the mental-illness issue and the insistence of the Democratic party hierarchy that someone without such a history take his place. Eagleton had not been damaged by Jack's charge for more than twenty-four hours. Then the allegation became a sympathy factor and actually helped him generate support. The person damaged by the episode was Jack. He had risen to a position of fame and credibility never before achieved by a muckraking journalist and, almost overnight, he had lost it. He had done hundreds of stories as controversial without a slip. And he would do hundreds more before the stain of the Eagleton case was removed, if, indeed, it ever could be.

TWELVE

On October 1, 1972, about two months after the broadcast of the Eagleton story, I quit working for Jack Anderson. In Washington, my move was widely viewed as an act of disgust with Jack. But it was hardly that. I had disagreed strongly with his handling of the Eagleton affair, but I still regarded Jack as the best and the bravest reporter I had ever known. At present, investigative reporting is all the rage in the news business. This was the main reason I could leave Jack Anderson without being in immediate danger of starvation. I was still in demand on the lecture circuit and I had been commissioned to write this book. But Jack Anderson had been an investigative reporter long before it was fashionable. He had endured years of litigation, suppression, and, among many of his colleagues, scorn, to keep at it while others scurried to cover safe topics such as foreign affairs and election campaigns. He had given me the opportunity to work with him and learn from him. More than that, he had given me credit, recognition, and support far beyond what I ever asked for or expected. Quite apart from professional respect and gratitude, I felt affection for Jack that a dozen Eagleton incidents could not extinguish.

The Eagleton affair had not left me disillusioned with Jack, but it had left me discouraged. Jack, and those of us who worked with him, had made a long climb up a slippery slope to achieve the credibility and impact the column had when the Eagleton affair occurred. In fact, it was this very standing that caused the story to be sent out all over America within minutes after Jack had recorded it. Now, it seemed, we had slid near the bottom of the greasy pole again and would have to start all over. It was demoralizing.

Besides, I had worked for Jack for the better part of three years, longer than I had ever worked at any other job. The future there seemed to hold more of the same and, although I enjoyed the work, it was not as exciting as it had been. After the ITT case, I found it doubly hard to crank out more routine stories to keep things going. I got into a rut. The feeling that it was time to move on became irresistible. So, late in September, I went in to Jack's office and told him I thought I wasn't doing my share and wanted to take myself off the payroll, but remain "associated" with him.

In his kind way, he urged me to stay on, but he knew I wasn't helping him as much as I once had. He needed another hungry young man. We agreed that we would remain associated, that I would contribute to the column whenever I could and that we would stay in touch. He told me he valued my advice and judgment and that he would need it. I thought that he was sincere, but I had doubts about how often I would be called upon to give counsel. I expected that things would be pretty humdrum around there for a while. It didn't turn out that way, though.

In the months after I left full-time work with Jack, the Watergate scandal emerged as the major story of the day and looked increasingly like one of the biggest scandals in American political history. Every major news organization scrambled to catch the Washington *Post*, which had broken the case open. Nearly every national investigative reporter was occupied with the story and other newsmen became investigative reporters overnight as they hustled to find fresh information about the scandal. Jack's column in these months had some important Watergate stories, but he did not lead the way, as he had on so many other stories about government misdeeds. All at once, though, Jack caught up. And in so doing, he got himself into a jam far more ominous than any he had ever been in before.

In mid-April, someone contacted Jack's office to offer some information. The person spoke to Jack Cloherty, one of two young reporters who had been hired after I left. Cloherty encouraged him to bring his information to the office. The source did. The information was a batch of official transcripts from the grand jury proceedings in the Watergate case. The Washington *Post's* remarkable investigative reports on the case prior to the election had made it evident that the five men arrested inside Democratic Party headquarters at the Watergate and the two others subsequently apprehended were not the only culprits in the matter. The *Post's* series suggested strongly that the chain of command for Watergate and related campaign misdeeds reached through the top levels of the President's re-election committee to the men closest to the President in the White House. The *Post's* reports made it seem that the original Watergate prosecuting team, members of the U. S. Attorney's staff in Washington, had snared the small fish and let the big ones get away. This was not especially surprising, since the U. S. Attorney's office is an appendage of the Department of Justice, which takes its orders from the White House. Now, though, the prosecutors were taking testimony again in what they insisted was a no-holds-barred effort to get at the truth. And the White House, with a nervous eye on the grand jury, was continuing its bitter and angry denials of the reporting on the case by the *Post* and other news media which dug below the surface.

In those circumstances, the acquisition of the grand-jury transcripts was an extraordinary coup. Grand-jury proceedings are, by law, secret. The secrecy is designed to protect innocent persons who may be investigated but not charged and to assure fair trials for those who are. It is also designed to protect witnesses from reprisals from those about whom they give testimony. Although grand juries were once considered a safeguard against malicious prosecution by government, they are hardly that today. In theory, a grand jury is a kind of citizen board of review which must determine if there is sufficient evidence to bring an official charge. In addition, the grand jury has considerable theoretical power to act on its own initiative, deciding what to investigate and which witnesses should be called and what questions they should be asked. In practice, however, grand juries almost invariably end up being rubber stamps for prosecuting attorneys and do whatever the prosecutors want them to do. Thus the grand jury ends up being, in all but the rarest instances, an instrument of government power. In this case, however, a conscientious job by the grand jury and an honest job by the prosecutors stood to cause those in power considerable problems. And the Administration wanted no one to know. Never had grand-jury secrecy been so devoutly desired at the highest levels of government.

The transcripts delivered to Jack's office contained some significant new revelations and provided sworn confirmation of a number of reports which had already appeared in the press. Here are the most significant:

—James McCord, one of those apprehended in the Watergate, testified that he and his crew of burglars had broken into the same premises three weeks before the night they were caught.

—McCord testified that one of the Watergate ringleaders, E. Howard Hunt, became afraid after he and his associates were caught that they were being abandoned by the President's top campaign officials. Hunt, said McCord, sent a three-page letter demanding "to contact someone in the White House."

—Hunt himself testified that he and Gordon Liddy, his co-captain in the break-in, traveled to Miami in December 1971 to set up a vast spy network against the Democrats. He got help, he said, from the CIA which provided him the name of a lockpicker.

—A top aide to presidential chief of staff H. R. Haldeman, Gordon Strachan, testified that his boss kept $350,000 in cash stashed in a White House safe during the 1972 campaign, then surreptitiously had the money delivered to a campaign staff member after the election.

This last revelation was of particular significance, because the Washington *Post* had reported earlier, and the White House had heatedly denied, that Haldeman had had control of a secret cash fund which was stored in a White House safe.

Jack stretched the contents of the grand jury transcripts out over eight columns, which began running on Monday, April 16. The columns quoted liberally from the documents, without saying explicitly that they were based on secret grand jury transcripts. By the end of the week, other newsmen were quoting the columns liberally and the prosecution sources had confirmed that, as the Washington *Post* put it, "Jack Anderson obviously is in possession of the minutes of testimony before the federal court grand jury."

On Thursday of that week, I got a call from my friend Len Appel, the lawyer with the firm which represented Jack. He was worried that the verbatim excerpts from the transcripts might get Jack into serious trouble. The law prohibits any court personnel, prosecutors, or grand jurors from making testimony public. Witnesses are not prohibited from revealing their own testimony, but everyone knew the witnesses weren't the source of Jack's information in this instance. Len said Warren Woods, the partner in the firm who represented Jack personally and was an old friend of Jack's, had sought to reach Jack without success to urge him to cease publishing the excerpts. Although the publication of the material was probably legal because of the First Amendment, Jack could be summoned before the grand jury himself and asked where he got it. If he refused to say, he could be jailed, under the Supreme Court's recent ruling on such cases. I also tried to reach Jack that day, but he was out of town. I talked to Les, who said he thought it was a close question, but that Jack had done the right thing. I told Les I didn't question the publication of the information from the transcripts, but merely the direct quotes. It was the kind of evidence of a breakdown in grand jury security that, in such a critical case, the court might feel the need to act upon. Les said he would pass along my advice to Jack.

On Friday, though, there was another column on the testimony, shot through with quotes from the transcript. The weekend passed with columns on another subject, and I thought the matter might blow over. But on Monday morning, the column again was devoted to the grand jury proceedings. And the entire fifteen-member bench of the United States District Court for the District of Columbia convened in a special session to decide what action to take to stop the blatant leak. Presiding at this meeting was Judge John Sirica, the chief judge, whose perseverance in the Watergate case and refusal to swallow the idea that the original seven defendants were the only ones involved had led to James McCord's decision to speak out. Sirica was, at this point, a hero in the Watergate drama, sharing the spotlight only with Carl Bernstein and Bob Woodward, the young Washington *Post* investigative team who had cracked open the case to begin with. The fifteen judges agreed to order a special, separate grand jury convened to investigate the leak, to find its source and to prosecute those responsible.

Now the issue was joined. There was going to be a grand jury investigation and the number-one witness almost certainly would be Jack. He would just as certainly refuse to identify his source and the court would either have to punish him or back down. The central figure in all of this, of course, would be Judge Sirica. Since he had taken such an aggressive position in trying to get to the bottom of the case, he could hardly stint at this point in acting to protect the integrity of the grand jury process. I didn't want to be a nuisance, but I couldn't resist calling Jack on the phone.

"What have you done now, you naughty boy?" I said when he came on the line, trying to keep it light.

He laughed. "I don't know why they're going after me," he said. "Every reporter in town is after the story of what's been going on in that grand jury room."

"For whatever it's worth, Jack," I said, "I urge you strongly to move as fast as you can to compromise your way out of this before it goes any further. Every day that goes by that brings you closer to a confrontation with that court brings you closer to going to jail."

"Well," he said, "I appreciate your advice and I've got Warren (Woods) and Betty (Murphy, another partner in Woods' firm) looking into it, now. We'll figure something out."

The next morning the column featured more slices of the grand jury transcript. And the news stories on the court's order that there be an investigation of the leak contained some bold words from Jack: "Reporters have been scrambling all over one another to find out what is happening in the secret sessions," he said. "The government is upset, apparently, because we nailed down the testimony precisely rather than relying on hearsay. It is significant that we began publishing excerpts from the grand jury proceedings on April 16. The next day, President Nixon announced a dramatic turnabout on Watergate. The factor that persuaded the President to throw open the Watergate investigation, say White House sources, was our access to the grand jury findings. Under our Constitution, we're free to publish any and all news generated by the White House, the Congress or the courts. No federal rule of criminal procedure supersedes the Constitution, which grants freedom of the press."

So Jack was not only saying publicly that he was being singled out for his accuracy, but that his reporting was responsible for forcing the President to abandon his stand on executive privilege and allow White House aides to appear before the grand jury. And he ended his statement with a little civics lecture. I winced at the thought of how Jack's statement must have been received by those fifteen judges who had voted to have him investigated. Their attitude toward him wouldn't be helped by the new installment in the column from the transcripts, although Les had told me on Friday that the column going out that day—for use on Tuesday—was the last one on the grand jury because Jack had run out of transcripts.

I assumed that Jack and the lawyers were busily trying to figure out a way out of this jam that Tuesday. After lunch, I was in the neighborhood, so I dropped by the office. A couple of reporters with tape-recorders were waiting in the reception room. And I couldn't get in to see Jack because he was already being interviewed on camera by Herbert Kaplow of ABC News. From the hallway, I could hear Jack's deep voice booming about the discriminatory nature of this grand jury investigation of him. I couldn't believe it. I asked Opal when I might be able to talk to him. She said he might be a while with Kaplow and that others were waiting. So I went into one of the offices and sat down at a vacant desk and began writing a memo to Jack.

The principal point of what I wrote was that there was no way Jack could come out a winner in a confrontation with Judge Sirica and the more he took credit for turning Nixon around on Watergate, the more he was taking bows for an achievement that Judge Sirica probably felt was his own. Before I had finished the memo, though, Jack happened into the office.

"Hi," he said, seeming glad to see me.

"I was just writing you a memo," I said, "but now that you're here, I'll just tell you what I was writing. You've just got to get off this collision course you're on with this court or I'm afraid you'll wind up in jail."

"I know what the risks are," Jack said. "But I believe it was right to print those stories and I'm willing to go to jail. I'll put the column out from a jail cell if I have to. It won't be any fun, but we'll come out of it all right."

"There's no way you're going to look like a hero," I said, "if you get into a confrontation with Sirica. His credentials as a hero in Watergate are already established. If you get into a fight with him, he'll take the view that you obstructed the investigation of the case, and perhaps endangered the success of the prosecutions. There's just no way that the public is going to think you're the good guy and he's the one that's trying to cover up for the White House."

"Well," said Jack, "what can I do?"

"The first thing you can do," I said, "is stop giving these interviews. When these people call up, you've got to just say, 'No comment.'"

There was a pause, as Jack shook his head. Then he said softly, "God, that's hard to do."

I laughed, knowing how he felt. He said he'd think about what I'd said. Then he left the room. I went back to the typewriter, took out the incomplete memo and threw it in the trash.

That night, I called Len Appel to tell him of my conversation with Jack. I asked him what Jack might do to extricate himself from this jam.

"Well, I don't know, Brit," he said. "Jack really doesn't have much to bargain with."

"Suppose he offered to cease printing the transcripts. Do you think that might help?"

"It might, but the prosecutors are under a court order to carry out an investigation. There's no way to turn back."

"Well, suppose he offered to quit printing verbatim excerpts and to turn over the transcripts he now has to the court. He could tell the court that his source isn't the ultimate source, so that getting his testimony wouldn't necessarily lead them to the leak anyway. My guess is that they're more concerned about the appearance of this thing and getting the leak plugged than sending anyone to jail."

"You might be right," said Len. "I don't know what else he could do. You know the court order on this contained some language urging anyone who might have knowledge of the matter to come forward. Jack could cite that as his reason for coming forward."

"The truth is that he doesn't have any more transcripts, but they don't know that. I think it's a good idea and Jack might very well listen to me. I'm going to call him."

"Fine," said Len, "but he's been working with Betty and Warren on this one, so there's no use getting me involved."

Jack was surprisingly receptive to my idea. He said he would call the lawyers first thing in the morning and propose it to them.

When I called the office the next morning to see what had happened, I learned from Opal that Jack had an appointment to see the Watergate prosecutors that afternoon. But it wasn't until the next day that I found out what had happened when Jack confronted them, with one leg already in the jailhouse door. From Jack himself and from Warren Woods and Betty Murphy, who accompanied him, I got this account of the meeting:

The three of them met prosecutors Earl Silbert, Seymour Glanzer, and Don Campbell in Silbert's office in the District court building. They were joined by Harold Titus, the U. S. Attorney. Everyone was polite but highly serious. Jack had been warned repeatedly by both his lawyers before going into the meeting that the law was against him and that he must take a penitent approach.

"Look," they had told him, "we are coming in as supplicants, not as aggressors."

"Don't worry," Jack had said, "you let me handle it."

Warren opened the meeting with a few introductory words in which he said the statute that makes revelation of grand jury testimony a crime did not apply to this case. Silbert's reply was that the Caldwell decision—the one requiring newsmen to identify sources if asked to do so by a grand jury—did apply.

Harold Titus made a lengthy statement to the effect that, "I regard my office as a sacred trust—we have a mandate from the entire court, to investigate these leaks and we intend to do so."

Jack reiterated the contention that the first amendment was not limited by the court's rules of procedure, but he added:

"I don't want anyone falsely accused. I have noticed that there have been some allegations that the prosecutors or others to whom the federal rules apply leaked the material. But I didn't get the material from anyone like that."

Back and forth it went, at times argumentative, at times agreeable, at times with each side talking past the other. At one point, Titus said, "As long as you keep printing the transcripts, people are refusing to come before the grand jury to testify. Suppose," he asked, "it were a Mafia case, with life and death of witnesses involved. Would you print transcripts then?"

"I use discretion," said Jack.

"We both have the same purpose," Titus went on. "We are investigating the Watergate case and we have been for a long time."

"I agree," said Jack. "I think you're really trying *now*."

"What do you mean, *now*?" asked Glanzer, irritated.

"I don't think you were before. I think you were using the grand jury process to protect the guilty. But I think you're trying to make an honest investigation now."

Glanzer started to argue, but Titus cut him off. "I would be glad to discuss the vigorousness of this investigation," he said, "but not now. We've got to stop the leaks and we've got to do it now."

"I think I have a right to print this information," Jack said, "and I don't think the case would have broken open the way it did this week if I hadn't had access to the transcripts. My White House sources tell me this was a factor in the President's decision. I have the right to continue to publish these documents if I please. And I have requests right now from the New York *Times*, the Los Angeles *Times*, the wire services for the full transcripts. My inclination is to give them to them. But before I do, I wanted to hear your case."

Jack was playing boldly with a weak hand, but I have watched him intimidate other formidable people with that booming voice, ringing with certainty, and that stern expression of his. Titus, however, is not a man easily cowed. He challenged Jack on his view that he was constitutionally entitled to protect his sources.

"Not only would it be a violation of my professional ethics," said Jack, "for me to divulge my source, it would be a violation of my religion. The Mormon faith holds that the Constitution of the United States is divinely inspired. So I could never consent to identifying a confidential source, no matter what."

Jack had earlier expressed his respect for Judge Sirica, so Titus asked:

"Would you reveal your source if Judge Sirica ordered you to?"

"No."

"What about the U. S. Court of Appeals?"

"No."

"The Supreme Court?"

"No."

"Now, how are we to reconcile your view that the Constitution is divinely inspired with the idea that you would not obey the order of the court specifically established to determine what the Constitution holds?"

Jack was in a box, but he never batted an eyelash.

"If the Supreme Court were to order me to reveal my source, I would only have to conclude that the Supreme Court was in error," he said.

At that point, Silbert began a lengthy explanation of the reasons secrecy is required by grand juries. They were reasons well known to Jack, as they are to any experienced reporter. But he listened most attentively. When Silbert was finished, Jack spoke again.

"You've convinced me," he said. "I have no desire to interfere with the investigation of the case. And so I will agree to stop publishing direct quotes from the transcripts."

The prosecutors were apparently glad to get that commitment, but Jack wanted to push them a bit harder in an effort to make sure they didn't come after him anyway. He looked Titus in the eye and spoke.

"Mr. Titus," he said, "I want you to know that I will never tell you any more before a grand jury than I am telling you here today. So, if you now call me before the grand jury, I can only conclude that the reason is that you want to put me in jail."

Titus replied that there was nothing personal about the case, and that the court had ordered them to make an investigation.

Earl Silbert asked if Jack would return the transcripts he had. Jack agreed, but Betty Murphy objected. Titus then asked if they would be returned if Judge Sirica asked for them. The answer was yes from Jack, but Betty objected again.

"Mr. Titus, we would have to resist a court order," she said.

"Mrs. Murphy is right," said Jack.

But Jack then agreed to have his lawyers voluntarily return the transcripts to Judge Sirica. The meeting ended with an informal agreement that Jack would stop publishing documents of which he had no more to publish and would return them to the court. In exchange, the prosecutors agreed that they would call Jack before the grand jury only as a last resort.

Outside the meeting, Jack encountered a battery of microphones and cameras. He made a statement explaining what had been agreed to. "I didn't want to hamper their investigation," Jack said, wearing his most sincere expression. "They made such a passionate point of it." He explained that he had not formally agreed to cease digging into the actions of the grand jury, but only to stop publishing the transcripts for the time being. "I have assured them," he added, "that the leaks were not in the prosecutor's office." Then who was his source? "A man with high connections in the Administration," said Jack. "I didn't ask and he didn't say where he got his information."

Although the columns based on the transcripts ended that day, the publicity Jack received from the incident continued for days afterward, largely because of Jack's agreement to stop. Even William Safire, the Nixon man who left to become a columnist for the New York *Times*, described Jack's action as "gallant."

Gallant or not, it was one of the most remarkable Houdini acts anyone in trouble with the government has ever made, to my knowledge. Jack ended up gaining recognition for breaking the story and nearly as much for stopping it.

I spent a month with my family at Rehoboth Beach, Delaware, that summer. One August afternoon, the beach was suddenly buzzing over the presence of a short, stocky man with black hair who was standing at the water's edge watching his young daughter play in the surf. It was Judge Sirica. It was the day after he had handed down his historic decision ordering President Nixon to produce for his inspection the White House tape recordings bearing on the Watergate case.

I had met Sirica a few months earlier at a wedding, where his daughter was the flower girl. We had talked briefly then, but I doubted he would remember. As I was walking by, however, Sirica looked at me as if he recognized me. I walked over.

"How're you makin' out?" the judge asked in his unassuming way.

"I'm fine," I said. "I guess you're tired."

"I sure am. This is the first time I've been swimming. I was here last weekend, but I didn't get to the beach. I had to spend the whole time working on this opinion I've been writing. By the way, how's Mr. Anderson?"

"He's fine," I replied, a little surprised to hear the judge asking after the health of a man who had published the transcripts of a grand jury investigation in his jurisdiction. "I was just heading down the beach to see if I could find him. He has a place down here and he's usually on the next beach."

"Well," the judge said, "give him my best."

That Jack, I thought. He'll be all right.

INDEX

ABC News, 225, 290
Abernathy, Ralph, 256
Adams, Sherman, 9, 31–32, 211
"Agency, The," 192–96. *See also* Central
  Intelligence Agency (CIA)
Agnew, James Rand (Randy), 49–59,
  60, 76, 165
Agnew, Mrs. James Rand (Ann), 51,
  52, 56
Agnew, Michelle Ann, 51, 56
Agnew, Spiro T., 23–24, 49–59, 60, 240
Aibel, Howard, 190, 237
Alabama, University of, 60–84
Allende, Salvador, 192–93, 195, 196
Alsop, Joseph, 102
Anderson, Jack, 1–11, 13–36, 37, 41,
  255–57, 258–81, 283–84; and Ag-
  new story, 49–51, 52, 54–59; and
  Al Capp story, 61–62, 64, 69, 70,
  71–77, 80, 83; Davidson and, 41–
  43, 44; described, journalistic style,
  personality, 1, 8–9, 13–17, 18–21,
  23–32, 33–34, 43–45, 47–48, 85–
  105 *passim*, 164–66, 273–74, 280–
  81, 283, 284–96; and Eagleton
  story, 258–81, 283; and FBI secret
  files, 256–57; and Fike-Laxalt-
  O'Callaghan story, 23–31; and hiring of Hume, 13 ff.; and India-
  Pakistan story, 89–105, 257; and
  ITT story, 110, 112–13, 117, 119,
  125, 126, 127, 131, 133–38, 139,
  145, 147–48, 151, 152, 154, 158,
  163–80, 181, 182–215 *passim*, 224–
  25, 233, 234, 236–37, 252; and
  Murphy-Technicolor Company
  story, 1–11; and Pentagon Papers,
  256; praised by the media, 255–57;
  receives Pulitzer Prize for national
  reporting for India-Pakistan disclosures, 104, 257; and Sherman
  Adams-Bernard Goldfine story, 31–

32; as successor to Drew Pearson,
  1, 8–10 (*see also* Pearson, Drew);
  and use of restricted informa-
  tion, 85–105, 256–57, 284–96; and
  Watergate story, 284–96
Anderson, Olivia (Mrs. Jack Ander-
  son), 43
"Anderson on Eagleton: A Charge That
  Didn't Stand Up" (Washington
  Post article by Maxine Cheshire),
  271–72
"Anderson Papers," 91–105
Anderson Papers, The (Anderson), 104
Appel, Len, 76, 186–87, 287, 291–92
Armed Services Committee, Senate, 86
Associated Press, 32, 95–96
Atlanta *Constitution,* 79
Atlantic (magazine), 14

Baez, Joan, 70
Baker, Bobby, 42
Baldwin, James, 256
Baltimore, Md., 49–59
Baltimore *Evening Sun,* 18, 53
Baltimore *News-American,* 56–57, 58
Baltimore *Sun,* 242, 243, 245
Baudelaire, Whitten's translation of, 35,
  36
Bayh, Birch, 137, 143–44, 227, 247–48
Bay of Pigs invasion, 193, 198
Beard, Bull, 119, 221, 224
Beard, Dita D., 107–38 *passim*, 197–
  218, 219 ff.; and affidavit denying
  authenticity of ITT memo, 197–
  218, 219 ff.; attempts by ITT to
  discredit, 153–54, 159–60, 161,
  169–70, 180, 181–82, 185–86, 189;
  in Denver hospital, 149–50, 151–
  53, 181–82, 198–99, 208–18, 219 ff.;
  described, 114–15, 120–21; disappearance of, 149–50, 151–52; and
  ITT memo, 107–38 *passim*, 149–